Praise for *Making Africa*

'At last, a book on 'How' rather ~~than What to do to improve the~~ of Africa's people. Leaders should read it, and learn.' **Mmusi Maimane, leader, Democratic Alliance**

'By understanding the intersection of people, policy, cities and states, *Making Africa Work* is the go-to guide to informed choices for a better Africa.' **Mondli Makhanya, *City Press* editor**

'I wish I had this handbook when I was president of Malawi. It not only offers convincing arguments on what to do, but practical examples and steps to how to get things done.' **Joyce Banda**

'This is a timely and important book. Africa's GDP per capita is now falling, and so the region is once again diverging from the rest of mankind. Africa's leaders face the choice between managing economic change, or being overwhelmed by political change. For those wise enough to choose the former, this handbook is a valuable guide.' **Paul Collier, Oxford University**

'Beyond the hype and clichés, a blueprint for a prosperous Africa.' **Donald Kaberuka, former president, African Development Bank**

'*Making Africa Work* enables thinking of countries as companies in outlining and illustrating practical choices for success.' **Neal Froneman, Sibanye Gold**

'This book provides essential hardware for every policy maker.' **Tendai Biti, former finance minister, Zimbabwe**

'*Making Africa Work* should be in the brief case of every African leader. It answers the *why's* and *how's* of Africa's development record, confirming what progressive voices have said: Africa has been in trouble because of the mediocrity with which it has been run. Fortunately, it illustrates that our continent is not beyond repair, in offering practical recommendations which we must now implement.' **Raila Odinga, former prime minister, Kenya**

'*Making Africa Work* is a guide for practitioners and scholars through the business of Africa. With comparative insights and on-the-ground experiences in sectors driving economic growth and development across the continent, while covering key structures and issues shaping the context of Africa's "new normal", this is an important and timely contribution.' **Lyal White, Gordon Institute of Business Science, University of Pretoria**

'Incisive insights, an invaluable synthesis of fieldwork and first-rate analysis.' **Gilbert Houngbo, former prime minister, Togo**

'This outstanding book persuades that democracy and development are indivisible: if the politics are broken, it's like trying to build a house on sand.' **Hakainde Hichilema, former presidential candidate, Zambia**

'If there is only one book you read this year, let it be *Making Africa Work*. In drawing on rich African and international case studies, this book's invaluable contribution is in illustrating exactly how and when to get the critical components of leadership, policy and governance right.' **Erastus Mwencha, deputy chairperson, African Union Commission**

MAKING AFRICA WORK

A handbook for economic success

Greg Mills
Olusegun Obasanjo
Jeffrey Herbst
Dickie Davis

HURST & COMPANY, LONDON

Published by arrangement with Tafelberg, an imprint of NB Publishers

This edition first published in the United Kingdom in 2017
by C. Hurst (Publishers) Ltd.,
41 Great Russell Street,
London, WC1B 3PL

Printed in India

Distributed in the United States, Canada and Latin America by
Oxford University Press, 198 Madison Avenue, New York, NY 10016,
United States of America.

A Cataloguing-in-Publication data record for this book
is available from the British Library.

ISBN:9781849048736

www.hurstpublishers.com

'lim' uze ushay'etsheni!' — Plough until you hit a boulder

Contents

Preface
The reason for writing now

This book is a guide to improving Africa's capacity for economic growth and job creation. Such a blueprint is especially needed at a time when African countries, many of them still poor, must prepare for a massive increase in population and, accordingly, the number of young people seeking employment.

We are hopeful about the prospects of African countries, but only if tough decisions are made now. The old 'business-as-usual' approach of governments and leaders has to change if they are to cope with Africa's pending population boom. Reform necessitates fundamentally changing the way in which African economies work. It means being open to international trade and capital rather than aid, being reliant on enterprise rather than personalised and patronage-ridden systems, while the aim of government should be private-sector growth rather than public-sector redistribution. Underlying all of these initiatives is the imperative for a sense of urgency to create jobs before the population wave overcomes African societies.

Even though the continent enjoyed impressive economic growth rates in the 2000s of around 5 per cent, not enough has changed. For one, this growth was in great part not the result of improved governance, but rather a sharp rise in commodity prices, underpinned by soaring Chinese demand.

Now with commodity prices in decline, there is concern that many African countries did not do enough during the 'fat' years to reform their political- and economic-governance practices. As Warren Buffett famously observed, 'Only when the tide goes out do you discover who has been swimming naked.'

This is not about economic growth alone. Another measure of the success of African reform is in the stability of its societies. The continent has been the site of two-thirds of conflict-related deaths worldwide since 1990.[1] The poor are also still with us. More than 40 per cent of Africans live in extreme poverty.[2]

Despite these realities, so far, it has proven difficult to change the old ways of running Africa's economies. The inertia reflects the contemporary retreat of democracy and 'misgovernance' – when government works efficiently, but only for an elite.[3] In this environment, the incentives for liberalising economies are outweighed by the benefits of keeping things just as they are, as elites are easily able to manage and deflect international or other disincentives designed to encourage change.

However, those leaders who, today, have the foresight and vision to make the necessary choices for change will, in the future, be renowned for the prosperity and stability that they brought to their countries. Meanwhile, those rulers who perpetuate the old ways will see the further impoverishment of their nations and their own rule threatened. The Arab Spring, when youths who perceived that they had no future overthrew leaders and destabilised countries in a matter of weeks, highlights how quickly such tensions can spill over, even into political collapse. The threat is particularly severe now that power is increasingly in the hands of individual citizens enabled by the rapid spread of mobile communications.

It seems inevitable that the number of failed states in Africa – already the largest in the world – will increase if leaders do not move to address the imminent challenges presented by the large population increases that are projected, with the concomitant suffering and chaos that accompany institutional collapse. Similarly, other critical challenges faced by African countries, including adjusting to climate change, improving the status of women and reducing inequality, can be addressed only if states grow their economies and generate more jobs. Otherwise, the demographic crisis will become all-engulfing and prevent action on anything else.

Our analysis is based on fieldwork across Africa that began 12 years ago, when the Brenthurst Foundation was established. Our book emphasises research conducted since the downturn in commodity prices that began in 2014. It uses both statistical analysis and case studies to describe the challenges to prosperity in Africa and the strategies undertaken elsewhere in the world that have been successful in reducing poverty. It takes account of the very real challenges facing government leaders across the continent as they try to make improvements in their countries. We also believe that reflecting on comparative international case studies is instructive because of the continued progress of the countries that we cite as examples. One of the starkest failings of postcolonial African governments has been their insularity. Africa's challenges should be understood in the context of universal norms and practices, and not as isolated or unique problems. Not so long ago, after all, many Asian and Latin American countries found themselves under circumstances that were very similar to much of Africa today. Whether devising industrial policy or trying to achieve equity through growth, Africa does not have to reinvent the wheel: a lot can be learnt from others.

We have chosen to structure the book by sector, including mining, agriculture, infrastructure, services, manufacturing, planning and delivery. This sectoral analysis is important because the governance record of a country is the accumulation of a large number of decisions made in different fields of activity. It is often easier to see how state actions affect economies by examining common economic challenges across the region. The sectors that we examine here are the most important for Africa. We analyse the critical aspects of African economies from the oldest and most traditional sectors to those areas where entrepreneurs are participating in the newest forms of technology.

At the beginning of each chapter, we include a brief digest of the key steps for success, as well as the challenges and opportunities Africa's states will experience. The concluding chapter collects all of the sectoral suggestions to provide a comprehensive blueprint for African leaders.

This structure and the solutions offered reflect the diversity of the authorship. One half of the team are long-time collaborators, Greg Mills and Jeffrey Herbst. They are joined for this project by Major General (rtd) Dickie Davis, who has had more than three decades of experience in implanting the decisions of politicians, much of it in difficult circumstances, from Bosnia to Afghanistan, and who has devoted much of his post-military career to sub-Saharan Africa. Finally, former Nigerian president Olusegun Obasanjo, who, arguably, has more experience at the sharp end of the challenges Africa faces than any other living African.

We have benefited greatly from a two-day seminar hosted by the Konrad Adenauer Stiftung in August 2016, when more than 30 policymakers, academics and private-sector executives – all from Africa or with considerable experience in different parts of the continent – reviewed the manuscript and made many important observations and suggestions. They have greatly enriched our findings. Although we certainly did not all agree on everything, this intensive workshop reinforced our view of the great opportunities for significant growth and poverty alleviation that are realisable if African leaders make the necessary difficult decisions, and of the conversely dystopian futures countries face if dramatic steps are not taken now.

Acknowledgements

The Brenthurst Foundation, our common institutional affiliation, was established by the Oppenheimer family in 2005. Its goal is to strengthen Africa's economic performance. Many of the experiences and lessons that are described in this book come from working with a large number of African and other governments as we have endeavoured to develop practical policy solutions and identify international best practice.

At the Brenthurst Foundation, we have been fortunate to work with many excellent people in producing this book. Their intellect, energy, professionalism and integrity have inspired us to get these words into print.

In particular, Nicky, Jonathan and Jennifer Oppenheimer have offered ongoing and invaluable support to the foundation and to this project. The Mandela-Machel Fellow at the foundation, Nchimunya 'Chipo' Hamukoma, was a constant and always cheerful source of reference material, tables and charts. Ghairoon Hajad was an invaluable logistics resource. The foundation's long-time institutional partner, the Konrad Adenauer Stiftung, kindly hosted a seminar to discuss an early draft. We are most grateful to the staff of the venue, the Villa La Collina, and to Holger Dix, Terence McNamee, Leila Jack and Andrea Ostheimer for their organisational roles in delivering the seminar.

Dr Driss Ouaouicha, the president of Al Akhawayn University in Ifrane, kindly organised and accompanied us on a research schedule in Morocco. David and Vicky and Peter and Lauren Horsey generously opened their homes to us in Kenya, and put up with researchers lounging and typing on their porch for hours on end. John Kollias pointed us towards useful material on the role of technology. Olly Stern organised a schedule in London, which offered an understanding into the reasoning behind investment decisions. Christopher Clapham provided, as ever, a home-away-from-home in Mepal to write up material, while Lyal White was a generous travel companion in Latin America. Thomas Vester and Dafydd Lewis organised an excellent itinerary in Vietnam and the Philippines, as did Ambassador Barry Desker in Singapore and Hery Saripudin and Pradono Anindito in

Indonesia. Rod Hagger fixed everything from field trips and seminars to broken wheels in Lilongwe, while Paul Norman, Mark Pearson and David Littleford, among others, ensured that our months in Zambia were both productive and comfortable. Our insights into the mining industry benefited from a round table held at the Royal Zambezi Lodge in April 2016, which generated the Zambezi Protocol. Paul Cluver generously gave both of his time and contacts in the farming community of the Western Cape, as did Lampie Fick in Caledon. Joe Siegle offered unique and helpful insights into the relationship between democracy and development. Branko Brkic kindly allowed reproduction of material that first appeared in the *Daily Maverick*, as did Ray Hartley from the *Rand Daily Mail*. Johnny Clegg not only made the time to comment on this volume, but also supplied the Zulu proverb at the opening, which perhaps best describes the tenacity required of authors and leaders alike.

Tom Alweendo, Isaac Kgosi Phillip Carter, Fidèle Sarassoro and Ahmed Shire all kindly helped arrange the interviews with, respectively, the presidents of Namibia, Côte d'Ivoire and Botswana, and the prime minister of Ethiopia. Ambassadors Louis Pienaar and Dahan Ahmed Mahmoud, along with Anthony Mukutuma and Matt Pascall, hosted a mission to Nouakchott, Mauritania, in October 2016.

Tafelberg's Gill Moodie and Erika Oosthuysen were fuss-free partners on this project, while Mark Ronan did a superb editing job.

The book also comes with a song, 'Mama Afrika', performed and written by Robin Auld and Greg Mills. It can be downloaded from the Brenthurst Foundation's website, www.thebrenthurstfoundation.org.

Last, and certainly not least, our respective families selflessly encouraged us to 'get this done' and allowed us the time and space to do so!

OO, GJBM, JIH and RRD,
Abeokuta, Johannesburg, Washington and Marlborough

About the authors

Greg Mills has directed the Johannesburg-based Brenthurst Foundation since its inception in 2005, and is author of the best-selling books *Why Africa is Poor – And What Africans Can Do About It* (Penguin, 2010) and, with Jeffrey Herbst, *Africa's Third Liberation* (Penguin, 2012). In 2008 he was deployed as strategy adviser to the president of Rwanda, has run strategic advisory groups in Malawi, Mozambique and Afghanistan, and has worked for heads of government in Liberia, Lesotho, Kenya, Zambia and Zimbabwe. He holds a PhD from Lancaster University and an honours degree in African studies from the University of Cape Town. A member of the International Institute for Strategic Studies and Chatham House, and of the Advisory Board of the Royal United Services Institute, in 2013 he was appointed to the African Development Bank's High-Level Panel on Fragile States. He is on the visiting faculty of the Royal College of Defence Studies, NATO's Higher Defence College and the South African National Defence College. His most recent books are *Why States Recover* (Picador, 2014) and, with Jeffrey Herbst, *How South Africa Works* (Picador, 2015).

Jeffrey Herbst is president and CEO of the Newseum in Washington DC. Previously, he was president of Colgate University, a leading liberal arts college in the US. Holding a PhD from Yale University, he has also served as provost and executive vice-president for Academic Affairs at Miami University. Dr Herbst started his career as a professor of politics and international affairs at Princeton University, where he taught for 18 years. He is the author of *States and Power in Africa: Comparative Lessons in Authority and Control* (Princeton University Press, 2014), and several other books and articles. He has also taught at the universities of Zimbabwe, Ghana, Cape Town and the Western Cape. A member of the Council on Foreign Relations, he has served on the Advisory Board of the Brenthurst Foundation since 2005.

Olusegun Obasanjo is a former president of Nigeria. He had a distinguished military career, including serving in the 1957 UN Peacekeeping Mission to Congo and receiving the instrument of surrender on behalf of the Nigerian government from the opposing forces in the Nigerian Civil War in 1970. Having attended various educational institutions, including Abeokuta Baptist High School, the Indian Army School of Engineering and the Royal College of Defence Studies in London, he rose to the rank of general and became the Nigerian head of state after the assassination of the then military head of state in February 1976. He handed over to a democratically elected government in September 1979. He was jailed for his pro-democracy views for three and a half years until the death of General Sani Abacha in June 1998. On his release, he was democratically elected as president in 1999 and served two terms. With over 30 books in print covering a variety of topics, he pursues a passion for conflict resolution, mediation and development through a number of institutions, including his chairmanship of the Tana Forum and the Brenthurst Foundation.

Dickie Davis is special adviser at the Brenthurst Foundation and managing director of Nant Enterprises Ltd. He served for 31 years in the British Army, which he left in 2015 with the rank of major general. During his military career, he served extensively on operations in Afghanistan, commanding the first UK Provincial Reconstruction Team in Mazar-e-Sharif (2003), leading the International Security Assistance Force's reconstruction and development effort as chief engineer of ISAF IX (2006–07), and as chief of staff, Regional Command (South) (2009–10). He is a vice-president of the Institution of Royal Engineers, chairman of the Royal Engineers' Museum and honorary colonel of the Royal Monmouthshire Royal Engineers (Militia). He holds a degree in civil engineering, a master's degree in defence technology, is a fellow of the Chartered Management Institute, and was appointed CB in 2015 and CBE in 2004. He is co-author, with David Kilcullen, Greg Mills and David Spencer of *A Great Perhaps? Colombia: Conflict and Convergence* (Hurst/OUP, 2015), which is based on extensive fieldwork in Latin America and sub-Saharan Africa.

Acronyms and abbreviations

ADMARC	Agricultural Development and Marketing Corporation (Malawi)
AGOA	African Growth and Opportunity Act
APRM	African Peer Review Mechanism
AU	African Union
BEAC	Botswana Economic Advisory Council
BSGR	Beny Steinmetz Group Resources
BRT	bus rapid transport
CAR	Central African Republic
CBD	central business district
CEO	chief executive officer
DRC	Democratic Republic of the Congo
DTC	Diamond Trading Company (Botswana)
ET	Ethiopian Airlines
EU	European Union
FAO	UN Food and Agriculture Organization
FDI	foreign direct investment
GDP	gross domestic product
GMO	genetically modified organism
ICMM	International Council on Mining and Metals
IMF	International Monetary Fund
IPO	initial public offering
IPPUC	Instituto de Pesquisa e Planejamento Urbano de Curitiba (Curitiba Institute of Urban Planning and Research)
MIT	Massachusetts Institute of Technology
NAFTA	North American Free Trade Agreement
NGO	non-governmental organisation
OECD	Organization for Economic Cooperation and Development
PAN	Partido Acción Nacional (National Action Party, Mexico)
PRI	Partido Revolucionario Institucional (Institutional Revolutionary Party, Mexico)

SAA	South African Airways
SADC	Southern African Development Community
SOE	state-owned enterprise
SWAPO	South West Africa People's Organization
SWOT	strengths and weaknesses; opportunities and threats
UAE	United Arab Emirates
UN	United Nations
UPND	United Party for National Development (Zambia)
ZNBC	Zambia National Broadcasting Corporation

Introduction

Africa faces a difficult, possibly disastrous future unless it acts quickly to consolidate democracy, liberalise its economies, invest in people and infrastructure, and ensure the rule of law.

Given sub-Saharan Africa's population is projected to double to 2 billion within a generation, without leadership taking these decisive actions to encourage long-term investments, the continent will be overwhelmed by the growth in people, especially in its cities. If the right policy and institutional actions are taken, however, they will help to create the conditions for a high-growth demographic dividend.

The nature of the challenge that Africa faces is on display on the Great East Road, which runs from the Zambian town of Chipata, on the Malawian border, to the capital, Lusaka. The journey along this national road is at best harrowing. Although the 570-kilometre road from Chipata has mostly been rebuilt, and the traffic speeds have consequently gone up, it is still a dodgem ride of four- and two-wheeled vehicles, tractors, trucks, herds of goats, cattle, oxcarts, donkey carts, pedestrians, dogs and even disabled carriages. Travelling along it, we braked to a near-stop no fewer than 20 times for errant goats. After that we stopped counting.

The trucks add further confusion, especially as the road descends towards the Luangwa River and its great 222-metre suspension bridge. Built with British aid, a plaque on the western end of the bridge commemorates its inauguration by President Kenneth Kaunda in 1968. The pinstriped paramilitary act as traffic police, allowing only one truck over at a time, whose loads consist of mainly processed food and fuel for Zambia and the Democratic Republic of the Congo, their cabs emblazoned with biblical treatises and other urgings, from 'God only Knows' to the intriguing 'Third Base'.

The road is a reflection of the situation in Zambia. There are ever-more people and they are on the move to the cities. By 2030, the population will grow from the current 16 million to about 25 million. An increasing number will be attracted to the urban areas because, despite the country's rich soils, agriculture has consistently performed below its potential, not least because of government interference in maize pricing, lack of land tenure, and difficult and expensive logistics.

Lusaka, built for 1 million people, houses 2.5 million today and will, at current rates of increase, be home to double that number in 15 years. Who will employ the young people looking for work in the next few years?

Zambia has yet to provide an answer. The presence of so much two-wheeled traffic reminds one of Kenneth Kaunda's attempts, as president of the First Republic, to spur economic diversification with the creation of a number of new domestic industries, including Luangwa Industries, which made the Eagle brand of bicycle in Chipata. Zambia also manufactured Mitsubishi trucks and cars, assembled Fiats, Peugeots and Land Rovers, produced batteries in Mansa, glass and clothing in Kapiri Mposhi and Kabwe, canned pineapples in Mwinilunga and processed cashews at Mongu. Dunlop made tyres in Ndola for export in the region; Serioes International stitched designer suits for export to the UK and Germany; Lever Brothers, Johnson & Johnson and Colgate-Palmolive manufactured household goods and toiletries; and ITT Supersonic produced televisions and radios in Livingstone.

Yet, while Zambian industries used to rank only behind Zimbabwe and South Africa in the region, by 2016, very few remained. The Chipata bicycle factory had become a beer warehouse, Livingstone Motor Assemblers (then one of only seven Fiat factories worldwide) a small timber factory, Kabwe's Mulungushi Textiles a piggery, and Kafue Textiles a maize-storage site. With the disappearance of tariff protection and the tax incentives once administered by the government's Industrial Development Corporation, the centrepiece agency for the import substitution industrialisation strategy, these industries left too. Local consumers voted with their money for cheaper, and often better-quality, imported goods.

The attempts at industrialisation were hampered not only by a lack of competitiveness and the size of Zambia's market, but also by the simultaneous nationalisation of key industries. In April 1968, Kaunda announced that the state would take control of all private retail, transport and manufacturing firms, in what came to be known as the Mulungushi Reforms. Eighteen months later, the Matero Reforms were announced, whereby the government purchased 51 per cent of shares from the existing mining companies,

Anglo American Corporation and Roan Selection Trust. In 1973 both companies were fully nationalised and transferred to the state's Zambia Consolidated Copper Mines (ZCCM). That year, the mines produced at least 720 000 tonnes of copper and employed 48 000 people.

Over time, however, burdened by poor state management, the copper industry collapsed and along with it the economy. As will be further explained in Chapter 5, ZCCM production fell to 257 000 tonnes in 2000, when it employed just 21 000 people. The contribution of mining to the economy fell from one-third of total output in 1973 to under 8 per cent 30 years later, before slowly recovering again.

And Zambia has not been able to grow other sectors that might employ new workers. For instance, the World Bank noted in 1966 that, 'There is considerable untapped agricultural potential and scope for further development of the tourist industry.'[4] This, as will be seen in Chapter 4, remains sadly the case – one of potential and promise rather than delivery and progress.

And, similarly, half a century later, tourism, a sector that should be able to generate a large number of jobs, is weighed down by continually changing regulations, a permit culture, and the cost and difficulty of getting to and around the country. Zambia's potential is poorly marketed and its national parks only partly developed. As a result, despite extraordinary offerings, including Victoria Falls, considered as one of the Seven Natural Wonders of the World, the country receives a maximum of just 150 000 international tourists a year.

Still, Zambia was a poster child for a new era of African growth in the 2000s, when its economy grew at 7 per cent annually from 2004. The country's performance was supposedly down to better governance and policies. But when the copper price went down, growth slowed, the effects worsened by an inconsistent tax policy and a spendthrift government. Zambia's economic growth fell to just 3 per cent by 2015.[5] This rate is barely enough to maintain current per capita incomes and wholly inadequate to generate the employment required by the large number of young people who will be looking for jobs in the next few years.

Zambia's particular challenges exemplify common problems across the continent.

The African reality

Africa has enjoyed an unprecedented (at least by the postcolonial record) economic growth period over the past 20 years. Since 1995, annual GDP growth across the sub-Saharan region has averaged 4.3 per cent a year, three percentage points higher than in the previous two decades.[6] As a result, (real) income levels have been lifted substantially, from $726 per capita in 1994, for example, to $984 in 2005.[7]

Such growth rates, however, have not been universal across the continent. In eight countries, income per person actually fell – starkly so in the case of Zimbabwe, by some 30 per cent. Moreover, growth has not been as pro-poor as in other regions. Whereas elsewhere in the world there has been a reduction of 2 per cent in poverty for each percentage point increase in average per capita consumption, in Africa such growth has caused a reduction of just 0.69 per cent.[8] In part, this is down to the source of Africa's growth, which is primarily the extractive (oil, gas, mining) sector, rather than agriculture or manufacturing.

This record reflects great disparities in accessing finance, education, healthcare and other basic services, and where formal employment prospects also vary greatly, including between rural and urban settings. And, in part, this slow reduction in poverty levels relates to a lack of appropriate skills and the presence of the system necessary to instil them. Whereas sub-Saharan Africa's primary-school education enrolment rates have improved in the region from under 60 per cent to 100 per cent since 1970, the rates of completion and mastery remain problematic, at just over 60 per cent compared to the global average of over 90 per cent. A high level of illiteracy results in widespread marginalisation from productive economic and social life, and is associated with poorer health and nutrition. While the official unemployment rate for the whole of sub-Saharan Africa is, at 8 per cent, only slightly above the global average of 6 per cent,[9] *underemployment* is much higher. Many of those denoted as having work are self-employed or in poorly-paying jobs. Africans are working to survive, but, by and large, they are poor.[10]

Moreover, the good times are now over because of the commodity-price slump and uncertainty in the world market. Growth in 2016 across sub-Saharan Africa was projected to be 1.4 per cent – less than half of the 3.5 per cent in 2015 and far below the growth trend over the previous two decades.[11]

Before the commodity collapse, observers had commonly exclaimed Africa as 'on the march' or, in contemporary parlance, 'rising'.[12] Not surprisingly, given the fog of despair that has frequently enveloped the continent, a small industry quickly developed around the better prospects for Africa, based sometimes on a combination of hubris, faith and anecdotal data. For example, *The Economist* has noted that 'Africa's 1.2 billion people … hold plenty of promise. They are young: south of the Sahara, their median age is below 25 everywhere except in South Africa. They are better educated than ever before: literacy rates among the young now exceed 70 per cent everywhere other than in a band of desert countries across the Sahara.' This, according to the article, is the continent exemplified by 'Nairobi's thriving malls and Abidjan's humming ports', as well as less conflict and improved healthcare.[13]

Africa's level of poverty has been falling (from 61 per cent in 1994 to 43 per cent 20 years later).[14] Nevertheless, Africa houses about half the world's extreme poor, and the bulk of the world's fragile states, where reform and recovery are tenuous. It has a long way to claw back on the lost decades of the 1960s, 1970s and 1980s when development in East Asia, to take a regional example, surged. As the World Bank estimated for Africa back in 2000, 'With the region's rapidly growing population, five per cent annual growth was needed simply to keep the number of poor from rising. Halving severe poverty by 2015 would', it noted, 'require annual growth of more than seven per cent, along with a more equitable distribution of income.'[15]

Even before the commodity collapse, there had not been a substantial transformation of the income structure in the vast majority of countries on the continent. As *The Economist* has argued:[16] 'Some 90 per cent of Africans still fall below the threshold of $10 a day,' while 'the proportion in the $10–$20 middle class (excluding very atypical South Africa), rose from 4.4 per cent to only 6.2 per cent between 2004 and 2014'. Moreover, 'over the same decade, the proportion defined as "upper middle" ($20–$50 a day) went from … 1.4 per cent to 2.3 per cent.' It notes that there may be 'only 15 million middle class households in 11 of sub-Saharan Africa's bigger economies (excluding South Africa and using a range of $15–$115 a day)'.

Africa's improved economic growth in this century was a significant achievement. However, more will have to be done for a sustained period in the future, especially as the commodity boom of the early part of the century is unlikely to be repeated.[17] The stakes will become even higher when the huge surge of population growth hits countries across Africa.

People: The fundamental challenge for Africa

This book asks the most fundamental question for Africa and for those concerned about significantly reducing world poverty. Can Africa follow East Asia and significantly reduce the number of people living on low incomes and reap the related gains in infant mortality, child and maternal health, education and well-being that other nations, once thought to be hopeless, have achieved in recent years? In particular, in light of the enormous increase in populations that will occur across the continent, will enough jobs be generated to employ the resulting massive number of young people?

We believe that these questions must be answered now in order to prepare economies for the coming demographic reality. Waiting until populations have substantially increased will mean that leaders will only be able to offer measures that come too late for their unemployed citizens. Africa's total population is expected to more than double by 2050 to 2.4 billion. According to the UN, Africa is expected to account for more than half of the world's population growth between 2015 and 2050. Nearly all of this growth will be among the 49 countries of sub-Saharan Africa, comprising 2 billion of this figure. This book is mainly focused on this demographic phenomenon.[18] Even the rapid expansion of Asia's population pales in comparison: that continent will have grown by a factor of 3.7 between 1950 and 2050, whereas Africa's equivalent factor is predicted to be 5.18 from 2000 to 2100.[19]

The Swedish statistician Hans Rosling has noted that, '[t]he reason the population is growing in Africa is the same reason that [saw] population growth first in Europe, then in the Americas, then in Asia. It's when the population goes from a phase where you have many children born and many who are dying. Then the death rate goes down and [some time later] the birth rate follows.'[20]

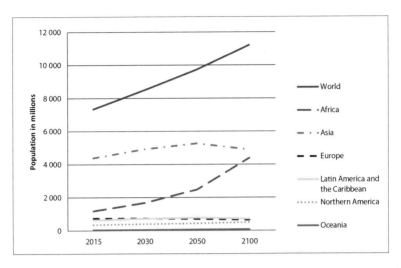

Figure 1: UN medium variant population predictions, 2015–2100

Source: UN Department of Economic and Social Affairs, Population Division. World Urbanisation Prospects: The 2014 Revision, https://esa.un.org/unpd/wpp/DataQuery/

Between now and 2050, the populations of 28 African countries are projected to more than double. By 2100, 10 African countries are projected to have increased their populations at least fivefold: Angola, Burundi, Democratic Republic of the Congo, Malawi, Mali, Niger, Somalia, Tanzania, Uganda and Zambia. There is a link between poverty and population growth, where the latter is especially high in the group of 48 countries designated by the UN as the least developed countries, of which 27 are in Africa. Africa's increases are projected despite an anticipated substantial reduction of fertility levels. The UN's medium variant projection assumes that average fertility will fall from 4.7 children per woman in Africa (in 2010 to 2015) to 3.1 from 2045 to 2050, reaching 2.2 by 2095 to 2100. After 2050, Africa is expected to be the only major continent still experiencing substantial population growth. As a result, the continent's share of global population is projected to grow to 25 per cent by 2050 and 39 per cent by 2100.

To highlight the disruptive nature of the population growth that Africa will experience, Figure 2 displays the growth of three countries: Burundi (relatively small), Ghana (a medium-sized country) and Nigeria (the continent's behemoth).[21]

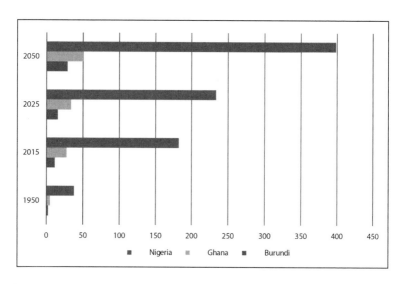

Figure 2: National populations in selected years (in millions), 1950–2050

Source: UN Department of Economic and Social Affairs, Population Division. World Urbanisation Prospects: The 2014 Revision, https://esa.un.org/unpd/wpp/DataQuery/

Each country's population will have grown by an order of magnitude between 1950 and 2050. In the relatively short period (by demographic standards) between 2015 and 2025, they will grow between 20 per cent (Ghana), 33 per cent (Burundi) and Nigeria by 31 per cent. Therefore, all three will certainly be radically different in 2035 compared to their populations in 2015.

Africa's population growth compared to the rest of the world's demographic decline means that it will be increasingly differentiated by the age of its population. Africa will be much younger than the rest of the world. As *The Economist* has noted, 'Africans will make up a bigger and bigger share of the world's young people: by 2100, they will account for 48 per cent of those aged 14 and under.'[22] Or, put differently, 10 of the world's youngest countries are in Africa.[23]

Niger is both Africa's and the world's most youthful country, with a median age of just 14.8, half the global figure of 29.6 years, a function of a high birth rate and low life expectancy. The average fertility rate in Niger is 7.6 children, compared to a global figure of 2.5, and life expectancy is just

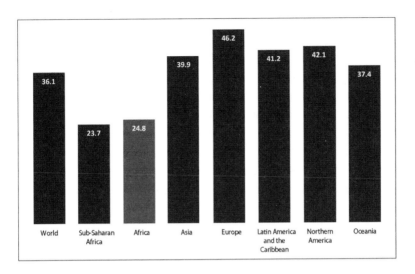

Figure 3: Projected median age of total population in 2050

Source: UN Department of Economic and Social Affairs, Population Division. World Urbanisation Prospects: The 2014 Revision, https://esa.un.org/unpd/wpp/DataQuery/

58 years. Uganda is the world's second most youthful country, and Chad the third, where the median age is 16.

By contrast, much of the rest of the world is ageing. In 2015 the segment of the population over 60 was equivalent to 12 per cent of the global population. At the current growth rates of over 3.2 per cent per annum, by 2050 all major continents of the world except Africa will have nearly a quarter or more of their populations aged 60 or over.

If properly harnessed, and properly planned for, Africa's population increase and the resultant proportion of so many young people present a tremendous force for change, providing opportunities to fill the resulting labour-force gap. (A similar situation is seen in other parts of the world where ageing populations create an opportunity to provide services for that age group.) Sixty per cent of Africa's population and 45 per cent of the labour force are under 25, with some 10 to 12 million youths entering the labour market every year. Youth as a proportion of the total population is projected at over 75 per cent by 2015, and is not expected to decline before another generation or more. The World Bank, for example, has estimated that the demographic dividend could generate 11 to 15 per cent GDP growth between 2011 and 2030. But such growth depends on providing improved education and skills, suitable infrastructure and the systems to employ young people, as well as efficient government to make it all happen.

Without such planning and a conducive set of policies for development, there could ensue a demographic disaster and a spur for social unrest and increased migration both within Africa, and to Europe and elsewhere. The choice is in the hands of Africa's policymakers.

Critically, the large number of young people who will come of age in the next few years will need jobs.

The International Monetary Fund (IMF) has estimated that, in order to maximise its booming population dividend, the continent will need to produce an average of 18 million high-productivity jobs per year until 2035. The surge in young people will necessitate an extremely rapid, possibly unprecedented, rate of job creation. The IMF also notes that over this period policies are required to gradually transition jobs from the informal sector, which accounts for about 90 per cent of the 400 million jobs in low-income sub-Saharan African countries, to the formal sector.[24]

To date, Africa's job creation has not kept up with existing birth rates. The *African Economic Outlook 2015*, for example, reports that only 7 per cent of the continental population aged 15 to 24 in low-income countries had a 'decent' job. In African middle-income countries, this figure increased marginally, to 10 per cent.[25] Underlining the challenge, the World Bank has forecast that, by 2030, despite major efforts, some 19 per cent of Africa's population will still live in poverty. Those 300 million people will then represent 80 per cent of the global population living on less than the (2005 equivalent of) $1.25 a day.[26]

The risks stemming from large numbers of digitally connected youths without jobs are high.[27] They are unlikely to sit idly by waiting for change: they will demand it. In the future, increasingly, the political focus will shift to the cities, the youth and to the technologies that they employ.

At the same time, where people live and work in Africa is changing. The countries south of the Sahara, are projected to constitute the most rapidly urbanising region on the planet. The percentage of people living in this region's cities will rise by 16 per cent to reach a level of 56 per cent by

2050.[28] Over this period, some 2.5 billion people will be added to the urban population worldwide, with almost 90 per cent of the increase occurring in Asia and Africa.[29] For example, Lagos – which had a population of 1.4 million in 1970, and 5 million in 1991 – will increase to 25 million by 2020, rivalling Cairo as the continent's most populous city. Africa's urban growth will far outpace the historical rate of developed and developing regions. While the population of London grew at 2 per cent annually from 1800 to 1910, doubling every 35 years, some African cities' populations are doubling every 10 years, with growth rates at over 7 per cent annually.[30]

So far, as will be seen, African urbanisation has not correlated with economic growth on a similar scale to that experienced elsewhere. As the World Bank has put it, African cities 'cannot be characterised as economically dense, connected, and liveable. Instead, they are crowded, disconnected, and costly.'[31] Urban migrants have largely moved from low-productivity jobs in rural communities to equally inefficient jobs in lower-income urban areas. Neither the migrants nor African economies have enjoyed the economic benefits of urban agglomerations, concentrations of labour, or economies of scale.

The inevitability of a fast-growing population increasingly concentrated in the cities is a game changer for Africa one way or the other.

The old policies that featured to varying degrees across the continent – state interference in the economy, corruption and a failure to concentrate on growth – will not only fail to serve the population but, worse still, if these policies remain unchanged, will condemn leaders to an increasingly restive citizenry. These conditions have the potential to destabilise governments and end the tenure of low-performing rulers. In a more crowded and urbanised Africa, the fate of leaders will, in the future, be much more directly tied to economic performance.

Commodities: Dealing with the bust

During the commodity boom there was considerable optimism that African economies were changing and that they were no longer dependent on exports of raw materials. In 2010, the McKinsey Global Institute claimed that the 'commodity boom explains only part of Africa's growth story.

Natural resources directly accounted for just 24 per cent of Africa's GDP growth from 2000 to 2008.' McKinsey argued that 'the key reasons behind Africa's growth surge were improved political and macroeconomic stability and microeconomic reforms.' However, hedging its bets, McKinsey believed that the continent would continue to benefit from 'rising global demand for oil, natural gas, minerals, food, arable land, and other natural resources'.[32]

This analysis informed McKinsey's upbeat 2010 *Lions on the Move* report about Africa.[33] This report states: 'We find that Africa's economic growth surge was widespread across countries and sectors and that its roots extend far beyond the global commodity boom', noting 'Africa's business opportunities are potentially very large, particularly for companies in consumer-facing industries (such as retail, telecommunications and banking); infrastructure-related industries; across the agriculture-related value chain; and in resource-related industries'. The report declares: 'Global executives and investors cannot afford to ignore the continent's immense potential.'

As China's demand has slowed, however, it is clear that the argument about Africa's minimal dependence on commodities as a driver of growth was wrong. McKinsey underestimated the influence that raw material exports had on the domestic economy as a whole. It is also clear that the report was off the mark about the pace and extent of improving governance and the appetite of African governments to pursue policy change. Six years later, McKinsey revisited its African thesis in *Lions on the Move 2*.[34] The second iteration acknowledged Africa's slowing growth and the divergent paths of its countries. 'Some countries have continued to grow fast while others have experienced a marked slowdown as a result of lower resource prices and higher socio-political instability,' concedes the report. Progress requires governments and 'Africa's companies to step up their performance'.

Whatever the value and accuracy of such bold predictions, it is clear that African economic growth cannot continue to rely on commodities, not only because the continued demand is questionable, but also because commodities do not provide the jobs that Africa needs. The price upswing was driven primarily by demand from China, which grew its share of worldwide metals consumption from 6.4 per cent in 1990 to 43.9 per cent in 2015. However, China's annual increase in metals consumption has slowed from 10.3 per cent during the period 1995 to 2008, to 3.2 per cent during

2010 to 2014.[35] China's growth rates are expected to continue to decline as it transitions from a manufacturing economy to one focused on services and consumption.

The end of the commodity super-cycle has been followed by the drying up of other funding sources. In the decade from 2005, 17 African countries issued dollar denominated bonds to foreign investors as investors looked to Africa for higher yields. Ghana's debut dollar bond was four times oversubscribed. Zambia's 10-year bond, issued in 2012, was 24 times oversubscribed, selling at a yield of 5.6 per cent.

Debt cancellation for 30 African countries brought down external debt in the region from a peak of 76 per cent of GDP in 1994 to 25 per cent by 2008, enabling African governments to take on fresh loans. While nearly $14 billion in debt was issued during 2014 and 2015, the market has slowed as a result of lower commodity prices and weakening African currencies, and as rising interest rates elsewhere took root.[36] Although the continent's median debt-to-GDP level is only 42 per cent, in some of the previous boom economies, including Zambia, it had risen through the 50 per cent levels and in Ghana to over 70 per cent. Unless things change, African liquidity is likely to worsen as the repayment date of these bonds, mostly after 2020, arrives.[37]

Furthermore, it does not appear that many African countries took advantage of the 'fat' years of high commodity prices to fundamentally change their institutions, policies and politics. The Heritage Foundation's Index of Economic Freedom is a comprehensive rating scheme that evaluates countries based on rule of law, fiscal performance, regulation and openness of markets. The index is not perfect – no system that seeks to rate all countries is – but it does allow for consistent comparisons across nations and across eras.

Between 2010 and 2015, according to this index, Africa did not make much progress. The average ranking of countries in the region increased from 54.07 to 54.95 (the highest, Hong Kong, is 89.6). In the rankings, the African continent moved from a position that would have been (in the 2015 table) more or less tied with Surinam, at number 129, to being about equal to Egypt at number 124.[38]

Africa's unimpressive improvement in governance is confirmed in other rankings. The 2016 Ibrahim Index of African Governance,[39] the 10th produced by the Mo Ibrahim Foundation, recorded a slight improvement in overall governance of one point over the previous decade. But underneath this headline sit some disturbing trends. In 2015 almost two-thirds of African citizens lived in a country where safety and rule of law had deteriorated over the previous 10 years. The continental average score for the corruption and bureaucracy indicator has also declined over the last decade, with 33 countries registering deterioration, 24 of them falling to their worst ever score in 2015. And two-thirds of the countries on the continent, representing 67 per cent of the African population, have shown deterioration in freedom of expression over the past 10 years.[40]

Regulatory and administrative processes are critical determinants in ensuring decent growth and providing jobs, as other regions illustrate. In fact, as Paul Collier has commented, when commodity prices are low is the ideal time to reset the rules because all actors will understand that they cannot just ride the tide of high prices, and that governance will therefore be critical to promoting growth.

Though no one can predict the future course of commodity prices, and many who have tried have ended up looking foolish, it seems that prices have returned to the 'old normal'. It would be reckless to believe that the high prices of the last decade will return any time soon, if ever.

Better practice: What development looks like

Despite the challenges Africa faces, we are still hopeful about the continent, because other countries have managed to overcome what seemed to be similarly insurmountable barriers. Poverty is not inevitable. An enormous amount is now known, worldwide, about how to grow economies and improve standards of living.

By the end of 2015, less than 10 per cent of the world's population lived in extreme poverty, despite the use of a new daily income figure of $1.90 to define this category, up from $1.25.[41] In fact, despite protestations about rising inequality between rich and poor, the last few decades have seen the largest reduction in poverty in world history. In the 20 years from 1990, the number of people living in extreme poverty fell by half as a share of the total population in developing countries to 21 per cent, a reduction of nearly 1 billion people.

Much of the reduction in poverty is due to developments in East Asia. China's economic progress has been responsible for three-quarters of this effect, by lifting 680 million people out of misery in the 30 years from 1980. It has reduced its extreme-poverty rate from 84 per cent to just 10 per cent in 33 years.[42]

Poverty rates have declined during the last 30 years, in large part, because growth in developing countries rose from an average annual rate of 4.3 per cent from 1960 until 2000 to 6 per cent between 2000 and 2010. It is estimated that around two-thirds of poverty reduction has been a result of growth.

But there is also widespread international recognition and support for the need to go much further, as highlighted by the adoption, on 25 September 2015, by the UN General Assembly of 17 'aspirational' Sustainable Development Goals, the successors to the Millennium Development Goals.[43] The extent of poverty in Africa is brought into sharper focus, too, as is noted above, by increasing urbanisation across the continent, where dearth and excess exist in close proximity, and by concerns about the rising inequality worldwide between generations. Whereas, in the past, subsequent generations had an expectation of higher incomes than those born earlier, this may no longer be the case.

Indeed, we do not for one moment underestimate the challenges that African governments face in promoting growth and reducing poverty. The book will, in some detail, describe the very hard choices that African leaders will need to make to change many of the standard operating practices that have developed during the half century or since the independence of most African countries.

At the same time, studies of developing countries worldwide illustrate the need for sustained efforts at promoting governance for extraordinary economic change. In the 1950s, for example, economic development in East Asia was thought to be a difficult, perhaps impossible, task, not least because of so-called 'cultural' aspects, including Confucianism. China for many years was similarly seen as hopeless.

Although no country or region is a complete analogue to any other, the East Asian experience does illustrate the astonishing results that a determined government can deliver.

Singapore, which obtained its independence in 1965, a year after

Zambia, illustrates a tale of two countries and continents. Zambia's per capita income in 2016 was, at $1 000, just over three times greater than at independence in 1964; Singapore's GDP per capita at $56 284 was over 50 times more than it was in 1965. It is difficult to think of contemporary Singapore as a fragile, poor backwater. Yet it was born in crisis out of the separation of the Malay Federation, amid the *konfrontasi*[44] with Indonesia, and riven with multiracial, ethnic and religious sensitivities and differences. While the state under Lee Kuan Yew was at the helm of this transformation, its actions were always guided by commercial principles, and balanced by a devolution of power and shared responsibility among fellow 'founding fathers'.[45]

Much can be learnt about Africa's prospects from what Singapore has accomplished. Despite many opportunities, however, the lessons from this and similar transformations have not been grasped.

Ironically, Africa appeared to go in the opposite direction. 'In 1968,' recalls the former prime minister of Kenya Raila Odinga, 'a team of Singaporeans came to Kenya to learn our lessons, since we were then a more developed country than they were.' Forty years later, Odinga says, 'As prime minister, I took a study trip to Singapore with six ministers. That was the latest in many trips taken by the Kenyan government, about which no report was ever written, and where the participants kept everything to themselves. I said that this trip had to be different, that we had to translate our findings into actions. On our return, I asked for a plan of action from each minister on the basis of what they had learnt from Singapore, since there was no point in reinventing the wheel. Each minister was tasked to prepare their action plan against our Vision 2030.' But after he left government in 2013, Odinga depressingly observes, 'nothing further happened'.[46]

Yet East Asia seemed to have few advantages over Africa at the point of decolonisation. Traditional East Asian societies were often characterised by ethnic disunity, frail institutions and limited governance outside of the capital, weak democracy, subsistence agriculture, fragmentary external trade linkages and acute social stratification. These conditions were prevalent, too, in many African states.[47] Both continents shared a history of colonial (and commodity) exploitation, where the conquerors were sharply divided from the conquered by race, though there was a tendency on the part of the colonial rulers to favour some local groups over others. And in both

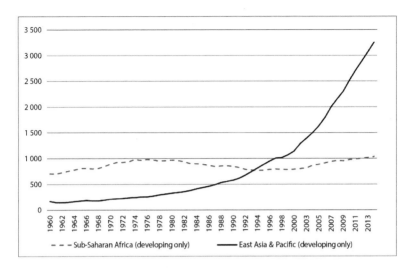

Figure 4: East Asia and Africa compared: 50 years of per capita income (in 2005 $), 1960–2013

Source: World Bank national accounts data and OECD national accounts data files, http://databank.worldbank.org/data/reports.aspx?source=world-development-indicators&preview=on#

continents settlers were imposed on the local groups, arousing intense hostility.[48] This left them not only with unnatural borders and poor terms of trade, but their people were also left with a devalued sense of their own worth, angry with outsiders yet lacking confidence in their own abilities and suspicious of their fellow country people.

Yet the East Asia region has prospered. As Barack Obama observed during his first visit to the African continent as American president in July 2009,[49] colonialism alone does not explain the tribalism, patronage, nepotism, corruption and self-destructive policies that have caused the continent's development to slip so far behind its people's needs and its peers in other regions.

While most East Asian countries had to accept a complex ethnic make-up as a result of colonial involvement, as with Africa, this has not in most cases resulted in endemic instability. East Asia, too, has had to cope with underdeveloped human capital, yet its states have, by and large, quickly turned their people into an asset through investment in education. While Africa's institutional capacity is cited as a structural developmental impediment, some countries in South East Asia have grown economically with institutions at independence far worse resourced than those in African countries.

In fact, in some respects, African countries were better off than their Asian counterparts at independence. Few African countries, after all, can claim the bitter cost and devastation wrought by the scale of conflict in Vietnam, Laos and Cambodia.

Despite the contemporary fad to bash aid as the explanation for all of Africa's problems, [50] Asian countries have also received comparatively large amounts of donor assistance. During the 1960s, aid per capita received by both regions was similar. Whereas some Asian countries enjoyed especially large aid flows (such as South Korea and Taiwan), and continue to do so (Vietnam), they did not allow themselves to become dependent on this single source of income. Asian countries have put aid to good use, because of improved governance, sound polices, effective planning and clearer, firmer local ownership of projects. [51]

East Asian states that attempted top-down, centrally planned economic control and development were a disaster, just as the model has, too, proven a disaster in those African and other nations that have tried to take this path, no matter how intellectually coherent and tempting it might have been to the postcolonial leadership. Both regions suffered from characteristic problems of socialist gigantism and exploitation. However, those Asian countries – China, Cambodia and Vietnam, for example – that moved off this system immediately prospered.

A better policy environment also helps to explain why some East Asian countries have used their significant natural-resource endowment to their advantage (Vietnam, again, or Malaysia, for example) without becoming overly locked into natural-resource production and hence vulnerable to price fluctuations.

The difference in development results between East Asia and Africa does not originate either in political systems, even though, for some, East Asia's development success has been used to justify authoritarianism, given that the region's economies have managed high economic growth rates without conferring full political rights on its citizens.

Democracy and development

Given Africa's historical, postcolonial experience, we suggest that democracy and development go hand in hand. It is not one or the other, democracy or growth, but these aspects are mutually reinforcing, however attractive African leaders (and some outsiders) might find authoritarianism as a system of government that 'gets things done'.

As described in Chapter 2, many African leaders have responded to the overwhelming wishes of their citizens by changing from autocratic regimes – the preferred system of government from the 1960s to the 1980s – to electoral democracies. There has been backsliding, inevitably, and many of the institutions and elections that have undergirded them have been imperfect. There are other very good reasons for maintaining these democracies over an anecdotal preference for a 'benevolent dictator'. For one, as is examined later, such benign autocrats committed to popular welfare, as in the East Asian model, have been few and far between in Africa. Moreover, the empirical evidence is clear: Africa's democracies develop faster, are safer for the incumbents and are richer than the alternatives.

So far, it has proven difficult to duplicate East Asia's model of soft authoritarianism in Africa. Because Singapore, for example, is a small and compact island, its leaders could argue that the population had to make sacrifices given the realistic challenges that Malaysia and Indonesia would pose if Singapore remained a poor country. Further, few African countries, given the challenges they face, have seen or can realistically expect the 'legitimacy through performance' that was central to gaining and maintaining the confidence that the island's citizens had in its impressive leaders.

There are many other aspects of East Asia's relative economic success that have been similarly overlooked by advocates for autocracies. These include high spending on education, bureaucratic responsiveness, creating an attractive policy for business investment, low wages, high productivity, investment in infrastructure, raised agricultural outputs as an initial spur to growth and an overwhelming focus on competitiveness.

Overall, the most notable differentiating factor between Africa and East Asia is, as highlighted in this volume, the relationship between government and the private sector. Private-sector growth in Africa has largely been an anathema, and not just in the period after independence. The colonialists

– be they British, French, Portuguese or Belgian – whatever their ideologies in Europe, established highly interventionist states that actively prevented indigenous African economic enrichment, while protecting white settlers, colonial companies and monopoly capital.

By and large, the African leaders that emerged after independence were comfortable with the economic systems they inherited (once stripped of racism), especially as state intervention offered many patronage opportunities. Expanding state control and intervention was one of the few levers open to them in the context of overall state weakness. This pattern was exaggerated by the failure of such liberators to have a plan beyond redistribution to their preferred constituents.[52] Subsequently, African elites have remained largely uninterested in major reform and liberalisation, apart from 'opening up' the system in piecemeal fashion (from cellphone companies to infrastructure investments), and in a way that has reduced any threat to the status quo.

Therefore, investment growth that diversifies the economies and creates jobs in Africa, notably in industry, has remained very low.

Instilling a sense of urgency and ownership

Beggars work the traffic lights in the city of Fes. They are sub-Saharans, our Moroccan colleague tells us. 'They are working their way through the country to get to Europe.' There were, in 2016, an estimated 1 million sub-Saharan African migrants waiting along the North African coast – mostly in Morocco, Algeria and Libya – intent on making their way to mainland Europe. In the Sahel, the city of Agadez in Niger (since the 15th century a gateway between West and North Africa) had become an epicentre in migrant smuggling, with more than 20 000 passing through monthly in 2016, most from West Africa, and Nigeria in particular.[53]

Given the continent's projected population increase, without economic growth Africa's poverty threatens to overwhelm Europe. While Europe will work to secure its borders, and to find and fund the means to keep Africans in Africa, Europeans cannot be expected to be more successful at encouraging and improving African economic growth than Africans themselves, or more committed to this task.

Yet, compared to East Asia, in Africa there has not been the same sense of urgency or the need to introduce reforms in response to this looming crisis, particularly those reforms aimed at radically increasing economic growth and numbers of jobs. In part, this reflects hostility to foreign capital. It also relates to lack of capacity and poor leadership. And it reflects a failure to learn from the experience of others.

The continent's ambitions should not be to duplicate the Asian path, but to learn from Asia and other fast-growing regions to create a vision to ensure that leaders and citizens can flourish together. Having a 'good' crisis – that is, using the opportunity crisis brings to usher in difficult and heretofore politically unpalatable changes – has been a key element in catalysing reform in Asia and Latin America, including, among others Colombia, Chile, El Salvador and Costa Rica.

While identifying and using a sense of crisis, African leaders will have to strive to escape the 'tyranny of the emergency' and instead create a common vision of how their countries will progress. We were reminded by one colleague that 'a disciplined nationalism is the secret sauce of development'. This can be interpreted as the deep commitment to popular welfare exhibited by East Asian leaders, whatever the system of formal government. Failure to develop a common vision by which societies as a whole can advance will mean that leaders will not be able to explain the actions in a wider context, critical constituencies will not understand why they are being asked to make sacrifices, and political stability will inevitably be endangered.

Just as the arguments for addressing this crisis go beyond statistics to a human story of hope and fear, so do the methods. Colonialism and racial exclusion left a deep scar of injustice and rivalry. This has left a legacy of suspicion towards business, and, in particular, foreign enterprises. In this environment, emotion is as important in appreciating the policy options as empiricism.

Leaders will need therefore, at the outset, to develop a 'growth ideology' beyond the vacuous vision documents that litter the policy landscape. Rather than employing more consultants, governments and ruling parties will need to drop their animosity towards business. Such an approach calls for government to come to an understanding with business, and to remedy stultifying attitudes that vary from benign neglect to ostentatious antagonism. Business, for its part, needs to clearly understand and deliver on its wider social responsibilities in an open and transparent fashion, designed to build and maintain trust. A failure to achieve this amid a rapid population increase brings the risk of accelerating a social and political crisis, and, ultimately, state failure and, thereby, widespread human tragedy.

The chapters that follow address the critical sectors that make up the economies of Africa's countries, and illustrate modes of reform and best practice.

Part 1

The state of Africa's people, institutions and structures

Chapter 1
People and cities

Five steps for success:
- Cities must be seen as drivers of Africa's diversified growth and jobs. Urban-centred growth represents a dramatic change from the export of natural resources, which has been central to most African economies.
- Urgent action is the only way to address the pending urban-population explosion.
- Focus on city-level funding and authority as a means to redefine the resources to enable local governments to meet the challenge of quickly expanding populations.
- Promote density of housing and cost-efficient transport solutions to realise the urban dividend.
- Focus on the provision of local security as the door through which much else follows.

Challenges and opportunities: So far, the rapid increase in Africa's population has not been matched with a growth in jobs. Urbanisation in Africa does not yet appear to be delivering the improvements in economic growth and quality of life achieved elsewhere, notably in Asia. Instead, African cities are growing in a largely unplanned manner, stretching existing infrastructure and services to beyond breaking point and failing to improve productivity and create jobs. Whether a population surge turns out to be a good or a bad thing depends, largely, on how government responds, enables job creation and improves the absorption of people into the private sector.

Key statistics: According to the 2016 Ibrahim Index of African Governance, 33 African countries have experienced a decline in safety and rule of law since 2006, nearly half of them quite substantially. Almost half of the countries on the continent recorded their worst ever score in this category in the period 2013 to 2015. The index has 'demonstrated a strong link between Safety & Rule of Law and governance performance'.[1]

Hillbrow is the most densely populated part of the City of Johannesburg. It's a potpourri of nationalities, customs, cuisine and language, a blur between informal and formal, legal and illegal. A dip into its labyrinth reveals a fable of the modern African city.

Our guide is Brighton.[2] He left the army in Zimbabwe in 2005 'for greener pastures,' he says, and has been working as a security guard at a school since 2009. 'No single group dominates the suburbs,' he says as we drive east, although, of course, there are pockets of ethnic flavours. 'More Somalis and Bangladeshis live in Mayfair,' he notes, as we drive down the high street. 'There are more students here,' he says, pointing at a young couple lounging on a balcony in Berea. 'But everyone is mixed up – Nigerians, Ghanaians, Zimbabweans, Malawians, Mozambicans. We all become South Africans to survive.'

The suburb of Hillbrow is a rectangular shape running north–south, covering a little over a square kilometre and officially housing 100 000 people, perhaps twice that number, compared to Johannesburg's average of just under 2 500 per square kilometre.

One of the 50 largest cities worldwide, and the wealthiest in South Africa, Johannesburg was founded on the riches beneath its soil. It is home to 7 million people, the bulk of the population of the province of Gauteng, the heartland of South Africa's economy.

Today, Hillbrow is synonymous with a collapse in governance in the 1990s and the flight of wealthy white South Africans to the north of Johannesburg or farther afield. There is in-your-face evidence of illegality – Brighton eagerly points out a queue of men waiting to buy drugs from a plain-clothes policeman who has hopped out of the back of a passing van in O'Reilly Road. When asked what sort of drugs, 'Marijuana, crack, [the heroin-based] *unga* … whatever you want' comes the reply. It seems drink is the greater devil, however, with constant 'watch out for him' references to the stone-faced drunk standing dead centre in the road or tottering off the pavement.

But it's not so much the illegality as the coexistence of informality and more formal trade that is striking. Food kiosks and vegetable sellers operate on the sidewalk in front of the ubiquitous pawn shops, shebeens, barbers' shops, surgeries, strip joints, electronics outlets and butcheries, no-name businesses alongside high-street brands. Hillbrow's businesses are, if anything, increasingly off the grid. A visit to the electronics traders in Esselen, Twist and Kotze streets, mostly run by Ibos and Bangladeshis, hints at a trend of increasing informalisation. No television licences are asked or quoted for, as is legally obligatory, or VAT, for that matter. For them, the cost of joining the formal sector, including paying tax, is greater than the advantages. It's all in the margin.

Further east, on Yeoville's Raleigh Street, is the relatively orderly Congo Market. Inside, stalls run by Congolese and Nigerians sell blackened, smoked vundu, mostly from Zambia, salted, eviscerated tilapia, yams, brightly coloured Congolese wax fabrics, orange chillies and chilli oil, aubergines, sundry tins of groceries and plastic packets of tofu, rice and semolina. The prices are all much the same from stall to stall, and competitive.

Overlooking Hillbrow is Ponte City, a 54-storey, 173-metre-high steel and concrete toilet roll, the tallest residential tower on the continent. It was built in 1975, when Hillbrow enjoyed the moniker the 'Manhattan of Africa'.

Designed by 29-year-old architect Rodney Grosskopff, as a symbol of 1970s skyscraper living and aspiration, Ponte was one of the first victims of inner-city decay as the middle class and their businesses fled for safer and more prosperous surrounds. By the late 1990s, rubbish had piled up five storeys high inside the building's inner cylinder as the tower found itself engulfed by an area rife with crime, drugs, prostitution and guns. There was talk of turning it into a prison. Fifteen years later, however, Ponte City has been renovated and revitalised, and is now home to 3 000 students, professionals and workers, including South Africans, Nigerians, Congolese and Zimbabweans, all carefully choosing to ignore the Nigerians washing cars at the entrance and holding their noses against the thick smoke from burning rubbish. The monthly rent for a large flat is R5 000 – it's good value and convenient, whatever the challenges of negotiating the vagaries of Primrose Terrace and Ponte's neighbourhood.

'Our residences have got to go up,' says Grosskopff, 'otherwise we'll never get to work with the commuting distances and traffic involved. The question,' he asks, 'is not whether it's the logical or scientific way to go; it's whether society prefers it and will allow it?'[3] And living where you work does significantly reduce the premium of transport.

Hillbrow is not an isolated case of unplanned African growth and unrealised development potential – far from it. Just past the signs declaring 'No Idling Allowed', a facsimile of two giant elephant tusks welcomes visitors to Mombasa's Daniel arap Moi International Airport. At the start of 2016, major construction was under way, widening Barack Obama Road first to four lanes and then to eight from the Changamwe roundabout to Mariakani, 36 kilometres north-west of Mombasa, on the road to Nairobi.

The route through Mombasa to the Makupa Causeway, linking Mombasa Island to the mainland, is lined with dusty roadside stalls, their tatty tin frontages offering similar items: food, vegetables, fruit, Pepsi, Coke, airtime, shoes, clothes, cosmetics, books, building materials, and just about anything imaginable. The truck in front, its tailgate emblazoned with the words 'Believe me I will be there', weaves to avoid the *tuk-tuks* (when you switch on the engine they pronounce their name), *boda-bodas* (motorcycle taxis) and *matatus* (minibuses), and works its way around the other trucks straddling the pavement and road.

The Vatican Hotel, despite its name, offers little divine guidance at the busy Makupa roundabout leading onto Kenyatta Avenue, named after the country's founding leader, where hawkers offer 10-shilling bags of peanuts, sliced pineapples, bananas and second-hand clothes. The traffic weaves to avoid the barrows laden with vegetables, fruit and household commodities, and their sweating human pushers. The four-lane Nyali Bridge, spanning the sea, provides the only route north and is next to the site of a new, top-end residential apartment development. To the south, plans are afoot to build a bridge to supplement the existing clumsy and time-consuming ferry service.

Visitors to Mombasa would have been astounded by the ease of the flow of traffic today, even without the new infrastructure under construction. Apparently, according to the driver, President Uhuru Kenyatta came to the coast for a month and things got tidied up. The solution was simple: increase the number of lanes depending on the flow of traffic, and allocate traffic officers to police key intersections.

As the primary port in East Africa, Mombasa is the centre of the coastal tourism industry in Kenya. Although it has the potential to serve as a motor of growth for Kenya and the East Africa region, Mombasa processes the same amount of cargo (780 000 containers[4]) in one year that the world's most active ports (Shanghai and Singapore) handle in a week.[5]

Beyond the port, Mombasa continues to struggle to develop its economy. It's a costly place to do business. Despite being the second-largest city in Kenya and one of its most prominent economic hubs, it ranked only sixth out of 13 Kenyan cities in the World Bank's Ease of Doing Business Index.[6] Access to finance is limited, and job and market information scarce.[7] About 80 per cent of Mombasa's population of 1.2 million live in informal settlements, which cover more than 90 per cent of the land area, and almost 40 per cent live below the poverty line.[8]

The majority participate only, or at least predominantly, in the informal sector, doing low value-added jobs.

There are also layers of insecurity, related both to Mombasa's role as a transit point for drugs and the legendary corruption among port officials and customs officers. The city's predominantly Muslim character adds further complexity. Between 2012 and 2014, for example, no fewer than 21 Islamic clerics were gunned down in the city. Radicalism and criminality have appeal in the absence of other opportunities.[9] Some of Mombasa's youth have, in particular, declared that they are 'no longer part of Kenya'.[10]

Given its strategic location as the gateway to East Africa, Mombasa is so far a missed development opportunity, where the downsides of crime and terrorism both demonstrate and exacerbate the costs of weak governance. Dealing with the root causes will demand action on a wide range of fronts, from improving the efficiency of the port, which requires hitherto unseen levels of political will, to breaking and reshaping corrupt systems, to investment in both hard and soft educational and vocational infrastructure. It's a big task.

Hillbrow and Mombasa are illustrative of Africa's looming urban and demographic challenges, though cities hold out the promise of accelerated development.

The advantage of cities

In Europe the focus is now on African migration across the Mediterranean. The International Organization for Migration estimates that more than a million migrants arrived in Europe by sea in 2015 and almost 34 900 by land, compared to a total of 280 000 arrivals by land and sea for the whole of 2014. And these figures do not include those who got into Europe undetected.[11] Migrants come mainly from West Africa, the Horn of Africa and, since 2013, those fleeing the civil war in Syria. The figures could be much greater, now and in the future. There may be as many as 1 million waiting in Libya alone to continue their often perilous journey across the sea to Europe.[12]

But, within Africa, for the last hundred years there has been a much greater number of migrants of a different sort – a number that is rapidly growing. These are the flow of rural Africans into cities, as Figure 1.1 illustrates, as well as the flow of Africans over their borders into other African states.

Historically, such urban growth has been good news for development and jobs. Urban agglomerations help provide economies of scale for people as a labour pool and ease the delivery of infrastructure and services. They also solve two major challenges to improved productivity: connectivity and energy.[13] As developed countries move away from manufacturing towards services as a source of employment, density may become less critical, given that many can work from home. By contrast, however, in those economies where jobs are driven by manufacturing, which some in Africa hope to benefit from, density of housing with efficient transport to the workplace is all important. Success in mass transportation requires density in accommodation.

Africa has so far missed out on urban-led growth. According to a 2007 study of 90 developing countries, Africa is the only region where urbanisation does not correlate with poverty reduction (as highlighted in the Introduction).[14] And, according to the Brookings Institute, unlike other regions, African urbanisation has not been driven by increasing agricultural productivity or by industrialisation. Rather, African cities are centres of consumption, where the rents extracted from natural resources are spent by the rich. Thus, African cities have largely failed to install the infrastructure that has made cities elsewhere places of prosperity.[15]

Instead of capitalising on the advantages of agglomerations, there remain acute problems in Africa (as will be explained in Chapter 7), notably in electricity generation and transmission, and where the effect of migration has been to produce more and more congestion, rather than enhanced connectivity. More than half of sub-Saharan Africans in cities live in slums, with just 40 per cent having access to proper sanitation facilities. These are the same ratios as in 1990. Africa's urban child dependency ratio is 40 per cent higher than in Latin America and 65 per cent higher than that of Asia.

Cities inhabit the space where implementation occurs, where the policy rubber has to hit the road, where policymakers come face to face with society's problems. Although the role of municipal actors is frequently overlooked, their direct influence is often greater than that of presidents. Indeed, the rise of national governments in policymaking and implementation is a relatively recent global phenomenon, spurred on by globalisation, the need to raise armies (especially given the last century's world wars) and the national importance of managing inequality.

City governments are inherently pragmatic and less partisan, since their job is to 'clean the streets' regardless of their political allegiances. Mayors are by necessity not legislative but executive. Or, as Teddy Kollek, who ran Jerusalem for 28 years, once put it in trying to negotiate between Israeli and Palestinian communities, 'Spare me your sermons, and I'll fix your sewers.'[16]

Still, for all their coalface responsibilities, cities mostly lack the policy tools. As Harvard's Edward Glaeser, an expert on urban development, said, 'Cities are the best path we know out of poverty. They are the best transformers of civilizations. But, there are also demons that come with density.'[17]

One challenge is that the political environment and boundaries have not kept pace with the rate and reality of expansion. There is a need for a clear

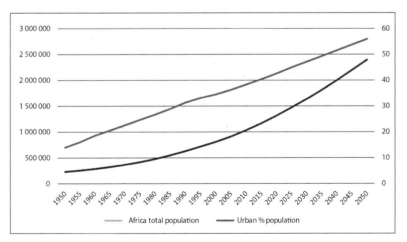

Figure 1.1: Africa: Urbanisation and population, 1950–2050

Source: United Nations, Department of Economic and Social Affairs, Population Division (2014). World Urbanization Prospects: The 2014 Revision, https://esa.un.org/unpd/wpp/DataQuery/

demarcation between city and national responsibility, combined with the appropriate delegation of authority and allocation of resources to city governments. In an era when mayors are supposed to 'rule the world', given the burgeoning size of their immediate constituencies, local authorities have limited authority and few funding tools and resources.

A second challenge is that of inequality, and the stresses and strains this presents. For example, the centrepiece of South Africa's tourism industry, Cape Town, is nevertheless a study in contrasts. Drawn by the backdrop of opulent coastal mansions, pristine beaches and 'old' wealth, visitors arriving at Cape Town International Airport are often shocked to pass through miles of squalid squatter camps where basic sanitation and electricity remain elusive luxuries. A reminder of the injustices of apartheid, the city's wealth inequality is mirrored by spatial divisions. The poor and gang-ridden suburbs of the Cape Flats and the townships spread interminably away from the heart of the city, with the consequence that the people who live in those areas have a long way to travel to their places of work.

Still, the city remains an attractive destination for migrants from all over the country and the continent. The result has been massive pressure on housing, basic service delivery and public-transport systems, and more than anything, jobs.

According to Tim Harris, former Head of Investment for the City of Cape Town government, the authorities have three priorities for tackling the new urban-migration challenge: connecting citizens through investments in public transport and information and technology infrastructure; maintaining a high level of delivery for basic services as the city expands (including free allocations of water and electricity for those unable to pay); and ensuring sufficient and appropriate human-settlement solutions.[18]

Yet, like most African cities, Cape Town has very limited scope to act independently of central government in dealing with its specific challenges – or, more positively, to play to its strengths. The reasons for this, as in other areas, come down to money and autonomy.

Currently, the city, with its population of 3.7 million, has an annual budget of R36 billion ($2.6 billion), which includes R6 billion for capital expenditure – compared to the national budget of R1.25 trillion for a total population of 52 million. Eighty per cent of the city's income comes from the premiums charged on utilities (especially electricity), property rates and other charges. The remainder comes from three sources: a tranche from the national government determined according to a countrywide formula; conditional grants from the Treasury (which remove the discretion for municipalities to spend as they may need to); and a portion of the fuel levy raised on sales within the municipal boundary. The vast proportion of these funds (like other municipal budgets) is spent on maintaining and expanding infrastructure, and delivering basic services, including water, electricity and refuse removal, on the back of that infrastructure. The shortage of funding is worsened by 'unfunded mandates', including library services and clinics, where the city is 'left out of pocket by hundreds of millions of rands for services provided which are not matched by income or allocations from higher structures,' says Harris.[19]

This fiscal and political environment severely limits the latitude of Cape Town, along with other South African cities, to act independently, for example, in designing strong investment incentives. It can offer 'non-financial' incentives: accelerated planning approvals, biodiversity offsets, an investment facilitation touch-point in the mayor's office, and the overall 'lifestyle' advantages. On the financial side to support investments, the city has been able to offer discounted electricity tariffs and waive various application fees and development contributions that would normally be incurred by infrastructure projects. It can also offer discounted rates and land leases, though this is controversial within the administration, not least given the budgetary funding imperative.

From the city's vantage, the most important reform allowing municipalities to shape their destiny would be the devolution from central government of the powers of taxation. Any intent in this regard on the part of the drafters of the constitution quickly ran afoul of the low capacity of many subnational governments and a move towards centralism by the national government. This has removed the potential for tax competition between subnational governments, a key tool in spurring development worldwide.

A common challenge for cities is to make full use of the potential for connectivity offered by high density of accommodation. But African cities generally expand by sprawling and not through increased density of the sort seen in Hillbrow, stretching out and not up.

But Africa can, again, learn from others. For example, the success of

Curitiba, a city in southern Brazil, demonstrates how, with clever thinking, thorough planning, continuity in leadership and determined execution, a city can deal with apparently insurmountable problems. Curitiba is famous for how its invention and application of a novel transport system changed its transport environment and therefore the city's connectedness. But a closer look reveals that it was just one element of a master plan that has delivered real improvement across the city and to the lives of its people.

Curitiba and bus rapid transport[20]

Curitiba, with a population of 2 million, is the capital of the Brazilian state of Paraná. In 2010 Curitiba was awarded the annual Global Sustainable City Award on account of its excellence in urban development. It deserved it, because it really did innovate and integrate.

'We have many visitors from China, South Africa, Colombia and other countries,' says Silvia Ramos of Urbanização de Curitiba, the transport regulator.

It's little wonder. Curitiba originated a surface transport system, known as bus rapid transport (BRT), which has become an international role model that others have sought to replicate. There are now more than 250 cities worldwide with BRTs.

Getting this to work involves more than just mobility. Curitiba has successfully used a relatively cheap surface public-transport system to transform the city, not just in terms of the movement of people, but also in terms of how it uses land and public spaces. Integration has been achieved by connecting people, and this has been key to the city's economic progress.

Back in 1966, when the city was drawing up a master plan, they looked at models from France and the UK, among others. But the cost of an underground was deemed prohibitive for the city, despite its agricultural-based wealth. So they opted for a surface transport system with dedicated bus lanes, which was about a 10th of the cost of an underground railway.

When the system was first implemented in 1974, it moved just 50 000 passengers annually. Today, the BRT carries 1.7 million people a day over a network of 85.6 kilometres, along six lines with an operating fleet of 1 368 buses, some capable of carrying 250 passengers, and pausing at 6 500 stops. The buses drive 328 kilometres each day and are supplied and run by private companies, which are paid by the kilometre. Passengers pay a standard fare of just under a dollar regardless of the length of the journey. This fee cross-subsidises those, mostly the poor, who live farther out from the city centre.

Jaime Lerner has been a pivotal figure in this system. He was part of the original team that decided on the winning bid for the city's master plan and, in 1965, helped create the Instituto de Pesquisa e Planejamento Urbano de Curitiba (Curitiba Institute of Urban Planning and Research – IPPUC), a research, monitoring and implementation body funded by the municipality.

Lerner was elected mayor three times, the first in 1971. Although he implemented a number of important changes in the city, including establishing more parks, creating an apprenticeship system for deprived young people, and launching a successful recycling scheme, the BRT remains his greatest achievement, and Curitiba's gift to the world.

'You need to think of the BRT,' he says, 'not just as a transport system, but as a city design. It has been the engine of the city's growth. We started small, but for each stage to solve each problem, we have used innovation.'

Not only have the number of lanes and buses increased exponentially, but the services have also radically improved. More than 90 per cent of the fleet is adapted for disabled users. Various feeder lines are fully integrated, with a range of bus types and sizes. Tubular stations improved the passenger experience. The three-lane systems of the BRT, the slow and fast car lanes, and staggered BRT alignment stations were introduced to reduce hold-ups. And now increasing numbers of buses use biofuel, while the electric and hybrid 'Hibri-bus' is imminent.

'Everything in Brazil is dedicated to the car,' says Lerner. 'For example, there are at least 5 million cars in São Paulo alone, each car taking up 25 square metres of space on the road and in parking. This is the size of a small housing unit. Even if half of this was dedicated instead to housing, we could house another 2.5 million people closer to their place of work. But to do this, we have to provide public transport, to turn the space for cars from private to public.

'Back in the 1970s, when we did it, it was said that every city which achieved a population of 1 million should have a subway. As we did not have the money, instead we asked: What is a subway? The answer was, it is a system that is fast and has good frequency, so you don't have to wait. So, since we did not have the resources to go underground, we asked, "Why not the surface?" So we took the existing streets, and linked them to the structure of growth of the city – where we linked and integrated living, working, leisure and mobility.'

'This is why Curitiba,' he notes, 'is different. It involved the renovation and evolution of the existing system.'

The BRT has resulted in an estimated reduction of about 27 million car trips annually. Given such efficiencies, Curitiba's growth has been above 7 per cent over the last three decades, while per capita income is 30 per cent higher than the national average. Ironically, Curitiba is now the second largest producer of cars in Brazil, and also has a lively services and high-tech sector.

Curitiba has been able to make dramatic inroads into the perennial and similar challenges facing Brazil's cities: transport, governance, infrastructure and security. Yet remarkably few other Brazilian cities have sought to emulate its success. The reason, says Lerner, is very simple: politics. The problem, he believes, is that 'decisions today are closely tied to having consensus, but democracy is not consensus, rather conflict wisely managed'. Rather than attempting a perfect solution, which will take time, if not for ever, to be implemented, there is a need for pragmatism: 'Improvement needs a start. You need to have a demonstration effect sometimes to get things moving.'

A key reason for Curitiba's comparative success has been consistency in planning and implementation.

Daniele Moraes is an architect at the IPPUC. She reminds us that the 1965 master plan was not the first in Curitiba's history. The first city plan was produced in 1853, which was followed 90 years later by the Agache Plan, which laid out a high-density city centre with suburbs radiating outwards – the design trend of the time – for the population of 180 000. The winning bid for the 1965 plan, by which time the city had 500 000 inhabitants, built on the Agache scheme but focused on a combination of land use, roads and public transport to deliver a better environment, and social and economic development. Since then there have been two further revisions, in 2004 and 2014.

It has not just been about plans, but continuity in terms of people as well, explains Moraes. She points out that 'Curitiba has enjoyed six mayoral terms – 24 years – of mayors from IPPUC. Jaime Lerner, who served for three terms, Rafael Greca, who still works at IPPUC, and Cassio Taniguchi, who served two terms. They were all also from the same political group which ran the municipality for 40 years.' She adds, 'Jaime Lerner was a shrewd politician and diplomat. He taught children about recycling, for example, and in so doing created a whole generation concerned about urban planning and the environment. He created a lot of support for change.'

Critical mass is important too. A municipal-funded institution, the IPPUC has a staff of 160, of whom half are architects and engineers.

Of course, there are challenges. Noted local economist Carlos Guimaraes of FESP (the São Paulo School of Engineering), a private Brazilian university with a focus on commerce, observes that there is a difference between the IPPUC team and the 'professors now in City Hall who are very theoretical about things, but they don't know how to make them happen'. And there are always funding shortages, reminds his colleague Luis Fernando Ferreira da Costa because Brazil remains a very centralised country. 'Taxes go from the cities to the states to the federal centre, but the amount that comes back depends partly on politics. It also reflects the size of the federal government: everyone in Brazil wants to work for the government. We need greater decentralisation and greater autonomy, like the United States, so that the states can raise and spend their own taxes.' Cape Town is not alone.

'Solving problems,' Lerner notes, 'is not related to scale, or the size of the city, or financial resources. The challenge is in organisation, and in creating shared responsibility between citizens and government, and the public and private sectors. Otherwise you won't get the outcome you need.'

Curitiba's success has been exported worldwide, including to towns in Nigeria, Tanzania, South Africa and Morocco. Oscar Edmundo Diaz worked to implement the TransMilenio BRT system in Bogotá, Colombia's capital, together with Mayor Enrique Peñalosa. The system started in 2000 with two corridors, 400 000 passengers and four private operators. By 2016 it had expanded to 12 routes, 2.5 million passengers and 10 operators. Some routes were carrying 52 000 passengers per hour in each direction, equivalent to the most efficient metros in the world. But this is still deemed insufficient for a city of 9 million, and reflects challenges, too, in opening up more routes.

Peñalosa returned to office after a 14-year absence in 2015. One of his challenges was to meet the 2015 target of 366 kilometres of corridors on the network and to ensure that 85 per cent of the population live within 1 kilometre of a mass transport system by 2030. Diaz also returned as a special adviser to the mayor, having spent time in the interim assisting African countries with their own BRT plans. He highlights, with the benefit of reflection, the importance of managing the politics of routes, providing security on buses and adequate ticketing facilities, and the need for density as prerequisites for the success of mass transportation systems. 'Build up', he says, 'or these systems cannot deliver.'[21]

Managing the challenges that allow full exploitation of the advantages of urbanisation is, however, not just a planning problem. Development solutions hinge on having appropriate skills and investing in creating such skills. They also require improving security and ensuring the rule of law. Poor security works directly against the advantages of urbanisation, since the answer to poor security in the cities is to keep people apart, behind high walls or on separate transport systems.

As noted in the Preface, Africa is the most violent continent in the world, experiencing two-thirds of non-state fatalities worldwide.[22] The Ibrahim Index of African Governance for 2016 notes that weaknesses in the provision of safety and the rule of law on the continent have 'held back further governance progress'. Some 33 countries 'have experienced a decline in safety and rule of law since 2006, 15 of them quite substantially'. As the index notes, all four subcategories within the safety and rule of law category show negative trends, with personal safety and national security showing the largest deteriorations at the subcategory level. Moreover, almost half of the countries on the continent recorded their worst ever score in this category within the last three years. The index concludes there is a 'strong link between Safety & Rule of Law and governance performance'.[23]

The on-the-ground reality of such statistics can be seen in parts of Cape Town.

The security dimension

Father Craven Engel has the stocky physique of a rugby player. Just like his famous namesake, Doctor Danie Craven, he represented South Africa at scrumhalf.

For 27 years he has worked in the once coloured-only township of Hanover Park, Cape Town, one of the most violent neighbourhoods in the world. The annual murder rate in and around its cinder-block two-storey flats has been as high as 100 deaths per 100 000 residents. Due to high rates of violence in other townships, including Nyanga, Langa, Khayelitsha, Kraaifontein, Delft, Bishop Lavis and Philippi, Cape Town is the most violent city in South Africa as well as Africa. In the reporting year from 1 April 2015 to 31 March 2016, the Philippi East police precinct recorded the highest murder rate in the country at 203.1 per 100 000 residents, followed by Gugulethu at 140.1 per 100 000, and Nyanga at 130.6 per 100 000 people.[25] Indeed, at 52 murders per 100 000, eight times higher than the global rate, Cape Town is among the world's most dangerous cities, in the company of Caracas in Venezuela, San Pedro Sula in Honduras, and San Salvador in El Salvador.

Hanover Park, at just two square kilometres, is formally divided by the police into two sectors. In reality, though, as the Google Earth map displayed in Engel's conference room illustrates, it is fragmented into several gang-run communities: Cowboy Town, Back Streets, The States, The Taliban Area, The Valley of the Plenty and The Jungle. Each is controlled by a grouping that is essentially an affiliate of two predominant major gangs, the Mongrels (under the 'British flag') and the Americans. The Americans have recently spawned another affiliate – labelled ISIS – though the pastor is understandably keen to downplay the religious dimension in an already fraught and volatile environment.

Father Engel runs a programme under the Pentecostal Church, funded by the City of Cape Town, to prevent violence, mediate between gangs and rehabilitate their members. Five 'interrupters', all former senior gang members, are employed along with the same number of outreach workers; there are also four data capturers and researchers. The team monitor security events using a system of 'shot-spotters', microphones installed on street lights linked to a Google Earth system and cellphones. This technology allows real-time monitoring of shootings, and immediate intervention and mediation. Although they share 'analytical' information, the police here are little trusted or used. Indeed, there are claims that the increasingly heavy weapons used here – including 16- and 21-shot Uzis – have found their way into Hanover Park from police armouries.

Father Engel has plenty on his plate, with an average of between 40 and 50 murders a year. During May 2016, for example, 325 gunshots were logged in the township, with five dead and eight wounded from 36 gang-related incidents, about 30 per cent of which were related to drugs and turf wars. The rest of the violence, the pastor notes, is 'sporadic' – often tit-for-tat attacks. The day before we visited Ceasefire, Father Engel's NGO, two gangsters were shot in retributive gunfights, one of them a bodyguard of just 15.

Gangs are a way of life, Father Engel admits, among Hanover Park's 55 000 people. Unemployment is endemic here, despite the city's relatively low overall rate of joblessness (21.1 per cent) compared to the South African average of 36.3 per cent. Gang members often leave school early, earning their 'rank' in prison – known as the 'University of Crime' – in a strict hierarchy defined by 'generals', 'captains' and 'shooters'. Violent activities centre on the borders between the ganglands, where there is little movement of people, or where lighting is poor at night.

He says that the proportion of high-risk individuals in Hanover Park is less than 8 per cent of the population. 'If you can get the violence out of the areas, just like you would use a toilet and sewer to remove waste, then a solution is possible.' This is not easy, however, in an area where confidence is low, transport to places of work costly and insecurity pervasive. Father Engel has stepped in where the state has failed, stabilising the situation. But, for this to stick, more than a civil-society initiative is required. Sustained policing that deploys available technologies is one aspect, increasing the police-to-population ratio, averaging 439 officers per 100 000 people in Cape Town (with some areas, such as certain townships, well above this figure) towards the international norm of 220 to 100 000.[26] There is an overlap between the lack of policing attention and the rates of violence, where just 15 areas of the city, says its mayoral security chief J.P. Smith, account for half the crime.[27] Still, more will be needed, says Father Engel, 'to create alternatives – jobs. If we can create jobs for just 10 per cent of them, then the rest will start dreaming.' It is not surprising that in those police precincts in the Cape characterised by high murder levels, there are high levels of socio-economic inequality and increasing unemployment.[28]

Africa is not the only continent that has grappled with such challenges. Seemingly hopeless situations can quickly be turned around, within a generation. The story of Medellín, Colombia, illustrates this promise.

What success looks like

The turnaround of Medellín, the second-largest city in Colombia, has in part been due to better leadership and city planning. But it has also been made possible by a changed security environment in the city once eponymous with the drug lord Pablo Escobar.

Medellín once boasted the highest rates of violent crime in the world, reaching nearly 7 000 murders a year at the peak of Pablo Escobar's reign in the early 1990s. By 2008, the figure was down to little more than 1 000 homicides, falling to 658 by 2014.[29] In 1991, to use a different measure, Medellín experienced 381 homicides per 100 000 residents, twice as much as the rate 20 years later in Ciudad Juárez, then the epicentre of Mexico's drug war. By 2015, Medellín had the same homicide rate as Washington DC.[30]

The spark for these improvements and the economic growth that followed came 20 years earlier, when Escobar was tracked down and killed by the authorities in a Medellín *barrio* in December 1993. His end signalled the advent of a new security and intelligence regime, a renewed war on drugs, and a whole-of-government approach to dealing with security and development.[31] The election of the government of President Álvaro Uribe in 2002 in particular saw a dramatic turnaround in Colombia's security situation by providing increased resources to the security services, greater spending on infrastructure and attention to detail by leadership to even the most remote areas of Colombia. This set in motion a process that enabled a truce to be agreed with the guerrillas of the Revolutionary Armed Forces of Colombia (known as FARC) by the end of 2016.[32]

Policing is now controlled from Medellín's high-tech dispatch centre located in the mayoral offices, where officers monitor feeds on giant television screens. The capabilities of the police have also grown hugely. By 2015, for example, there were 10 211 police officers for the estimated 3.5 million citizens living in the wider metropolitan area around Medellín,[33] virtually double the number deployed 15 years earlier.[34] At the same time, the quality of policing has improved, notably because of a higher percentage of graduate officers in the force[35] and improved cooperation with the military.

Medellín is now a global trendsetter in urban development. For the city, as for Colombia as a whole, security has been the door through which much else has followed. There have also been important changes in the planning and infrastructure of the city, along with a realisation that security, like growth, depended on a different operating system, using public spaces better and linking outlying areas with the central business district (CBD). The Integral Urban Project provided the city's so-called 'gondola' transport system of cable cars, which now connect various outlying informal settlements across extreme topography to the metro system and thus to the city centre. The project also encouraged development around the metro stations in the form of libraries and green spaces.

Line J of Medellín's Metrocable network now passes over La Comuna 13, one of the city's toughest *barrios*. Inaugurated in 2007, the funicular transport system connects the 28 000 inhabitants of the *comuna*, and others, to the centre of the city. The journey, which would once have taken hours of travelling up and down winding, narrow roads, takes 10 minutes, and costs just $1.

Looking down at the rusted tin roofs and red-brick dwellings perched on the hillside, a local policeman observed in 2014: 'We had a problem at the start of the cable car. The locals were shooting at it from the ground.' The security problem was solved by improved patrolling. Line J, one of three spanning the city, carries 30 000 people a day, the cable cars travelling quickly over the *barrios* at 16 kilometres per hour, dispatching people efficiently to San Javier Station, at the bottom, and at La Aurora, on the top of the hillside 2.7 kilometres away.

Once at San Javier Station, commuters hop onto the Metro, first opened for service in 1995, and built by a Spanish–German consortium. Smart and litter-free, the system's 27 stations and modern carriages are a symbol of the change in Medellín's fortunes. Once the town of Escobar, the city is now the epicentre of Colombia's mining and manufacturing industries. The Metro carries half a million passengers daily, including 350 000 residents from the north-eastern quarter, where many of the working class live. It is breaking down the barriers between once disparate poor and rich areas, and enabling new business growth.

With construction costs for the Metrocable at $10 million per kilometre and the Metro itself costing $2 billion, developing the city's transport system was a bold step. The use of the Metro as a development axis was recognised by Medellín's planners as critical in meeting the city's modern needs in a period of social change and instability. Medellín's urban growth since the 1960s had filled the entire Aburra Valley with communities, where harsh living conditions were heightened by drug trafficking, joblessness and violence.

In this positive cycle, improved security has led to economic prosperity, which, in turn, has cemented stability. Medellín boasts some 1 750 export businesses, the largest number of any Colombian city, from textile manufacturers to services. They are supplemented by mining, electricity generation, construction and, increasingly, tourism. Medellín's success is connected to openness, both between its own communities and to international markets.

These developments have helped change local attitudes and integrate communities into city life, merging the formal with the informal. Medellín gained the Urban Land Institute's Innovative City of the Year award in 2013, beating New York and Tel Aviv in the process.

Moving up and with the times is not something most African cities have yet managed, at least not in quite the same positive way.

Conclusion: A new urban agenda

Medellín was, not that long ago, synonymous with a level of anarchy that even the most challenged African cities have yet to achieve. However, a dedicated government with a comprehensive security, economic and infrastructure plan was able to turnaround a situation that many had deemed hopeless. The critical ingredients were the recognition the severity of the situation and the leadership taking responsibility for both the problems and the solutions.

The positive lesson for African leaders from Medellín is that change can happen and even extraordinary difficult situations can be addressed in a relatively short period of time. There is another dimension too. Positive change in an urban environment affects proportionately greater numbers of people than in the rural areas, and in so doing releases considerable entrepreneurial dynamism and economic growth.

Achieving this demands a concerted effort by the state and its leaders. Sometimes, as in the case of Father Engel, there are heroic individuals who try their utmost to improve their neighbourhoods. However, they cannot ensure the security of even small areas, let alone highly complex and combustible African cities, and it is difficult for them to sustain their programmes. The dynamics of high population growth, lack of employment and rapid urbanisation can create large areas where government rule is not apparent, and criminals and others can move freely. As a result, the future, as long as 'business as usual' continues, is of increasingly anarchic urban areas where people attempt to pursue lives under great stress and insecurity. Given current policies, governments in Africa will not be able provide either the conditions or resources needed for cities to make best use of their inherent advantages of density and scale.

The solutions have to be vested in the overall political economy if urban environments are to provide an answer to Africa's extreme challenges of social and economic exclusion. Within this framework, can a solution be found that links housing, financing, security, internet connectivity, transport and governance to education, economic growth, healthcare and job creation? Key in this is certainty in the rule of law and avoidance of corruption.

There is little gainsaying the extent of the African challenge. Africa's current urban frameworks, as will be seen in Chapter 6, are less a product of positive push and pull factors than of desperation. Using this opportunity to deliver a different future involves an acceptance of, on the one hand, the need for density in housing and, on the other, the role that informal communities and business can positively play. Planning, governance and architecture, in this way, become less about building afresh and more about inserting structures into the informal sector and building on the resources and resourcefulness already present.[36]

Whatever the scale of these challenges, and the constraints of time and resources, Medellín illustrates that 20 years is long enough to fundamentally break the negative patterns of the past if good leadership and the right sets of incentives are in place. The challenge to African leaders is that such dramatic results require a sharp deviation from the status quo that gave birth to these conditions.

The security aspect cannot of course succeed alone. Committing substantial military and financial resources to contexts as diverse as Iraq and the DRC illustrates that there is no such thing as a security solution to a country's problems. Security crackdowns might provide space, but a political and economic solution is required for longer-term stability.

Chapter 2
Democracy and development

Five steps for success:
- Democracy and development are indivisible. Democratic government represents the interests of the general population, and not just an elite.
- The bouts of stability that authoritarians can bring must be viewed sceptically, given the superior global economic performance and stability of democratic governments over the long term.
- Democracies must be crafted to address the particular political, economic and demographic challenges that countries face.
- Democracy is vital to the empowerment of cities because only democratic leaders are able to devolve power.
- A 'democracy playbook' is necessary to meet the threats to democratic elections and institutions.

Challenges and opportunities: The fundamental challenge to improving African economies is to develop structures and incentives that promote private-sector growth and the enrichment of the population. Correspondingly, the interests and considerations of elites across the continent must be devalued. Democratic systems, broadly defined, are best able to enrich whole societies because they are driven by the voters and their interests. Empirical evidence shows that democracies tend to govern better. It is the accountability of institutions – the hallmark of democracy – that promotes both political participation and good economic governance. Yet democratic progress, and even consolidation, appears to have stalled or even gone backwards in parts of the continent.

Key statistics: Despite the challenge of building institutional democracies, and the uneven progress in this domain across the continent, 70 per cent of Africans in 34 countries surveyed preferred democracy to 'other kinds of government' by 2013. The number of African electoral democracies increased from just two in 1980 to more than 40 a quarter of a century later. But the number of countries that are considered 'not free' outnumbers those considered 'partly free'. Although the continent has the youngest population in the world, with a median age of 19.5 years,[1] the average age of the 10 oldest African leaders is 78.5, compared to 52 for leaders of the world's 10 most developed economies. By 2016, Africa's five longest-serving presidents had been in power for between 29 and 36 years.

'One of the asymmetries of history,' wrote Henry Kissinger of Singapore's former prime minister Lee Kuan Yew, 'is the lack of correspondence between the abilities of some leaders and the power of their countries.' Kissinger's one-time boss, Richard Nixon, was even more flattering. He speculated that, had Lee lived in another time and another place, he might have 'attained the world stature of a Churchill, a Disraeli, or a Gladstone'.[2]

Singapore has been used an excuse not to fully democratise by Rwanda's president, Paul Kagame, among others. It is the case that the island nation's economic success is inextricably tied to Lee's style of rule. However, superficial references to Singapore as an alternative to democracy miss some important truths.

Like other nations in East Asia – including South Korea, China, Indonesia and Taiwan – Singapore modernised under a system of rigid political control. Nevertheless, the island state has enjoyed extraordinary freedom of individual choice and economic openness, a gentle autocracy quite distinct from sometimes violent and corrupt African eras of authoritarian rule, of which Lee himself was critical. Moreover, while some dictators might like Lee's 'big man' image, the reality of Singapore was far more than reliance on one person; it was fundamentally about reliance on institutions, and improvements in policy and governance in the pursuit of development.

Although Lee presented the articulate public face and adroitly managed the politics and personalities, his was a formidable team. Lee's memoir, *From Third World to First*, is testament to how highly he regarded the opinion of his colleagues and how often there were differences of outlook within government on key issues.[3] Differences of opinion were tolerated, the competition of ideas producing an improved outcome.

Additionally, Singapore made sure that the best and brightest were attracted, that they were paid properly, and they were given full support by leadership to do their job. As Lee observed, '[W]e stand a better chance of not failing if we abide by the basic principles that have helped us progress: social cohesion through the sharing of the benefits of progress, equal opportunities for all and meritocracy, with the best man or woman for the job, especially in leaders in government.'[4]

In contrast to the xenophobia and identity politics suffered in certain African countries embracing ethnic diversity and attracting global talent is another key factor in Singapore's success. The country had a population of a little over 1 million when it gained independence. Out of Singapore's current population of 5.3 million, around 1.5 million are expatriates, permanent residents or migrant workers. The injection of immigrants has been part of a strategy to maintain GDP targets, and this syncs with Singapore's need for continuous innovation and efficiency.

All this has been underpinned by Singapore's determination to globalise rather than nationalise. African goeverments routinely make it difficult to move goods in and out of their countries and are inherently suspicious of the motives of foreign investors. In contrast, Singapore has capitalised on its strategic geographic location by matching it with policies and the focus of institutions. There is a zero tariff on imported goods, low tax rates, a range of free-trade agreements, and vigorous trade and export promotion, with nearly 40 000 international corporations on the island, including 7 000 multinationals. Singapore has avoided trying to buck the markets or the needs and sensitivities of multinational companies and international finance. In fact, it has always acted to strengthen regulatory institutions to negate any perception of developing country risk.

The argument in favour of more authoritarian rule would have it that a combination of low literacy levels, the distraction and financial cost of regular domestic election cycles and the lack of strong, capable alternative leaders makes Western-style democracy ineffective in Africa. Proponents of this argument state a preference for a tough figure, presumably like Lee, 'who can just get things done' over the long term – a form of benevolent dictatorship.

Until now the problem with such a model is that many African states have already experienced such one-party or one-man leadership, and it has worked less like Lee's Singapore than a caricature of a tin-pot and often extremely brutal dictatorship. In Africa, but also farther afield, dictatorships tend not to be benevolent. Just as they use repression to keep their citizens in check, they also often end violently. The problem has been that the African authoritarians have not adopted the laser focus on economic growth, the emphasis on talent and the global perspective that were critical aspects of the Singapore miracle.

We, therefore, believe that long-term economic success depends on African countries becoming more democratic. That is the only way that will force governments to create institutions that benefit the majority. Depending on the goodwill and wisdom of a small elite has failed for decades in dozens of countries. Without the imperative to be re-elected, there is no obvious system that will force African leaders to encourage the private sector and create jobs in the face of Africa's extraordinary population growth.

African democratic progress

During the Cold War, much of Africa was locked into systems of single-party or authoritarian rule, which by their very nature suppressed competition of ideas and systems.

Before the fall of the Berlin Wall, only two countries had what could be considered institutionalised democratic systems: Botswana and Mauritius.[5] Then, as superpower competition fell away, along with the military and economic aid that had sustained many African dictators, between 1990 and 2005 the number of countries that held regular, competitive multi-party elections increased dramatically to over 40. Ivory Coast had a multi-party poll in 1990; Benin and Zambia followed in 1991; Kenya in 1992; and Tanzania in 1995. Ghana and Nigeria reverted to civilian rule with multi-party elections in 1996 and 1999, respectively. Since 1991 there have been 36 peaceful transfers of power from incumbents at the ballot box in sub-Saharan Africa.[6]

During this time there was a nearly fourfold increase – to 11 – in the number of African countries judged as 'free' by US think tank Freedom House.[7] Arguably, the bigger shift was marked by countries labelled 'not free', which represented 70 per cent of the continent in 1990 but only 33 per cent by 2005. Most of the countries that moved out of this category migrated to the 'partly free' category, which grew from 24 per cent to 44 per cent in 2005.

The major surprise in the decade from 2005 to 2014, however, is seen in the limited progress – and arguably regression – when it comes to political reform. The number of countries rated as 'free' in 2014 is one fewer than in 2005 and there have been some significant disappointments, especially Mali. Perhaps even more notable is that, after a decade when the 'partly free' category outnumbered those in the 'not free' category, the number of countries that are considered 'not free' now clearly outnumbers those that are considered 'partly free' (21 to 18).

Of course, African regime transitions tend to be fluid. Of those where progress has stalled, including those reversions mentioned above, 80 per cent get back on the democratic path typically within three years, some countries more than once. These regimes involve often complex changing coalitions, with institutional as well as ethnic partnerships, sometimes including the military. Of the 91 presidents and prime ministers to have held office on the continent in civilian regimes since 1989, nearly half (45 per cent) either served in the armed forces or were once guerrillas.[8]

The threats to democracy in Africa vary from relationships with outsiders who are more interested in short-term profits, including revenue derived from minerals and oil, than in helping develop the institutions of governance, to deep-rooted problems of weak institutions, faltering nationalism and enduring poverty, which can result in votes being bought for a meal or a T-shirt.[9] Democratic institutions (i.e. parliaments, courts and public prosecutors) have often been nascent and weak, simply because it is very hard to create such resilient structures. Financial probity and transparency invariably improve, too, with such institutions, as is suggested by the growth rate differential indicated in the next section, though the relationship between governance and democracy is not linear. Electoral threats manifest in various ways. The 2002 African Union (AU) Declaration on the Principles Governing Democratic Elections in Africa highlights some of the challenges in calling for elections to be organised by 'impartial, all-inclusive, competent, and accountable national electoral bodies'. It also calls on member states to prevent fraud, rigging and other illegal practices.[10]

Compounding these challenges has been an apparent change in the engagement of the international community in its role in promoting democracy. Since the early 2000s, the focus appears to have shifted to preventing the spread of radicalisation and terrorism across the continent. The response of the US to the 2016 elections in Uganda was to temper its criticism because of the need to maintain Ugandan troops in the AU Mission in Somalia. Acknowledging the difficulties faced by the Ugandan opposition in the face of evidence of government rigging, harassment and lack of transparency in the East African nation's February 2016 election, Zambia's 2016 presidential candidate Hakainde Hichilema remarked, 'We can only help ourselves.'[11] Or, as Raila Odinga, the Kenyan opposition leader and former prime minister, put it in 2016, 'There is an assault on democracy on the continent. Elections are now held as rituals designed to perpetuate the rule of the incumbent, a predetermined constitutional requirement.' Odinga says this is down to 'the emergence of China as a dominant economic player. The US was once the defender of democracy on the continent, but now it is reluctant to play this role. Perhaps,' he suggest, 'it is operating in its strategic self-interest, out of fear of being dislodged by China.'[12]

Partially as a result of these changes in the international appetite for democracy, Kofi Annan, the former UN Secretary General, has observed that 'after an initial period of genuine change, rulers learned that elections did not necessarily have to mean democracy: elections could be gamed to remain in power, sometimes indefinitely.' The result, he says, is that 'some elections are merely the lip service that undemocratic leaders pay to democracy', in the process confusing 'legality with legitimacy' even if courts certify the results. The consequence of 'repression with stability', particularly in the long run, and of 'an electoral mandate with a blank cheque' is the closing of the political space. 'Healthy societies rest on three pillars: peace and security; sustainable development; and human rights and the rule of law,' Annan writes. 'Many states today believe they can have the first two without the third, which includes elections with integrity. They are wrong.'[13]

What emerged from both the 2016 Ugandan and Zambian elections, as will be seen below, is a template for incumbents to manage an election process in their favour: close down the democratic space, run interference, misuse state resources, control the diet of information and, if necessary, alter the numbers.

These events demonstrate that holding elections is in itself insufficient to claim a democracy. Indeed, they may even reinforce authoritarianism if they permit the subversion of democratic process through electoral malpractice.

In recent years this has been shown by numerous 'constitutional coups', whereby leaders consolidate their power by means of elections. For instance, Sam Nujoma, Namibia's founding president, introduced in 1998 a bill allowing him to serve a third term despite a constitutionally mandated two-term limit.[14] Zambia and Malawi followed suit in 2001 and 2003, respectively, though the incumbents, Frederick Chiluba and Bakili Muluzi, failed to secure their bids. Referenda changed the constitutions in Chad, Guinea and Niger. Uganda's Yoweri Museveni combined the scrapping of term limits with the promise of a return to multi-party democracy in 2005.[15] In December 2015 the Rwandan constitution was changed, by a referendum, to allow Paul Kagame to extend his rule. He had already effectively ruled since 1994. Until that amendment, Kagame was ineligible to run for the office of president in 2017 because the Rwandan constitution limited the president to two terms. A referendum approved the change with a majority of 98.3 per cent, thus freeing Kagame to run for an additional seven-year term and then two further five-year terms, potentially until 2034, by which time he would have spent 40 years in office.

It is habitually the practice of authoritarian rulers to make themselves indispensable. Kagame's answer to the question, 'Why pursue a third term?' – asked by former UK Prime Minister Tony Blair in 2016 – elicited the response that he was simply respecting the wish of the Rwandan people. 'I didn't ask for this thing,' Kagame said. 'I said, maybe you need to take a risk with someone else. But they kept saying, no, we want you to stay.'[16]

Yet, by comparison, the average tenure of the CEOs of America's largest 500 companies is 4.9 years, about the length of a single presidential term. The average duration of all CEOs is 8.1 years.[17] Although there are exceptions to this, companies tend to fear the role of the 'imperial' CEO.

A democracy that helps with the economic empowerment of the citizenry must, therefore, be more than just an electoral moment. It is about ensuring a separation of powers between the judiciary, legislature and executive. It is about guaranteeing meritocratic appointments across government, but especially in key governance watchdog institutions; it is about the need for procurement reform to ensure contracts are clean; and, within all of this, a free and vigorous media. It requires politicians to focus on policy choices, not identity politics. Where institutions lack teeth or independence, and governance is weak, the stage is set for the 'capture' of state institutions and the resultant redistribution of favours, jobs and contracts.[18]

Sub-Saharan Africa's capital cities can in this regard be expected to become larger than those in other countries due to the need for the appropriation of government largesse, or rents, stemming from such resources. By contrast, non-capital cities in Africa exhibit not only reduced population concentration, but higher rates of growth.[19] The nature of the political system can also influence urbanisation. One study published in the 1990s found that dictatorships had 50 per cent larger cities than those found in democracies.[20] The reasons for this relative level of concentration were given as high external tariffs, high costs of internal trade and low levels of international trade. Even more clearly, the study notes that politics, such as the degree of instability, 'determines urban primacy'.

The strength of a democracy is not just about the nature of the public institutions but also extends to the manner in which government engages with those institutions and with political opposition.

Three reasons why democracy is important to Africa's economic future

The first reason for supporting democracy in Africa is that the continent's democracies have typically posted economic growth rates that are one-third faster than its autocracies. They are, therefore, better equipped to create the numbers of jobs required as their populations expand.

This matches what has been seen globally and over a longer time frame. For example, as the work by Joseph Siegle and colleagues illustrates,[21] since the end of the Cold War, only nine out of 85 autocracies worldwide have realised sustained economic growth. Moreover, 48 of these autocracies had at least one episode of disastrous economic experience (defined as an annual contraction in per capita GDP of at least 10 per cent) during this period. There is a link between democratic and economic performance in this regard. Of the top 47 countries in the UN's Human Development Index – i.e. those classified as having 'very high human development' – 41 are deemed as 'free'; two (Singapore and Seychelles) as 'partly free'; and just four (Brunei, Hong Kong,[22] UAE and Qatar) as 'not free'.

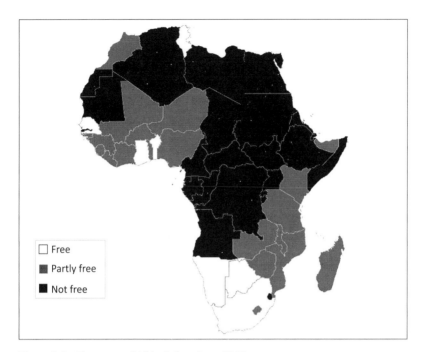

Figure 2.1: The state of Africa's freedom, 2016

Source: Freedom House, Freedom in the World 2016, https://freedomhouse.org/report/freedom-world-2016/table-scores

Analysis by Nicolas van de Walle and Takaaki Masaki substantiates further the link between democracy and growth.[23] In scrutinising 43 (out of 49) countries in sub-Saharan Africa for the period 1982 to 2012, the authors found 'strong evidence that democracy is positively associated with economic growth', and that this 'democratic advantage' is more pronounced for those African countries that have been democratic for longer periods of time.

Figure 2.2, which is calculated on the basis of the Freedom House classifications, shows that GDP growth in those countries classified as 'free' is substantially higher than growth in the 'partly' and 'not free' categories.

As can be seen, the performance of the 'not free' group is considerably worse if the oil-producing states (Sudan, Equatorial Guinea, Angola, Gabon and DRC) are omitted. Although, in the short term, commodity endowments can push up growth rates, over the medium to long term, the quality of governance becomes more important because commodity prices are

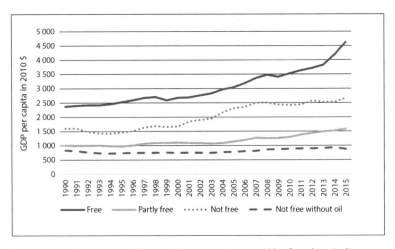

Figure 2.2: Sub-Saharan African GDP per capita sorted by freedom indicators

Source: Based on classifications that used Freedom House's Freedom in the World Report (https://freedomhouse.org/report-types/freedom-world) as well as GDP data from the World Development Indicators (World Bank national accounts data, and OECD National Accounts data files)

cyclical and good governance is necessary to garner investment.

Not only do democratic regimes improve accountability, but the great asset of democracy is that it also enables a test of philosophies in the marketplace of the political consumer. One of the inherent strengths of democratic systems is their flexibility and pragmatism. They enable consensus – that aid is no longer a panacea, that regional integration needs to be promoted, that investing in education and skills is essential – to be implemented and institutions to work.[24] Democracy makes politics and policies more competitive, something particularly lacking under autocratic regimes and, to be successful, businesses and economies need a competitive edge. Thus, a 'benevolent dictatorship' comes with a cost to potential economic growth.

This argument is reinforced by the poor performance of military regimes. Since the end of the Cold War, the number of military regimes and the frequency of coups have significantly declined. Even though there has been a revisionist literature on the impact of 'good coups' in Africa,[25] the record of economic management and political violence of the coup era speaks for itself, as African militaries have been worse at managing countries than their civilian counterparts.

Figure 2.3 illustrates the difference in economic performance between those governments in sub-Saharan Africa where the military has abstained from a role in politics (Botswana, Cameroon, Cape Verde, Djibouti, Gabon, Kenya, Malawi, Mauritius, Senegal, South Africa, Swaziland, Tanzania and Zambia), and those elsewhere where it has been involved since independence.

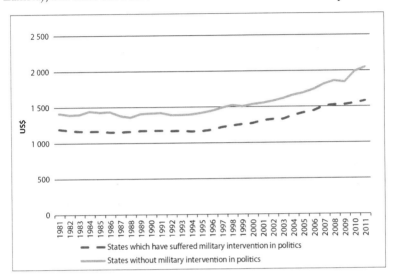

Figure 2.3: Economic performance of sub-Saharan Africa's militarisers versus non-militarisers (GDP per capita in constant 2000 $), 1981–2011

Source: World Bank Databank, http://databank.worldbank.org/data/reports. aspx?source=world-development-indicators&preview=on#

Autocracies are typically three times more likely to have sharp economic declines leading to regular periods of crisis. This volatility is partly, though not entirely, due to autocracies' greater reliance on revenues from natural resources. Moreover, analysis shows that autocracies are more likely to recede in periods of economic stagnation (i.e. when there is per capita growth of less than 1 per cent). Indeed, this matches a wider pattern – globally, the degree of fluctuation of growth in autocratic regimes is substantially higher. The coefficient of variation (standard deviation over mean) for the autocratic growth rate since 2000 is 4.28; for mixed regimes it is 2.11; and for democracies it is 1.48. In other words, democratic growth has been about three times less volatile than that of autocracies. In practical terms, this means that autocracies vary far more widely from year to year and among one another in their growth than do democracies. Consistency matters in growth and development; such volatility undermines the compounding impact of steady growth.[26]

As noted above, a key component in democratic reform is the role played by the private sector. Where this is weak, it limits economic opportunity and the potential for job creation needed to help turn around a stagnating economy.[27] These periods challenge autocracies' claims of 'performance legitimacy' – or, essentially, legitimacy through delivery despite an absence of human rights – and can lead to more abrupt transitions.

Democracies are more peaceful

The second reason for supporting democracy is that, historically, democracies have proved to be much more effective at resolving tensions and conflict within societies peacefully. Therefore, paradoxically, it is entirely in the self-interest of the leaders of authoritarian regimes to move towards democracy because authoritarian regimes often end violently, with serious consequences for the incumbent. Peace and stability, or lack of it, have economic as well as social consequences, as outlined above.

Before 1990, sub-Saharan Africa had experienced 19 democratic elections, 14 undemocratic or contested elections and 77 incidences of undemocratic regime change. Seventeen heads of state died violent deaths in office or shortly after having been deposed in a coup. The post-1990 reality of the continent is starkly different. Since then there have been significantly more elections. By 2016 there had been 118 democratic elections, 77 undemocratic or contested elections and 34 undemocratic regime changes. Eleven leaders suffered violent deaths in office. When the data is further disaggregated into the most recent Freedom House categories of free, partly free and not free countries, it's possible to see how different trajectories of regime change affect the levels of freedom within a country.

This should not be surprising. 'Democracies,' notes Annan, 'have far lower levels of internal violence than non-democracies. In an era when more than 90 per cent of wars take place within, not between, states, the import of this finding for conflict prevention should be obvious.'[28] Democracy produces orderly changes of leadership. It enables people to be patient for their turn, rather than revert to a coup. In this regard, the 1991 Organisation of African Unity Conference on Security, Development, and Co-operation in Africa identified lack of inclusive democracy as the primary cause of insecurity on the continent.[29]

A viable democratic dispensation offers the possibility of alternative government, and avoids government complacency.

Finally, and probably the foremost good reason for having a democratic system of government in Africa is that it's the style of government that the citizens favour. The Afrobarometer Index of Demand for Democracy climbed 15 points in 16 countries surveyed between 2002 and 2012, from 36% to 51%. Seven out of 10 Africans in 34 countries surveyed preferred democracy to 'other kinds of government' by 2013. The demand for democracy is strongest in West Africa. Africans also see elections as the best sign of a democratic regime.[30] There are good examples, too, where democracy has worked in spite of a difficult inheritance.

Ending coups: A personal reflection on Nigeria, by Olusegun Obasanjo, former Nigerian head of state

The military's intervention in Nigerian politics in January 1966 went on like musical chairs for 33 years, fouling the political air, causing instability and uncertainty, causing destruction of lives and properties, resulting in a civil war and leaving the country divided internally and isolated externally. This peaked when General Sani Abacha ruthlessly and recklessly pursued his programme of self-succession and life-presidency. Nigeria was impoverished economically, politically, intellectually and culturally. It became a pariah state. Nigerians deserted in droves and sought refuge all over the world. Nigeria was left prostrate. Those who raised their voices were either assassinated or put in jail, myself and my second-in-command as military head of state, Shehu Yar'Adua, included. We were arrested for a phantom coup and sentenced to long imprisonment. But for international intervention, we would have been killed. All the same, Chief M.K.O. Abiola, who was considered the winner of the aborted election of 12 June 1993, died in jail.

The sudden death of Abacha was providential, opening the gates of prisons and political reform, reversing the exodus out of Nigeria. General

Abubakar Abdulsalami, who succeeded Abacha, lost no time in releasing political prisoners and created a conducive atmosphere for Nigerian exiles to return home. He also opened the way for another attempt at democratic dispensation. It was in this new democratic experiment that I was persuaded to contest for the presidency of Nigeria.

I joined one of the three political parties, the People's Democratic Party. Since the advent of the military in the political life of Nigeria, there had been debate on how to put an end to the recurrence and persistence of *coups d'état*. Coups had become more and more destructive and destabilising. No matter the excuses, they had a major negative impact on democracy, governance and unity of the country. Nigeria needed to put an end to its perpetual coups.

The often prescribed solution of specifically putting a ban on coups in the constitution was not the answer. A coup is treason punishable by death only if it fails, and yet it puts the plotter in the State House if it succeeds. It was a destructive and destabilising practice, wasteful for the military itself, and undermining in terms of discipline, good order and military conduct. A junior officer takes a gun and looks at his political boss and senior officers through its sights, bumps them off and puts himself in the State House. He instantly becomes superior and senior to all political and military officers. Such was the situation existing in Nigeria between 1966 and 1999.

On assuming office as president, I decided to put an end to these incessant coups. I asked the military to submit the list of all officers who had either participated in coups in the past or benefited in the dividends of coups by being appointed to political office as governors or ministers. Not knowing what the list was meant for, the military faithfully compiled it and submitted it to me as the commander-in-chief and chairman of council of each of the arms of service. Ninety-three officers in all were given six hours' notice of retirement on a Friday, and ordered not to spend the Friday night in uniform or in barracks to prevent adverse reaction. The following Monday, the service councils met to ratify the retirement of all the officers. From my vantage position and background as a battle-tested and war-victorious general, I knew that an officer out of uniform and barracks is like a fish out of water, and their power and influence would be greatly diminished.

The retirement of these 93 officers all in one day was salutary. It meant that taking part in a coup or benefiting from one could catch up with you, no matter how long it would take, and for as long as you are alive. Their retirement did not stand in the way of any of them entering public life or making progress in it. Some of them later entered politics and became elected governors; some went into parliament; others got appointed as ministers or ambassadors. The idea was not to punish them for life but to exclude them from positions in the military where they could be coup planners, coup plotters, coups executors or coup beneficiaries. And once an officer has tasted the trappings of a political life, of living in a government house, with free food and so on, he would easily look for excuses to want more if he is in a position to make it happen.

The fact that since 1999 there has not been a coup or an attempted coup in Nigeria speaks of the effectiveness of the measures taken to put an end to the destabilising influence of coups on the political life and dispensation of Nigeria. Before 1999, and since independence, the longest that a democratic dispensation had lasted was six years – from 1960 to 1966.

It has neither been easy nor perfect, but there are improvements and evidence of learning among the political class. Any bad signs and misconduct would have to be carefully monitored. For those countries with similar experiences to Nigeria's, there is a need to find an effective and relatively painless way of curbing the incidence of coups and corruption by the military.

Preventing civilian coups, developing a democracy playbook

There is a meaningful debate to be had about the value of democracy to African countries and their leaders as they wrestle with the serious development challenges that face the continent. This is moot, given that we are seeing a pause in democratic progress and consolidation, as evidenced by Freedom House data, including how constitutions have been changed to allow incumbent leaders to serve for longer and increasing allegations of rigged elections.

One argument used to delay democracy is that it distracts from difficult development decisions but that, over time, with increased national income, it becomes a luxury that can be afforded. Put differently, this is sometimes rendered as the view that dictatorship can be optimal for poor countries until they reach a particular development benchmark, sometimes registered in terms of per capita wealth.[31] However, econometric analysis does not support the view that 'democracy becomes a hindrance to economic growth below a certain threshold of development'.[32] Neither does this argument explain why Africa has slipped towards increasing authoritarianism despite more than a decade of high economic growth.

The slide towards authoritarianism is less about a binary choice, as noted above, between autocracy and democracy, but entails more subtle interventions to change the course of an election or institutional process. Such interventions are seldom considered significant enough by the international community to warrant censure, let alone intervention. But usurping the democratic process has become an art form in Africa, where the losers and victims have little voice and, in the words of former Zambian president Guy Scott after his country's controversial 2016 election, can 'be picked off one by one'.[33]

In that election, for example, an external team was brought in to audit the voters' roll for discrepancies. But the audit happened much later than initially scheduled, giving rise to suspicions that it had been delayed to prevent inspection by the opposition and any legal challenge regarding its integrity. Although the process was supposed to take place at the Electoral Commission of Zambia's headquarters, the official audit, and the laptop containing it, were reportedly moved under the direction of the Office of the President and taken to a safe house around the corner from the electoral commission and given to consultants working for the Office of the President. The opposition, the United Party for National Development (UPND), said: 'The government's objective was to access to the main Electoral Commission of Zambia server room and to insert favourable numbers during the counting process based on the information from the electoral roll.'

The UPND learnt about this scheme through an informant, who provided them with pictures from within the safe house. One option considered by the opposition was to raid the house and destroy the equipment. This, however, would have put the UPND source in considerable danger while providing the 'auditors' enough time to relocate to another safe house. The UPND team also thought about releasing the images to the international media, but realised the likelihood of a tepid response, while it too would have compromised their sources. Instead, the UPND identified the route of the underground cables from the safe house to the electoral commission building and, without anyone knowing, had the wires cut just as the counting process began. 'This gave them no more time to move,' recalls the UPND officer, 'and eliminated incorrect numbers being put into the system. In a panic, one of the consultants [to the Office of the President] tried to enter the ECZ building in an attempt to fix the problem by entering numbers manually. He was spotted by one of the UPND members and wrestled to the ground before being arrested.'[34] After the failure of this plan, the Patriotic Front apparently resorted to more basic, but no less effective tactics, including deploying armed thugs at various polling stations to hound out UPND agents.

What is emerging from Zambia's and other African elections, including those in 2016 in Uganda and Gabon (where a claimed 99.9 per cent turnout in President Ali Bongo's stronghold, the province of Haut-Ogooué, just tipped the balance in his favour by 5 000 votes) is a winning template for incumbents: close down the democratic space, run interference, misuse state resources, control the diet of information and, if necessary, don't let the numbers stand in your way.

In the build-up to Zambia's election day, no media were available to disseminate pro-opposition news, despite the fact major sums of money and international subsidies were paid to the state broadcaster, the Zambia National Broadcasting Corporation (ZNBC), to assist its programming. This created an environment where only pro-government broadcasting was heard. The International Press Institute found that hindering opposition media cast a 'shadow' over Zambia's democracy.[35]

The ZNBC refused to air favourable opposition coverage, including Hichilema's UPND political campaign documentary, until ordered to do so by the High Court days before the election.[36] The documentary was aired once, well outside of prime time. Following the court ruling that it should be aired, the ZNBC claimed that there were no programming slots left. When *The Post* newspaper, MUVI Television and Komboni FM continued to cover the opposition, they had their offices raided and staff were attacked. They were forced to close. Limitations were placed on the opposition's public rallies and restrictions were enforced to curtail the free movement of opposition leaders.[37] These restrictions were a huge blow to the opposition given that so much of African political campaigning is about meeting the candidates and receiving memorabilia.

From the opposition's perspective, police intimidation and violence were also far more apparent during the 2016 poll than any previous elections in Zambia's history. Opposition supporters were killed, many others were beaten by hired thugs in full view of the police, and women were assaulted and stripped. The apparent purpose was widespread intimidation. The arrest of opposition leaders on suspect charges was commonplace throughout the campaign, its aim to cause disruption. According to the opposition, extra ballot papers were printed before the election. Registration of foreign voters on the electoral roll also became an issue, with a high number of these voting in key border towns. There was little the opposition could do, however, given that access to the voters' roll was denied them until the 11th hour. On the actual day of the election, 11 August 2016, the voting process went smoothly in most areas. Afterwards the UPND claimed that ballots had been binned, and that there had been widespread intimidation, tampered results and systematic bias in counting. The opposition alleged that the 'Gen 12' forms – those that certified the outcome of the count at every polling station with agents and representatives from all parties present signing – were withheld from UPND agents, so that they were not able to verify the results. The delay, they say, enabled the Patriotic Front to fiddle with the numbers, notably in the capital, Lusaka, where nearly one in six of registered voters resided. Certainly, the vote counting and the issuing of results slowed over the weekend following the election, despite being expected much earlier, a tell-tale sign of a fix.

Despite – or *because* of all this – the Patriotic Front achieved its 50.1 per cent winning margin by only 5 000 votes out of nearly 3.8 million cast.[38] Even if all the allegations of election malfeasance are discounted, the margin to avoid a run-off was suspiciously small, just 0.13 per cent.

These events demonstrate that holding elections is by itself insufficient to claim a democracy. Indeed, elections may even reinforce authoritarianism if they permit the subjugation of democratic process through electoral fraud.

Even before the results were made public, various international observer teams found the voting and counting process, in the words of the Commonwealth report, 'credible and transparent'. The European Union Election Observation Mission said 'voting was peaceful and generally well administered' despite being 'marred by systematic bias in the state media and restrictions on the [opposition] campaign'. There were other international missions from the Carter Centre, the AU, the Southern African Development Community (SADC), the Common Market for Eastern and Southern Africa, and the Electoral Institute for Sustainable Democracy in Africa.[39]

With their eye on preventing violence, the international community encouraged the UPND to seek legal recourse rather than take to the streets. 'Any challenges to the process at any level, from the president right down to district level, should be taken through legal means to the courts, with evidence, not to the streets,' said Janet Rogan, head of the UN resident office in Zambia, shortly after the final results had been announced.[40] Hichilema's party petitioned the results to the courts within the prescribed seven-day period. They were then given 14 days to compile and present their case to the Constitutional Court, which ruled that the hearing would start on 2 September 2016. Thereupon the full bench (which had been nominated by President Lungu) decided that the hearing would continue on Monday 5 September. On the Monday, three of the five judges decided that the 14 days stipulated by the constitution for an election petition hearing had expired on 2 September and therefore threw the case out.[41]

It would be tempting for international observers and outside governments – and investors likewise – to believe that their interests are best served in such fractious circumstances by doing nothing, a cliché-ridden policy choice of 'keeping your head down', 'not rocking the boat', 'letting them get on with things', and 'waiting and seeing'. The benchmark for a successful election is set very low by international observers: it is about preventing violence more than anything else, even if the books are obviously cooked. And their unwillingness to shake the system has a strategic competitive aspect, since other international actors are unlikely to do so, and may profit from any bilateral upset. There is a need to develop a 'democracy playbook' for elections.

To counter fraud and intimidation, opposition forces have to generate their own sophisticated processes of election monitoring, including parallel voter tabulation, and ensure their results are tallied and published before those of the government agency. This is something that the victorious campaign of Muhammadu Buhari managed to do in Nigeria in 2015 when up against the huge resources behind Goodluck Jonathan's campaign. Here, the spread of digital technology in Africa presents a paradox. Technology offers the means to quickly mobilise mass movements, especially in cities. At the same time, it can be used, in the absence of institutional norms, and checks and balances, to spread outrageous propaganda and the government can turn off communications at the flick of a (cellular) switch.

Countering these trends requires vigilance, but also alternative media outlets, free from government interference, and an opposition capable of advertising on radio, television, print and the social media. It demands extensive – and expensive – polling to assess and target such messaging. It requires the free movement of party campaigners, canvassers and election monitors alike.

All this requires funding – lots of it. It is estimated, for example, that the Zambian presidential candidates had, before the 2016 contest, spent as much as $15 million each on their earlier 2011 and 2015 campaigns. Jonathan's failed attempt to retain the election in Nigeria in 2015 is rumoured to have cost more than a billion US dollars. The eventual winner Muhammadu Buhari's campaign was closer to $200 million. The Buhari victory shows that money is not everything, however, and can be countered by clever alliance politics and electoral tactics.

Hichilema says that international observers were 'absolutely useless' in supporting the democratic process in his country.[42] However well meaning they may be, their role might instead be pernicious, since they are unlikely, by their mere presence, to accept that they have presided over a fraudulent event. For many of them, that would be an inconvenient truth. Of course, they could play a more useful role. For example, rather than allowing an incumbent to facilitate their supply from Dubai, why not provide ballot papers that can't be tampered with; rather than paying for observers to live it up at the Intercontinental, why not finance private-security companies to secure polling stations? That's how observers can be useful and taxpayers' money can be used to good effect.

If they lack political teeth, or resources, or both, observers would do better in such cases by not pretending, and just staying away.

Even so, history shows that the keys to domestic political power, like peace, are held by local actors, not foreign, whether from Africa or farther afield. For example, African governments established the African Peer Review Mechanism (APRM) in 2003 as a voluntary self-assessment of countries' governance. To date, there are 34 members, while 18 countries had, by November 2016, completed the assessment process.[43] Although it started well, like other institutions, the APRM fell afoul of a 'laundry list' approach, setting a lengthy list of governance priorities without the necessary means or will to address them. This was compounded by a lack of political will 'by African leaders, especially following the exit of presidents Mbeki and Obasanjo,' explains one official, who worked in the secretariat, and following the demise of Prime Minister Meles Zenawi of Ethiopia.[44]

This failure of African governments – and investors – to take the APRM seriously and the lack of tough engagement around elections are indicative of a difficulty in changing domestic political dynamics, of generating leverage over the elites and their ways of doing things. As a result, the record of outsiders improving governance and democracy in Africa is poor, not least because African leaders routinely resist such 'conditionality' on external assistance. Donors have consequently soft-pedalled on democracy and rule-of-law interventions, preferring less controversial initiatives, such as infrastructure assistance and the development of skills. But being firmer and more outspoken on democracy is the right thing to do, for reasons of long-term economic growth and because it means taking the side of the majority of Africans.

Conclusion: The need for institutions and urgency

Frustration with the pace of African economic reform can encourage populism and excuse authoritarianism in the interest of 'getting things done'.

But democracy is not only about results. It is about fair results and fair process. The latter includes open elections, inclusive governance and respect for the rule of law. The problem, as Nic Cheeseman reminds us, with populist politicians is that they rarely follow due process.[45] Rather than building up institutions, they break down old barriers to achieve their goals. Because they shake things up, they often receive immediate high praise for making changes. But their refusal to follow institutional rules and adhere to accepted norms leads, invariably, to the hollowing out of already weak systems, the erosion of checks and balances, and their substitution by political theatre and personality cults. This creates even greater space for abuse. It often starts with the corruption of the electoral system, and the harassment and persecution of the opposition. Over time, as it becomes more difficult to maintain momentum, authoritarianism inevitably creeps in.

Democracy and development are not a trade-off of one against the other. 'In the long-run,' Cheeseman says, 'efforts to promote development and fight corruption will not be successful unless they strengthen the institutions of the state.'[46] Ad hoc efforts to stop corruption may attract attention and look effective, but by being highly personalised, they only serve to compound the problem. The aim of governance is, after all, to allow for less personal discretion, not more. And it's not a question of whether individual leaders steal that defines the political economy, even though their example can be morally important. It's about whether their actions serve to strengthen or undermine institutions and their checks and balances. As Cheeseman says, what populists tend to do is rarely sustaining for either democracy or development.

There is one other aspect worth highlighting for those regimes unreceptive to their citizens' needs and demands, those happy with muddling along, serving the interests primarily of elites. The Arab Spring and, subsequently, Brexit and the rise of Donald Trump teach of the removal of previous barriers to politics, especially of money and access to traditional media. Tweeting 10 million followers, after all, costs nothing. Blogging and the internet are also powerful tools, free from traditional media-house filters. This is a trend that African electorates are exposed to through ever increasing mobile-connectivity rates. The possibility of greater political upheaval may also reflect the stake younger generations perceive they have in this status quo.[47] Of course, the use of technology is not one way – on the contrary, sophisticated media messaging by the Russian government and the manipulation of internet access by certain African governments illustrate that the authorities also understand, and know how to harness, the power of digital technology.

The population growth forecast for sub-Saharan African countries presents an enormous challenge, and stresses the need for urgency. To manage it, countries need to rapidly create jobs, while controlling the social tensions that such growth will produce. A democratic system of government with strong institutions has historically proven to be the most effective style of government for dealing with these challenges, and it is what African people want. Ultimately, truly strong leaders are comfortable with the challenge, competition and accountability that democracy brings. They do not need to suppress opposition with force or election fiddling: they win with better, more effective policies, underpinned with a track record of delivery.

Chapter 3
Infrastructure

Five steps for success:
- Infrastructure development requires a long-term approach to support projects that may take many years to complete, and to maintain the confidence of investors.
- Clear revenue models for capital infrastructure projects must be developed at the outset.
- The critical role of the private sector in infrastructure development will be influenced by the extent of public-sector monopolies.
- Infrastructure must be carefully linked to policy on trade, connectivity, skills and openness.
- The construction of housing can be supported by giving local authorities greater autonomy, pursuing a policy of increasing density in cities, simplifying the procedures for land title and supporting initiatives for affordable housing.

Challenges and opportunities: Functioning infrastructure – the roads, railways, ports, electricity and water networks, and other basic systems that make a country run – is an absolute precondition for development and growth in the sectors that subsequent chapters examine. African infrastructure is so poor at the moment that even slight improvements can dramatically affect the business climate of many countries and signal the beginnings of a turnaround. The current condition of basic infrastructure and regulatory systems in Africa pose a more-or-less absolute constraint to growth. To take just one example, it is hard to see how Africa can grow its manufacturing sector without improving its capacity to generate the electricity that such businesses rely upon.

Key statistics: Two-thirds of the population of Africa – 600 million people – are without access to electricity. By comparison, 75 per cent of the population of East Asia have access to power. Two-thirds of sub-Saharan Africa's installed electricity capacity is in one country, South Africa, which itself is beset with shortages and blackouts. Just one-third of Africans living in rural areas are within 2 kilometres of an all-season road, compared with two-thirds of the population in other developing regions. It is estimated that Africa requires $93 billion in annual spending to address its infrastructure backlog, nearly half of which is for power. More than 90 per cent of Africa's trade is moved outside the continent by sea.

'*Sklikktery klak … screee … sklikkerty klak.*' The Tazara Railway shook, rattled and rolled along the route between Kapiri Mposhi, in central Zambia, to Dar es Salaam, 1 860 kilometres away on the Indian Ocean. Tazara was the brainchild of presidents Kenneth Kaunda and Julius Nyerere, a shared centrepiece of African solidarity, development and anticolonialism. Today, Tazara is only just operational, with four scheduled weekly passenger services and infrequent freight trains.[1] In 2015 Tazara carried just 88 000 tonnes of freight, a long way from the 5 million-tonne capacity installed by the Chinese in October 1975, when they built the line, and the lowest recorded annual figure since freight operations started.[2]

There are good reasons why Tazara doesn't work very well.

The statue outside the railway terminal at Kapiri Mposhi, 200 kilometres to Lusaka's north, tells a story about the railway's hopes, blood, sweat and tears – and failure. The track alone incorporates a third of a million tonnes of steel rail, all shipped from China. A giant spade remembers the labour and sacrifice of the 50 000 Chinese and 60 000 Africans who built the 320 bridges, 22 tunnels and 2 225 culverts that dot the route. More than 160 workers, including 64 Chinese, died in accidents along the way. Taming the terrain was a feat of engineering, hardship and bravery.

At the time, Tazara was the largest Chinese aid project in Africa, costing at least $500 million in 1970s prices. Nyerere had turned to the Chinese for support, given that the US, among others, had declared the railway as being without commercial sense. The motive was the need to find another shipping outlet for Zambia's copper other than via white-ruled Angola, Mozambique, Rhodesia or South Africa. Add a large dollop of pan-Africanism and Nyerere's *uhuru*, not to mention a pinch of anti-Western salting, and Tazara was a done deal.

By 2016 the passenger coaches were old and worn out, the ablutions a vigorous assault on the senses, the continuous fight to stay upright made grimmer by the smell, and their location advertised only by a trail of wet footprints. 'You should see third class,' said the senior conductor. 'They don't even have the water bucket.'

The train clatters its way slowly down from the harsh, dry, brown highlands and across the green coastal plain towards Dar, dotted with banana and palm trees, and rich grasses. Passing 93 stations along the way, the line links otherwise cut-off, exceptionally poor rural communities. At Kapwila, for example, two hours from the border with Tanzania, people throng around the train hawking everything from water to beef. The scenes are sometimes pitiful. One small girl was unsuccessfully trying to sell the water she had decanted into old Fanta bottles.

Inside the train, more complex trade is going on. One of the conductors explained that, while she has not been paid her $90 salary for five months, the privilege of her position allows her to trade. For example, she picks up rice in Dar for 300 kwacha a bag and sells it at Kapiri for 400 kwacha. Others are doing much the same with second-hand clothes, known in Bemba as '*salaula*' (to 'pick' or 'rummage'), and bananas and sweet potatoes, thereby integrating the central and east African regions in spite of government.

Our journey took 50 hours, averaging under 40 kilometres per hour, but for more than 10 hours we had been stopped at stations along the way, shunting, loading people and produce, and getting through the border. A further hour or more was added by a faulty brake diaphragm, repaired by many men with big, loud hammers. There is no money to pay salaries and sometimes just enough for half a tank of fuel for the journey, leaving trains stranded en route. Delays are also due to software, human and organisational glitches, not just shortages of equipment.

Despite the overturned wagons and broken rolling stock littering the lines, as well as the declared 48 decayed sections where a speed limit has been imposed and the coaches bounce and lean more than normal, the line is generally in good condition – unsurprising, since it is almost brand new in railway-use terms. In a few places the Chinese-inscribed concrete sleepers have been stolen. Tazara also has 90 virtually new Chinese wagons among its working rolling stock of more than 500, and 14 serviceable giant General Electric locos.

The Chinese remain only half interested in keeping the railway dream alive. By 2015 they were into the 15th assistance protocol but they don't seem to want to commit to fixing it. Beijing's Africa policy is no longer driven by misty-eyed sentiment and mutual socialism as much as hard-nosed self-interest and commerce. The policies of other donors have also not generally helped. Over the last 15 years, Western aid has focused on improving the roads, especially in landlocked Zambia. Aid flows have gone hand-in-hand with graft on road contracts, some of the money to eventually wind up funding political campaigns. And when donors have tightened up on governance, the money has gone unspent. For example, half of the 2014 European allocation of €140 million for road funding in Zambia was returned to Brussels.

As a result, traffic has been diverted from the railroad to highways. While 60 per cent of the traffic leaving the port of Dar es Salaam went by rail down the central and Tazara lines 25 years ago, in 2015 this figure was less than 0.7 per cent.

By 2015, Tazara carried less than 2 per cent of its designed freight capacity. The cost of moving things by road, via Tanzania, Mozambique, Namibia or South Africa, should be higher given the relative load efficiencies of rail. But it is not. Both are around $145 per tonne. And whereas a truck from the Copperbelt to Durban will take around a week, the train to Dar has been known to take as long as two months. As one of the larger copper producers in Zambia noted, every day a tonne of copper is halted, it costs the company 60 US cents per tonne.

Tazara can be turned around, but to do so will require dollops of political will. At first, it will necessitate recognition that its current state is not adequate, even though it suits several key actors to keep it down and out. Among other aspects, it will also require the recently deconcessioned Zambia Railways to improve its own service to link between the mining areas and the Tazara line through Kapiri Mposhi.

The benefits of improvement would be huge, and would extend beyond mining. For example, Zambia has the potential to double its annual maize output, with ease, to 4 million tonnes. To date, the most Zambia has ever managed to export in one year has been 600 000 tonnes because of logistics constraints. It costs $180 per tonne to move fertiliser by road from Beira, and just $50 to Beira from the outside world. Hence its high cost at $400 per tonne. Zambia uses 400 000 tonnes of fertiliser for its annual requirement of 2 million tonnes of maize. If this input cost is reduced, yields will shoot up.

At the end of the Tazara line, the port must work; at the moment it does not. In 2014 Dar did 14.5 million tonnes of trade, including 642 000 containers, up from 3.8 million tonnes and 124 000 containers in 2000. Of this, just 1.8 million goes to Zambia. One World Bank report has shown that, on average, each vessel waits for 20 days in Dar, compared to three to four days in world-class ports.[3] With the port creaking under the strain of handling 1 250 trucks each day, the railway sits idle. In the port manager's words, 'In order for us to be efficient … the railway has to be efficient. The railway has failed us.'[4] Fixing the system requires champions for rail more powerful than the opposing trucking lobby and those who profit from endless delays and demurrage. It was both unsurprising, but at the same time encouraging, that one of Tanzanian president John Magufuli's first acts in office was to disband the port authority's board of directors over its failure to take action against the port's long history of poor performance.

If Dar were to become as efficient a port as Mombasa today (and that is hardly a global leader), Tanzania would earn approximately an extra $2 billion a year, or 7 per cent of its GDP, with a further $800 million annually flowing to neighbouring countries. There would be obvious benefits from increased flows to port operators and tax authorities, much greater than the $300 million, which is currently estimated to be the amount made from fees by slowing things down.

The African infrastructure challenge

There is a tremendous backlog in Africa's infrastructure. Africa's spending on infrastructure nearly halved, to just over 1 per cent of GDP, between 1980 and 1998. And whereas African defence spending (as a percentage of government expenditure) averaged 10 per cent in 1998, spending on infrastructure was just 4 per cent. Take the example of Ghana. With less than a quarter of China's road density (and just 4 per cent of India's), it was no wonder that road transportation costs in Ghana were between two and two and a half times higher than in Thailand, Pakistan and Sri Lanka in the mid-2000s.

The World Bank estimated in 2009 that Africa, compounded by the effects of population growth, required $93 billion in annual spending to address its infrastructure backlog. The report, *Africa's Infrastructure: A Time for Transformation*, estimated that fragile states would need to devote around one-third of their GDP to a catch-up infrastructure programme. 'The conundrum is that countries with the greatest infrastructure needs are often the countries that are least attractive to investors,' says the report.[5] Of the $93 billion, almost half was needed to boost the continent's power supply, around seven times the rate of the annual average financing over the last 10 years. It also noted that a quarter of Africa's installed power-generation capacity is not operational. The report calculated that improving the operating efficiency of existing infrastructure, collecting bills, trading across regions, reducing excessive staffing and other savings could reduce the annual funding gap to $31 billion.[6] African governments already spend $45 billion annually on infrastructure, of which 40 per cent is allocated to power alone. So, in theory, through the effective, efficient allocation of resources, a solution is within grasp. But the reality is somewhat different.

If the work to catch up already looks daunting, it is worth noting that the electricity requirement of the continent is expected to double by 2030 and treble by 2040.

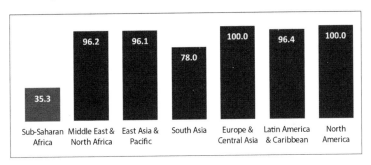

Figure 3.1: Access to electricity (% of population) in 2012

Source: World Bank, Sustainable Energy for All, Global Electrification database, http://databank.worldbank.org/data/reports.aspx?source=world-development-indicators&preview=on#

Yet in 1970, sub-Saharan Africa had three times the generation capacity of South Asia. Now the population without access to electricity in sub-Saharan Africa is the highest of any region in the world (see Figure 3.1). Africa's average residential electricity consumption per capita is equivalent to

73

around half the average level of China's or one-fifth of Europe's. Put differently, 12 countries in sub-Saharan Africa account for 90 per cent of capacity; 30 countries have power systems smaller than 500 megawatts; and 13 have systems less than 100 megawatts.[7]

Roads and other basic infrastructure are similarly inadequate. The World Bank points out that only one-third of Africans living in rural areas are within 2 kilometres of an all-season road, compared with two-thirds of the population in other developing regions.[8] Freight charges in sub-Saharan Africa were on average 200 per cent more expensive during 2010 than elsewhere in the world, according to the World Bank. In South Africa, which is more developed than its neighbours, costs were still 40 per cent higher than in other countries outside the continent.

Much of this situation can be explained by a failure to reinvest, poor policy and a (deliberate) lack of competition perpetuated by monopoly practices. For example, South Africa's rail network is the 10th largest worldwide and represents about 80 per cent of Africa's total. Yet South Africa's rail services are so inefficient that just 13 per cent of all freight is transported by rail (compared to 48 per cent for Australia, or 21 per cent for Brazil[9]). This pushes up transport costs, particularly for bulk mineral exports. South Africa's transport costs amounted to 57 per cent of overall logistics costs in 2014,[10] well above the global average of 39 per cent.

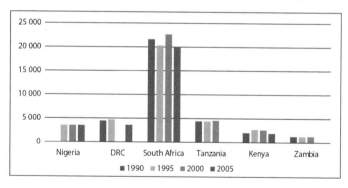

Figure 3.2: Railway lines in Africa, route km, 1990–2005

Source: World Bank, Transportation, Water, and Information and Communications Technologies Department, Transport Division. (Information available only for select years.) http://databank.worldbank.org/data/reports.aspx?source=world-development-indicators&preview=on#

Low investment is not just a South African problem. In the 1970s Zambia was considered to have one of the best African rail and road transport networks. Yet 20 years later, the government itself estimated that 80 per cent of the road network had deteriorated. Out of total road assets valued at $2.3 billion, $400 million had been lost through neglected maintenance. Tazara was beset with avoidable problems, notably vandalism of the infrastructure, a backlog of maintenance and lack of investment. Trains were often forced to stop because fishplates and sleepers had been removed from the track. The concrete sleepers were taken and crushed to extract the reinforcing steel for scrap.

Although infrastructure development is difficult, the root of the infrastructure failure is in the political economy. Limited competition along trucking trade corridors in the sub-Saharan region has kept road tariffs unnecessarily high. Links between the ruling elite and the trucking companies have resulted in unbalanced policy preferences. As the World Bank notes, the profit margins, however, range between 60 per cent (in southern Africa) and 160 per cent (West Africa), 'shared between bribes, regulatory rents, and transport company profits'.[11]

'Despite the commercial and economic imperative for making investments in infrastructure,' one investor with experience across a number of countries and sectors observes, 'African governments seldom exhibit a burning urgency to get things done. This reflects,' she says, an experience repeated across the sector, 'lack of government capacity, specialist skills, a robust legal system where international conventions are converted into domestic law, financial acumen, and the overall enabling environment for business.' When it comes to the debate around power, for example, there are challenges in securing a long-term power-purchasing agreement. 'A lack of understanding about the basics around royalties and contracts,' she notes, 'leads to lots of negotiating time, even for the smallest investment, and lots of "binary" brinkmanship in the process.'[12]

Success thus requires more than just financing for development. The Panama experience illustrates the importance of focusing on the need for an overall policy environment – infrastructure software – in addition to the provision of hard physical infrastructure.

Panama: A delivery package

Both Dar es Salaam and Panama have it but only the latter truly uses it: location, location, location.

Not only is this the estate agent's maxim, but it is said to be one that also applies to development success. Think Singapore, at the trading crossroads of South East Asia. Or Morocco, just across the Strait of Gibraltar from Europe. Or Panama.

The completion of the canal just over 100 years ago, breaching the Central American isthmus was, even by contemporary standards, an extraordinary achievement. It took the excavation of more than 150 million cubic metres of earth, two decades and two attempts: first by the French from 1881, and then by the Americans.

The French effort went bankrupt in 1889 after they spent nearly $290 million, and cost the lives of 22 000 of the 63 000 workers, mostly from malaria and yellow fever.

Starting up the project again in 1904, the Americans finished the job 10 years later. They completed the Gaillard Cut, built the 1 000-foot-long locks with their 50-foot-thick concrete walls and 88 pairs of 700-tonne steel doors, in the process creating Gatun Lake, at the time the world's largest man-made reservoir. Building the canal cost $375 million, about $9 billion in 21st-century money, and the lives of another 5 600 labourers. Though still shockingly high, the fatality rate was significantly reduced with the discovery of the link between malaria and the mosquito, as a result of research led by Drs Carlos Finlay and Walter Reed, and the sanitation projects to mitigate the disease that ensued.

This amazing technological achievement, which raises vessels 85 feet in three chambers each on the Pacific and Atlantic sides through giant gravity-fed 6-metre-diameter spigots, has been an extraordinary money-spinner for both the US government and, since the handover of control in 1977, for the Panamanians.

Each day 45 to 50 ships make the 77-kilometre voyage, at an average cost of $85 000 per ship – the maximum cost being $490 000 – depending on their size. It was originally estimated that the canal would carry around 80 million tonnes of shipping traffic annually. By 2016, it was over 300 million tons.

But geography alone is no guarantee of success. Panama could have been Nicaragua, a country with its own plans for a canal. Now the former has an economy of $8 200 per capita; the latter $1 450. It is just that Panama took advantage of its location.

Panama has been one of the fastest expanding economies worldwide during the last 15 years, growing at an average of over 7 per cent between 2001 and 2014, over double the regional average in Latin America.

A University of Chicago-trained economist, and former World Bank vice-president, Nicolás Barletta served as president of Panama from 11 October 1984 until 28 September 1985, when he resigned over the military's increasingly violent role. Barletta, who later served as head of the canal authority, identifies several drivers in the Panamanian economy: geography, regional and global connectivity (including the regional airline, Copa), the canal, its sophisticated telecoms, and a healthy policy environment.

As a result of these factors, says the former president, '83 per cent of the economy is made up of services, including tourism, the trade zones, medical health, the ports, ship bunkering and repair, and banking'. The results have been significant: 'On the demand side of the economy, exports have grown by an annual average of 14.5 per cent for the last 12 years; and on the supply side, investment makes up 27 per cent of GDP, comprising equally the state, local private sector and foreigners.' This rate is well above the regional average of 20 per cent of GDP.[13]

In terms of complementary policy, the use of the US dollar offers monetary stability (Panama has no central bank), while tax reforms have reduced rates and brackets, simplifying filings and improving collection. The corporate tax rate is a flat 25 per cent.

There was always a danger that an earner like the canal, which brings in $1 billion annually in profits to government, could have led to government apathy and national laziness. Yet the Panamanians have not stood still on all manner of inherited infrastructure.

At either end of the canal, the two ports have been run by a Hong Kong-based company since 2000. And in 2007 work began on a $7.8 billion canal expansion to allow vessels with a beam of 180 feet to pass, such as ships carrying 13 000 containers. The expansion was opened in June 2016.

The old canal could take vessels of up to a maximum of 80 000 dead-weight tonnes carrying up to 4 400 containers (termed Panamax). The canal expansion enables it to handle vessels of up to 120 000 deadweight tonnes, carrying up to 13 000 containers. The charge per vessel through the new locks is estimated at $1.5 million each. This is still less expensive than the alternative of a trip around the Horn.

The expansion is not the only sensible long-term investment Panama has made. While others talk about special economic zones, Panama has created six. American troops were based in Panama across 14 locations until 31 December 1999. Although their presence was an affront to some Panamanians, many realised the financial benefit these 'hidden tourists' brought. Rather than lamenting the financial loss after the Americans left, the government and private sector set about converting the old bases into productive centres and economic communities. The former US Air Force base at Howard is now Panama Pacifico, a special economic zone, just a 15-minute drive from Panama City across the Bridge of the Americas. This special economic zone hosts 248 companies, two-thirds of which are in manufacturing. Most are foreign, including big names such as 3M, BASF, Caterpillar, Dell and SAB Miller.

Panama Pacifico aims to attract businesses that will ultimately employ 40 000, with residential space for 60 000. Its motivation was to 'find ways,' says Frank Terracina, the director of marketing, 'of adding value to the goods shipped through the canal'.

Past the Pacific end of the Panama Canal Railway sidings, where 40-foot containers are loaded onto 50-wagon double-decker trains, is the City of Knowledge on the site of the old Fort Clayton US Army base, where now 5 000 people work. The brainchild of two visionary businessmen, Gabriel Lewis and Fernando Eleta, the City was created as an innovation centre.

If the land was the endowment for the City of Knowledge, the rentals from the 200 buildings on the 120-hectare site provide the cash flow. The types of businesses, non-governmental organisations and research institutions are carefully selected on account of their technology and knowledge component.

The attraction to businesses and others of both Panama Pacifico and the City of Knowledge lies in a combination of excellent connectivity, simplified bureaucratic procedures, liberal visa laws, and no taxes.

Hence the City of Knowledge has 15 times as many applicants as available spaces. Although Panama's minimum monthly wage is $600, the average pay for those working on the site is more than $1 500.

Of course, Panama has its problems. Its politics remain fraught and there are ongoing concerns about the rule of law and corruption. For example, former president Ricardo Martinelli, who stepped down in July 2014, has been accused of bribery, and has decamped to Florida. A quarter of the country lives in poverty, which is notably high in the rural areas, although this has come down significantly from 40 per cent in 2008. And the country's role as a tax haven was thrown into the spotlight by the Panama Papers, the leak of 11.5 million incriminating documents from the files of the world's fourth-biggest offshore law firm, Mossack Fonseca.[14]

However, in just five years nearly half a million Panamanians have escaped poverty principally as a result of faster economic growth. There has also been an overall decline in inequality. As former president Barletta notes, 'If we do the right thing, Panama's potential is to grow at six per cent for the foreseeable future.'

A key element of the 'right thing' has been to take the development of infrastructure seriously and to turn ambitious plans into action.

The critical housing and construction component

The township of Khayelitsha, isiXhosa for 'our home', was set out 35 kilometres from the Cape Town CBD in the mid-1980s. It represented a last attempt at apartheid spatial planning and a solution to the then burgeoning problems for the authorities presented by inflows of migrants, especially from the Eastern Cape, which had resulted in the creation of informal settlements, such as Crossroads, near Cape Town Airport. The pressures increased with the scrapping in 1986 of pass laws, which had been designed to limit the movement of black citizens, as the apartheid system unwound.

Housing has a central role in development, both as a social 'glue' and a personal financial investment.

Despite recent upsets with speculative housing bubbles and financial instability, in developed economies housing is often the largest personal tangible investment. Oxford University's Paul Collier and Anthony Venables illustrate that property makes up more than one-third of the total private wealth of households in Britain of $15 trillion. National asset accumulation is thus 'fundamentally bound up with investment in housing'.[15] Furthermore, housing construction creates employment, particularly given its labour-intensive nature, which is added to by the construction of transport and other related infrastructure.

As Figure 3.3 shows, there has been a significant increase in spending on infrastructure projects in Africa. However, only a very small percentage of this figure is spent on housing – estimated at just 10 per cent of public and private expenditure allocated to real estate and social development. In 2015, for example, 37 per cent was spent on transport, 28 per cent on energy and power, and just 6 per cent on real estate.[16]

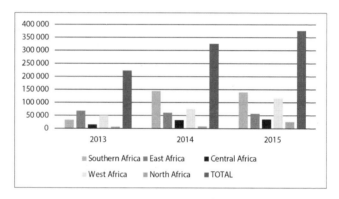

Figure 3.3: Africa's infrastructure projects ($ millions), 2013–2015

Source: Deloitte, Africa Construction Trends Report 2015, https://www2.
deloitte.com/content/dam/Deloitte/za/Documents/manufacturing/ZA-
ConstructionTrendsReport-2015.pdf

Yet, in much of Africa, from Khayelitsha to Kibera, and Makoko to Manenberg, the typical household lives in a low-cost shack, or worse. According to the African Development Bank, while sub-Saharan Africa has the lowest proportion of urban dwellers worldwide, it has the highest proportion of slum dwellers, at 65 per cent. Only about half of the continent's urban dwellers have access to sanitation, and one-third to electricity. Consequently, as rural–urban migration and population growth further stretch these resources, inequality in African cities remains the second highest in the world, with an average Gini coefficient of 0.58, well above the global average of 0.4.[17]

In the developed world, including in North Africa, housing is mostly built by private firms to acceptable standards, with discernible market value, and available for a mix of renting and ownership, both public and private. The scale of construction has generated formal jobs, and investment and ownership incentives for subsequent maintenance.[18] African houses, by contrast, which are often self-built, often lack compliance with building regulations, frequently rely on informal and unclear rights of occupancy, and are commonly not serviced with roads, electricity, street lighting, water or sewerage by the local government, especially in low-income areas.

Khayelitsha is spread over several sites – from the arrival station for new migrants to the south-east at Nkanini, to the outlying areas of Harare and Monwabisi. The total population is 800 000 but the township was originally designed for 250 000.[19] It has a young population (just 7 per cent of residents were over 50 in the 2011 census), mostly comprising recent migrants (nearly two-thirds are rural-to-urban migrants), lending the township the moniker 'Rural in an Urban Setting'. Set out across 43 square kilometres, it is one of the poorest areas of Cape Town: the average annual income per family is R20 000 ($1 250) – about half of the average for the city. Half of the settlements are informal shanties. It costs a worker R40 each day (about a fifth of a daily casual wage) to commute to the Cape Town city centre, where most of the work is found. This high cost reflects the geography: most people don't live near to where they work. Even so, this daily commute is shorter than the norm across South Africa, where workers travel for an average of two hours a day, and 40 per cent of their wages are spent on transport.

There are several initiatives funded by the city government to try to improve skills, security and business opportunities around Khayelitsha's key arteries. In the adjoining Harare and Kusaya townships, for example, this has involved building a series of rental sites close to the train station, which house some of the township's 3 000 spaza shops. There is also a well-patronised library at the centre. As one official said, it is like an 'externalised shopping mall'.

These initiatives have been enthusiastically taken up by business people, if at considerable financial cost to the city. Nearly R200 million ($13 million at the time of writing) is being spent on these improvements in Harare and Kusaya alone, and a further R627 million is earmarked for Hanover Park. But the initiatives remain complicated by issues of trust and leadership within the local communities (in terms of who speaks for whom, and with what agenda), and by the cultural baggage of rural life – an example being people's preference for single-storey dwellings. There is also the realisation that the city requires 400 000 new dwellings, some in so-called 'integration zones' closer to the city, along the commuting corridors and through more efficient use of existing urban land and dwellings. 'Over the next generation,' estimates one city official, '80 per cent of the population increase will be among the urban poor.'[20] Without action on housing, poverty will become ingrained in these townships, where houses are sublet and 'backyarders' build their own shelters among existing properties.

Spending on housing in Africa is likely to increase through a combination of population growth and increased aspirations. More than half the budget of an average African family is spent on food; housing, healthcare and education account for a further 24 per cent of household expenditure in 2015. With a projected 1.2 billion urban residents by 2050, Africa is acquiring 4.5 million new residents in informal settlements each year, thus doubling the slum population every 15 years.[21] The UN estimates that more than 200 million people will live in sub-Saharan African slums by 2020.[22]

For example, it is estimated that there is a backlog of 2.5 million units in South Africa alone and that the figure for Egypt, Nigeria and South Africa combined may be as high as 23 million, at an estimated market cost of $350 billion.[23]

There are considerable benefits to improving housing provision and access – benefits that go beyond having a comfortable, easily accessible and warm place to stay. There has been a global correlation between urbanisation and GDP growth. This is due to higher rates of productivity achieved through increased population density, economies of scale and provision of better infrastructure and services, such as education. This is evident, for example, at Khayelitsha's Site C Nolungile Station, where the Japhta K. Masemola and Solomon Tshuku roads intersect. Near the 'Kuwait' taxi rank, it is a hubbub of activity. 'Mamas' stand shrouded in smoke, fanning braais of chicken, offal, tripe and other cuts, amid containers housing funeral services, hair salons, surgeries and tailors. Despite its poverty, the area is, relatively safe because it's busy, not least because the vendors continuously keep an eye out for their own goods. Business inevitably congregates around the flow of feet and money.

Nevertheless, generally, Africa has, so far, failed to take advantage of urbanisation in economic growth terms to the same extent as other developing regions. As noted in Chapter 1, this is partly because urban migration has not been a result of the pull factor of industrialisation but rather the redistribution of rents, and partly because the push factor is low agriculture yields rather than agricultural improvements and efficiencies. For example, sub-Saharan Africa's urban population reached 40 per cent in 2013, and its GDP per capita was $1 018; East Asia and the Pacific reached this level of urbanisation in 1994 at a GDP of $3 617 per capita; the Middle East and North Africa in 1968 at $1 806 per capita; and Latin America and the Caribbean in 1950 at $1 860 per capita. Given the high percentage of personal wealth tied up in housing worldwide, the comparatively low growth in per capita income limits the resources that African households have to consume or to invest in housing.[24]

This is a double whammy, as the construction sector also offers the possibility of jobs, especially in the unskilled and semi-skilled categories. At the start of the 21st century, there were 111 million people worldwide in the construction industry, of which 75 per cent were in lower-income countries, though the construction output per worker in richer countries was nearly 10 times greater.[25] In South Africa, the best documented case in Africa, spending on construction works in 2013 amounted to R310 billion ($200 million), employing 820 000 people in the formal sector (8 per cent of the national total), and another 340 000 (17 per cent) in the informal sector. Of this, residential construction expenditure amounted to R50 billion, a sector that employed (formally) 150 000.[26] The building of a single house in Africa creates an estimated five jobs.[27]

To realise these job and other advantages demands, at its core, investment. It requires creating the right conditions, it demands planning, and it requires dealing with several aspects at once, including traffic congestion and pollution, which, as McKinsey points out, are among the other perils of unmanaged growth.[28] It requires partnerships to bring in expertise, technology and funding, and it demands dealing with policy impediments.

The simple acceptance of the principle and practice of densification offers some of the solutions. Many of the townships are already jam-packed: the density of the 150 000 inhabitants of Delft, for example, near Khayelitsha, is 14 000 per square kilometre; the density of the 17 000 people of Sweet Home Farm, one of Cape Town's 323 informal settlements, located near Hanover Park and started on a rubbish dump, is estimated at 33 000 per square kilometre.[29] Mumbai, to make a comparison, has a population density of 21 000 per square kilometre.

Acceptance of the need for high-density housing, land availability, the provision of effective services on a large scale, especially electricity, and the capacity of construction companies to build in volume are all required to manage the backlog.

Three other things are also needed. First, given the complexity of land ownership and the need to prioritise funding, there needs to be a political push from the top. Local authorities need greater autonomy, both to generate and spend revenue. Without this, they will have little interest in promoting economic growth, nor will they be able to afford the much needed essential infrastructure, without which 'sensible plans become idle dreams'.[30] This means that the banks, developers and government need to come up with a funding scheme that shares risk and reward.

Secondly, housing needs to be made affordable. The Centre for Affordable Housing Finance in Africa has calculated that the price of the least expensive newly built house by a formal, private developer is $31 085, while the mean per capita income is $1 764. This compares to the standard global affordability measure of three to five times the annual household income.[31] Little wonder, then, that most buy instead into the informal housing sector, where costs range from 2 per cent (in Malawi) to 15 per cent (in Zambia) of the cheapest formal unit. Making housing more affordable requires both building in a manner that keeps costs down, as well as providing innovative financing models, including subsidised houses and loans. Moreover, Africa's mortgage market, for example, is hopelessly underserviced. Typical terms on African mortgages are an interest rate of around 22 per cent and a term of only 10 years, catering to a 'tiny income-rich elite'.[32]

Thirdly, there needs to be clarity on legal title and rights. Here, the government has to commission innovation. There are a number of positive ways in which it could become involved – either by relaxing by-laws to allow residences to legally become businesses, or by making land available for high-employment businesses in tough neighbourhoods at peppercorn rentals or for building high-rise blocks. There is also a related need to address not only the ownership of land, including the promotion of sectional title, but also its availability, through state intervention. Currently, most cities are locked into a 'straitjacket of insufficient space'.[33] Opportunities that do not require large amounts of regulatory oversight or financial burden are preferable.

In so doing, governments have to improve the efficiency and skills levels of their bureaucracies. The average waiting time in Africa for a construction permit is 162.2 days, while registering property typically costs 8.3 per cent of the value.[34]

Job creation in Africa will, in particular, be greatly assisted by making it possible for people to live in places with easy access to their work. By definition, low-tech, high-labour manufacturing cannot be done virtually, and as China moves up the development scale, properly developed African cities can realistically aim to capture some of this work. Equally, the arrival of Africa's middle class will occur through home ownership, and the stake that this affords in economic, policy and political stability. To achieve this future, the provision of housing in Africa will have to involve both the private and public sectors. It will unquestionably be a marathon with no finishing line, a self-licking lollipop, since the more one gets things right in the city, the more people will come, and the bigger the challenge. Success will be closely tied in with effective land title and banking systems, and the establishment of credit through careful profiling.

Conclusion: Minding the gap

Turning the political economy of protecting privilege, plunder and survival into one of prosperity will lie at the heart of Tazara's transformation, as with any infrastructure project in Africa. It demands leadership letting go of control, and finding the means and structure to incentivise those operating nearer the bottom of the hierarchy. It requires managing the politics as much, if not more, than the economics.

The infrastructure deficit is a problem for all African countries, reflecting years of neglect, politicisation and underdevelopment. The costs will be high if this situation continues. According to the World Bank, the low quality of infrastructure constrains economic growth by around two percentage points every year, reducing business productivity by as much as 40 per cent. Innovation in financing and design, and better systems of usage of the existing infrastructure, are key to solving the African infrastructure deficit.

Attracting private finance is a vital part of plans to cut the deficit. Since the World Bank report of 2009 identifying the $93 billion annual infrastructure funding gap, capital funding for African infrastructure reportedly totalled about $328 billion between 2009 and 2014, or an average of $54 billion each year. In 2013, for example, flows from development institutions were $44 billion, with Asia accounting for the greatest share of the public money, at some $15.9 billion (China accounted for $13.4 billion of this amount, and Japan $1.5 billion). African development banks provided $2.2 billion, multilateral development banks $9.2 billion, Europe $6.3 billion, Arab donors $3.3 billion and the Americas $7.2 billion. Commercial lending accounted for only an additional $9 billion that year. [35]

Innovation in financing, as will be seen in Chapter 10, can help, but the answer does not lie only in new projects. More efficient use of existing infrastructure can reduce the expenditure gap to perhaps as little as a third of the estimated capital requirement. Technology might also offer some of the answers to the backlog. The cost of solar power, for example, continues to come down, offering energy alternatives for Africa. These costs have reduced by 75 per cent between 2010 and 2016, and wind by 25 per cent, challenging the primacy of fossil fuels, which currently generate 85 per cent of world energy. [36]

Maintenance of infrastructure is also especially important, but also difficult, as it is not a 'new thing' and therefore lacks kudos and money-making potential. There are positive signs, however. For example, Ethiopia has maintained a laser-like focus on infrastructure delivery, including mega-projects, like the Grand Renaissance Dam and its Djibouti–Addis rail link, generating much of its funding locally. Others have struck out on a new privatisation process to help catch up. The success of these initiatives will be determined by the extent to which, as Panama shows, they are followed through not only by delivery of the infrastructure assets, but the extent to which a whole package of reforms is put in place, including space for the private sector to operate free from regulatory overburden. In developing infrastructure, a long-term approach is vital, as is the political will to drive reform.

Part 2

The state of Africa's economy

Chapter 4
Agriculture

Five steps for success:
- Eliminate government distortions of agriculture pricing.
- Deal with fears of food shortages through better market forecasting.
- Ensure government policies embrace modern farming practices, including mechanisation, economies of scale and greater yields.
- Ensure security of long-term title for farmers, whether by leasehold or freehold.
- Improving logistics is critical to success in both food production and non-food agriculture exports.

Challenges and opportunities: Agriculture is a story of immense unrealised African potential. Other regions of the world have doubled or even tripled yields, whereas Africa's cereal yields, to give one example, are estimated by the UN Food and Agriculture Organization (FAO) to be 66 per cent below the global average.[1] Forty of the 55 African economies are net food importers, with some of the worst-performing agricultural sectors worldwide, while 300 million Africans suffer from malnutrition. The reasons for Africa's agrarian stagnation are clear: war, instability, lack of clarity about land title, low investment in people and management systems, government meddling in food prices, and the absence of economies of scale and technology. With 600 million Africans engaged directly or indirectly in agricultural production, an estimated 70 per cent of whom are women, improved performance can spread the benefits of economic growth to a marginalised section of the population.

Key statistics: Africa has 874 million hectares of arable farmland, 60 per cent of the world's total.[2] However, the continent uses only 43 per cent of its arable land with rain-fed potential. Less than 4 per cent of an estimated 39 million hectares of suitable agricultural land is currently irrigated.[3] Africa's use of fertiliser per hectare is just 13 per cent of the global average. The continent is relatively unmechanised: its farmers have only one tractor per 868 hectares, compared to the global average of one per 56 hectares. Food imports to sub-Saharan Africa total $25 billion annually.[4]

The joke, often endearingly told by Argentinians against themselves, goes that when God made Argentina, he gave it the best lands, climate, mineral endowment and much else. When the rest of the world complained, God evened things out by giving this new, bountiful land Argentinians.

The last 70 years of Argentina's economic story has been one of cycles: short boom followed by increasingly lengthy bust, followed by austerity reforms. In 1990, for example, Carlos Menem took office and introduced a series of reforms, stabilising inflation, and things started, once more, to improve. Yet, by the early 2000s, the country was once more in crisis, with serial changes of leadership and capital flight. Néstor Kirchner was then elected president in 2003 and his government stabilised the situation, presiding over a dramatic fall in both unemployment and poverty. Despite his policy populism, a semblance of economic stability returned, though this had much less to do with government policies, which included a massive debt default, than with private-sector ingenuity.

During the 1990s, the private sector in Argentina made considerable investments in new farming techniques, notably 'no-till' injected seeding along with the extensive use of herbicides and genetically modified seeds. By the mid-2000s, Chinese demand for soya, driven by a threefold increase in meat consumption per capita, fostered an Argentine export boom. 'Soya', said one Argentinian agricultural expert, 'is meat.' As a result, crop production increased from 20 million to 93 million tonnes between 1995 and 2010. Over the same period, exports rose from 2 million tonnes of soya to 56 million tonnes. This was largely driven by a surge in yields, as the area under cultivation (around 40 million hectares) increased only by 25 per cent.

Argentina is now the third largest soybean-producing country (the leaders are the US and Brazil) and the biggest exporter of processed soybean products, including meal, oil and biodiesel.

This agricultural production and export revolution has been replicated in Brazil, which grew soya exports to 54 million tonnes in 2014/15, over half of its annual production of 98 million tonnes, with China absorbing nearly 75 per cent of the total.[5] In 2000 Brazil's entire production had been just over 30 million tonnes.

Such moments of rapid agrarian change are not confined to Latin America. The term 'Green Revolution' was coined to describe what occurred in India during the 1960s and 1970s.

The Bengal Famine, the world's worst food disaster on record, occurred in 1943 in British-ruled India, when 4 million people died of hunger, caused mainly by a failure to prioritise food supply. This tragedy forced food security to be high on the agenda for postcolonial India and led to the Green Revolution between 1967 and 1978. Agricultural production increased during that period through expansion in farming areas, double-cropping, improved technology and better seeds, most notably seen in the so-called K68 high-yield-value wheat variety. These changes increased grain output from 72 million to over 130 million tonnes by 1978.[6] But the Green Revolution had shortfalls – not least, in the mind of some, because it did not create food self-sufficiency. However, not only did the Green Revolution improve food security and create agro-processing jobs, but it also allowed for industrialisation directly through the building of irrigation dams and hydropower facilities, and, indirectly, by ensuring urban food supplies.[7]

Similar stories can be told about other crops and in other countries.

At the time of the unification of North and South Vietnam in 1975, rice production amounted to 10.3 million tonnes for a population of 48 million people. Therefore, imports were required to meet shortfalls. These became bigger, as increases in production were not enough to match the growth in population. By 1980 there was a rice import requirement of 2 million tonnes. After a famine in the mid-1980s, the land-reform process was accelerated and the state monopoly relaxed, giving producers a greater stake in improving yields. As a result, by 2008 Vietnam was producing a surplus of 7 million tonnes, allowing it to become the world's second largest exporter of rice after Thailand.

A similarly impressive record exists in other areas in Vietnam's agriculture sector, notably fish farming and coffee production. The country's share of global coffee exports grew by more than 20 per cent a year during the 1990s, jumping from 0.1 per cent to 20 per cent in 30 years. Exporting 1.2 million tonnes in 2015,[8] Vietnam has become the world's second-largest coffee exporter. It is an industry that now employs about 2.6 million people, with beans grown on half a million smallholdings.[9]

In essence, Vietnam's increased output – in agriculture as in services and industry – has been due to the *doi moi* (or 'renovation') package of economic reforms, which aimed to create what is styled as a 'socialist-orientated market economy' by relaxing central control and through market liberalisation, thereby unlocking the investment and initiative needed for rapid growth. The results are impressive: in 1994, some 60 per cent of Vietnamese lived below the poverty line; 20 years later the figure was less than 10 per cent.

Africa has had its successes too. Kenya and Ethiopia are examples of progress in floriculture. Those countries now have 2 000 hectares and 600 hectares under cultivation, respectively. Their wage rates are low, they are close to European markets (compared to other regions), and their climate and altitude allow them to grow all year round. While both enjoy regional airport hubs with plentiful flights, Kenya has even established a dedicated terminal at Jomo Kenyatta International Airport to support the flower business.

Kenya's cut-flower exports increased twelvefold to 137 000 tonnes between 1988 and 2014, making it the world's third largest flower exporter. The country now supplies one-third of the European Union's (EU) flower imports. Half a million Kenyans are dependent on the sector and it brings in $600 million annually.

Further north, although its floriculture industry started with just one hectare of summer flowers in 1995, Ethiopia today ranks among the top five global suppliers. Among African producers and exporters of flowers, it is second only to Kenya. Revenues were over $265 million in 2015 and the sector is responsible for 75 000 direct jobs, most of which are occupied by women.

The first dedicated load, in 2005, recalls Tsegaye Abebe, founder of the Ethiopian Horticulture Producer Exporters Association, and the farmer who planted the first hectare, 'filled just 19 tonnes of the 36-tonne capacity of that Boeing 757. Then we filled it, increased aircraft numbers, and later moved over to a 75-tonne capacity MD-11. Today,' he smiles, 'we use two 777s daily, with three at peak, to Europe, plus passenger belly cargo to the Middle East. In all, it totals about 300 tonnes average a day over the course of the year.'[10]

Addis Ababa has offered low-interest loans to woo investors, a duty waiver on inputs and capital goods, and a five-year tax exemption for exporters. The lease of government land is 'almost free', at $7.70 per hectare annually, and concessionary loans are available with long pay-back periods.

The cut-flower industry is as much a logistics as a land business, where success is reliant on sound management and a responsive government, carefully tending to markets and pruning costs. When logistics costs are cheaper than the cost of heating European greenhouses, it makes sense to import flowers.

In South Africa the agriculture sector remains a big employer, with around 700 000 workers, approximately 5 per cent of the labour force.[11] For all of the concerns about land restitution and redistribution, the sector stands out as a model African exporter, especially of beverages, nuts and fruit, which account for two-thirds of agriculture exports. Wine exports alone brought in nearly $500 million in 2012/13.[12] These also represent highly beneficiated goods with a significant multiplier value.[13] The total direct and indirect benefits of the wine industry through tourism and other impacts are calculated to make up no less than 1.2 per cent of South Africa's GDP.[14] In the Western Cape province alone, agriculture provides more than a third of all export earnings.[15]

But, despite these success stories, overwhelmingly, the agriculture sector in Africa is characterised by not only unrealised potential, but also considerable cost in terms of nutrition, high prices and lost revenue.

The problem with African agriculture

The FAO's Rome headquarters is housed in the former Department of Italian East Africa. However, the outwardly clean lines of Mussolini's colonial headquarters, opposite the Circo Massimo, are not replicated inside. The internal layout is a confusion of alphabetically designated areas cutting across eight floors – an apt metaphor for the FAO's frustration in Africa. Its mission is to defeat hunger by acting as a problem-solving forum and a provider of technical information. Much of the focus of its 10 000 staff is on Africa, a net recipient of food aid.

Despite much effort, until now organisations such as the FAO appear to be largely powerless to do anything about this condition. By 2016, of the 37 countries worldwide that required crisis support for food shortages, more than 28 were in Africa.[16] Although world cereal production in 2016 was expected to remain constant, at around 2.5 billion tonnes, this was anticipated to fall by more than 10 per cent in Africa to 156 million tonnes.

Such extreme vagaries – and poor performance – reflect both weather patterns and conflict. However, overall, they illustrate Africa's very poor agricultural performance since independence. While other countries have revolutionised their yields to feed their people, as has been highlighted above, Africa has overwhelmingly stagnated. Undernourishment in Africa remains one of the highest in developing regions, at nearly a quarter of the population. This has a lasting effect on children and their cognitive development, setting the stage for generational problems, and exacerbating already formidable healthcare challenges.[17]

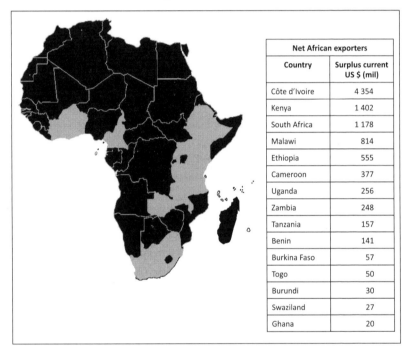

Net African exporters	
Country	Surplus current US $ (mil)
Côte d'Ivoire	4 354
Kenya	1 402
South Africa	1 178
Malawi	814
Ethiopia	555
Cameroon	377
Uganda	256
Zambia	248
Tanzania	157
Benin	141
Burkina Faso	57
Togo	50
Burundi	30
Swaziland	27
Ghana	20

Figure 4.1: African net agricultural exporters (in grey)

Source: World Bank, Africa Development Indicators, http://databank.worldbank.org/data/reports.aspx?source=africa-development-indicators#

This poor performance is also a driver of other costs. The vast majority of African countries are net food importers, which means that food pricing is at parity with imports, including the costs of transport and mark-up. There is also a huge impact from the loss of potential revenue from agriculture exports. And there is the distortive, diversionary effect of high prices on the household economy. Whereas the average American spends just 6.7 per cent of his income on food, tying with Singapore in first (i.e. cheapest) place, the first African country of the 92 surveyed by the US Department of Agriculture is South Africa, in 47th place at 19.4 per cent of income; Kenya and Nigeria fill the last two places, at 47 per cent and 56.9 per cent, respectively.[18] Little surprise, then, that more than one-third of Kenyans are considered to be malnourished. The level in Nigeria is over 40 per cent.[19] This high cost of food has a knock-on impact on the ability of citizens to invest elsewhere – for example, in healthcare, clothing, housing and education.

American food costs are low because of constant improvements in productivity, spurred by developments in mechanisation, technology and the increasing availability of chemical inputs, which have led to ever increasing economies of scale. Even as the amount of land and labour inputs used in farming in the US declined, total farm output more than doubled between 1948 and 2013.[20]

The FAO's analysis as to the reasons behind such systemic failure is refreshingly clear. There is, it says, no shortage of land and water in Africa. What is in short supply, however, are attractive and stable policy regimes, security of land tenure and a competitive approach.

However, the FAO's analysts puzzle about why the deeper problems – like the costs so clearly identified – are not then resolved. Low population density – around half of the global average and a 10th of that of Vietnam for example – hinders trading and market access, where farms and farmers are comparatively isolated. And everyone knows about the poor state of African infrastructure, especially irrigation practices and systems, and weak and expensive extension services. All these factors reflect and reinforce a lack of economies of scale. Habitual government meddling in pricing is another reason given.

Addressing these issues requires, however, an element of political will and policy granularity hitherto lacking. These failures reflect historical lack of interest by most African elites in transforming agriculture. Low population densities mean not only that there has been lower investment in fixed agriculture systems and greater propensity to physically migrate in times of stress, but also that the rural African population is so lightly scattered over the land that their political influence at the centre is limited.

This has translated into high subsidies for the urban population and low prices for rural producers. Such subsidies were often closely tracked to the timing of elections. 'Rather than farmers being seen as entrepreneurs,' says the FAO's head of trade and markets, Ben Belhassen, 'they are viewed as the rural poor.'[21] He describes this as being the cost of a tension between short-term political impulses and the need for a long-term development vision, of which farming should form part.

The solution, he says, needs to start from 'having the political will to prioritise agriculture in national development'. It also means the need to support farmers in their entrepreneurial endeavours. With both the problems and solutions known, once the political will is there, improvements will rapidly follow.

There is little doubt that improving agriculture performance offers great advantages for all African states; it has the potential for huge revenue generation and creating employment. Today, the agriculture sector in Africa is pivotal in providing employment for half the total workforce. It is also the primary source of livelihood for perhaps as many as one-quarter of urban households.[22] But the sector has remained largely stuck in low-yield, low-return smallholder agriculture. In the case of development success stories, notably those of Asia, the richer the countries and their people have become, the smaller the share of agriculture in the overall economy. Seen this way, the problem for Africa is that it has not stepped out of low-yield smallholder agriculture into something else.

There are therefore three key challenges that need to be met for agriculture to improve across Africa. First, the continent needs to improve its yields of staples, not least given the cost of moving goods across great distances; secondly, it needs to diversify crop types and access cash markets, at home and abroad; and, thirdly, to add greater value to agricultural produce.

The policies needed for greater yields are well known: improve inputs, introduce new seed varieties, provide better extension services, make investments in skills and basic infrastructure, introduce land reform, develop rural finance and insurance, and assure predictability both in pricing and the role of government.

Despite the fact these needs are understood, the reforms needed still do not occur. It seems that this has more to do with politics and the choices that politicians make.

Production, systems and technology

At the end of the 19th century, nearly half of all US workers were employed in agriculture; a hundred years later, that fraction had fallen to below 2 per cent. The same is true for the UK, where the share of the workforce employed in fishing and farming fell from 22 per cent of the workforce in the middle of the 19th century to under one per cent in the 21st.[23]

This was the result of mechanisation and improvements in technology. There is no reason to believe that an African path to agricultural productivity will not bear similar results, with an overall cost to employment on the farms as outputs rise. But there will be other opportunities along the way.

Equalizer is a manufacturer of seed and agricultural planting equipment. Its founder, Gideon Schreuder, started out by making a 'grain sieve' for his family farm in Hopefield, on the West Coast, north of Cape Town. 'The models on the market,' he reflects 16 years later, 'were not very efficient. And the screening and pre-cleaning was important, as it would get us a better price when we delivered to the co-op.'

One thing, inevitably, led to another, and by 2000 the mechanical engineering graduate was in the agricultural equipment manufacturing business. With more than 80 production staff, Equalizer has focused its efforts on designing and manufacturing minimum- or no-till planters and seeders. 'Developed for Africa, made for Africa, rough, tough and sturdy' is the mantra for the design of Equalizer's equipment, but this belies the cutting-edge sophistication of its automated machines, which are towed behind auto-steered tractors, spraying herbicide, cutting a narrowing furrow, dropping by air pressure seed and fertiliser carefully metered by depth and quantity on grids aligned to the soil conditions, before closing it all up again. The efficiency of the machinery illustrates the scale of the farming operations it is designed for. An 18-metre, 60-unit seeder machine for wheat can sow 12 hectares an hour; the 24-metre maize planter handles 14 hectares in the same time.[24]

With Australia and Canada among its international markets, by 2016 there were more than 800 Equalizer planters and seeders in the field. The company was producing one a day, overtaking John Deere as the preferred South African supplier.

Equalizer's success not only shows that manufacturing opportunities exist for African companies, but also signals the direction of farming: towards larger, commercial, capital-intensive operations offering economies of scale. There is also a tendency towards better farming practices driven by improved soil and water use to raise productivity. Heinrich Schönfeldt, a wheat farmer from the Overberg area, 100 kilometres from Cape Town over the Hottentots Holland Mountains, summarises the challenge for farming in the area: 'The bottom line is that we need to produce more of a better quality for less to compete with the rest of the world.' Or, as Lampie Fick, a former provincial minister for agriculture, whose family has farmed in the same area for more than 200 years, puts it, 'You can't talk about more food on less land without changing practices.'

The world's leading agricultural exporters are the US ($175 billion in export produce in 2015), Brazil ($90 billion), China ($70 billion), Canada ($65 billion), India ($47 billion), Indonesia ($43 billion) and Argentina ($41 billion).[25] All use genetically modified organism (GMO) crops. These are seed types that were introduced commercially in the mid-1990s. All of the top three maize producers (i.e. US, China and Brazil) and soya producers (US, Brazil and Argentina) use GMOs.[26] Although there is global concern about, and some opposition to, the use of such hybrid varieties, they are much more resistant than normal seeds to herbicide use, especially in the case of soya and maize, but also canola, cotton, alfalfa and sugar beet.

The introduction of GMO maize has led to a significant increase in South African production, nearly doubling average yields in just 10 years, driving up the national maize production this century by more than 40 per cent to 14 million tonnes in 2014, even though the area under cultivation fell by more than 50 per cent to under 2 million hectares. Average yields countrywide went up from 2.9 tonnes to 5.3 tonnes per hectare during this time. Similarly, soya production rose from 282 000 tonnes in 2007/08 to 1.1 million tonnes in 2014/15, the result of both a fourfold increase in areas planted and the availability of hardy soya varieties.[27]

But not all of the progress is down to new seed types. The Western Cape farming areas of South Africa produce slightly more than half of the country's annual output of 1.7 million tonnes of wheat, with another 500 000 tonnes that are produced in the Free State and the Northern Cape. The average yield per hectare in the Overberg area of the Southern Cape, around the town of Caledon, is 3.5 tonnes per hectare, double what it was in the mid-1980s.

A drive down the N2 from Cape Town towards Caledon offers a picture of rural bliss: carefully scalloped fields to both sides of the national highway, a quilt of green barley and wheat, and yellow canola are punctuated with neat, bright-white farmhouses.[28]

There are no GMO wheat seed varieties available here, at least not commercially. Wheat yields have increased by more than half in the Caledon area as a result of conservation farming methods. By avoiding continuous ploughing to remove weeds, and by leaving straw and other wastage in situ, biodiversity and carbon richness in the soils are improved, as is water retention and usage. In the Southern Cape region, where more than 90 per cent of farmers practise such conservation methods, the yield per hectare to water usage ratio has improved from between 6 and 8 kilograms of wheat per millimetre of rainfall to between 13 and 15 kilograms.

Richard Krige is an executive member of the industry body Grain SA. He farms over 2 600 hectares of wheat, oats, canola, lucerne, clover and barley, along with livestock, at Boontjieskraal, a farm south of Caledon. 'The farming community has gone from the era of mechanisation,' says Krige, 'where we ploughed all the time to get rid of fungi, disease and weeds, but which depleted the grounds of organic material and structure, to a focus on the chemical make-up of the soils, particularly the extent of phosphates and nitrogen compounds. Now we are concerned with the biological soil component as the source of nutrition. This means improving the soils, but also the varieties which allow for greater use of herbicides to control weeds, the greatest competitor to the crop.' For example, in the case of maize, using only fertiliser allows for an average yield, he says, of 3 tonnes per hectare; with only herbicides, 5 tonnes; and with both, 7 tonnes.

Despite such improvements in yield, however, South Africa has to import more than half its annual consumption of wheat. Even greater productivity is now achievable – perhaps as much as 50 per cent higher with a combination of new seed types and better farming methods. Gaining this benefit will require better cooperation between producers and consumers, as there has been in barley production, enabling co-funding of new varieties. It also means, says Krige, having to cut 'input costs, where we pay import parity prices on fertiliser and chemicals'.[29]

Though it will help meet the increasing demand for food from an increasingly urban population, this surge is unlikely to be a big source of employment. Heinrich Schönfeldt farms more than 5 000 hectares with just nine people, where once 45 were employed. Across the Southern Cape, farm employment has fallen by nearly half as big machines and intensification have taken over. The number of farmers has similarly fallen, as farms have become bigger. Indeed, from wheat to maize, there has been a productivity revolution in South Africa, with less than half the number of commercial farmers in 2015 (32 000) than there were in the late 1980s, while there has been a nearly 30 per cent increase in farming output since 1994.[30]

'While we have seen tremendous increases and improvements from new practices,' says Schönfeldt, 'there is huge potential in the rest of the Africa, where we could do three crops per annum. But to do this,' he adds, 'we need to make agriculture a sexy investment possibility, a business, and not just a passion, driven by the realities of global markets, the latest production methods and new technology. This means ultimately getting rid of a subsistence-farming mindset.'

In contrast with past production increases in sub-Saharan Africa, which were driven by an expansion of the area farmed, an increasing share of future production growth will have to come from improved productivity. Assuming rapid population growth, 'complemented by rising incomes and continuation of current policies and market structures,' the OECD warns, however, that 'the production of food crops in many countries is projected to grow more slowly than demand'. As a result, without 'productivity-enhancing investments', imports of commodities into Africa can be expected to grow.[31]

Malawi's 10 oxcarts' worth of development

Michael Kamzawa's situation perfectly illustrates Malawi's challenge and the challenges to growing African output.[32]

Surrounded by children in the village of Chikasauka, 50 kilometres north of Lilongwe, Mr Kamzawa, 64, tells us that he would like to be selected for the Integrated Production System – known universally as the 'IPS' – to boost his tobacco farming. Participation in the IPS would raise both the yield and quality of his burley tobacco leaf, and hence his income.

As a programme member, he would be able to use fertiliser and seed supplied by the local tobacco trading houses, and benefit from the expertise of 'leaf technicians' criss-crossing the country on 125cc Chinese-made motorbikes.

His immediate problem is that he had not been selected as part of the programme. The world tobacco market is just too small, and there are too many tobacco farmers in Malawi to accommodate everyone in the IPS. His problem is that government intervention in the maize market means he cannot get a commercial price for that crop. Between the two crops, he is thus condemned to a life of hard work and poverty.

Mr Kamzawa, and many like him, is impoverished because Malawi is not getting its agricultural act together.

At independence in 1964, Malawi was a bit player in the world tobacco industry. By the 1980s, it had become a major producer of air-cured burley tobacco, popular in American-blend cigarettes, complementing the Virginia flue-cured type produced in Zimbabwe. Relations between the farmers, government and buyers were carefully regulated by Hastings Banda's regime in Malawi to ensure control of both quality and quantity. Malawi's burley production grew by almost 500 per cent to 100 million kilograms between 1980 and 1992.

Then it all fell apart. As Banda's dictatorial rule faltered in the early 1990s, and as Malawi's burgeoning population sought to grow more to survive, overproduction followed, matched by a dramatic fall in the tobacco price. The likes of Michael Kamzawa will be paid as little as 25 per cent of the market value given his production of inferior grades.

As a result, the harvest and the price see-sawed dramatically, from a peak of 208 million kilograms in 2011 (when the price paid was $1.13 per kilo) to 65 million kilograms in 2012 (when the price recovered to $2.05 per kilo).

The global demand for Malawi's burley brand is approximately 140 million kilograms annually. Any more than that and the price paid for the crop edges perilously low to the estimated cost of production at around $1.50 per kg.

As a result of these wild swings, and in trying to get a grip on the industry, in 2012 the government agreed to allow 80 per cent of global tobacco sales (based on the 140-million-kilogram figure) to be contracted directly between the trading houses and the farmers. Under this scheme, the IPS, for a small deposit, enabled farmers to receive fertiliser, seed and technical knowledge from extension officers. In return, the farmers would sell for a pre-guaranteed but market-related price to the trading houses. This scheme was deemed a win-win, not only on grounds of quality and quantity control, but also because the tobacco industry was interested in improving compliance. Through careful screening of the farmers, wider issues have been tackled, including eliminating child labour, ensuring good agricultural practices, weeding out any non-tobacco-related material, such as plastic, from the product and improving environmental sustainability through, for example, the widespread planting of forests.

The big benefits to the farmers were higher yields and more stable prices, leading to higher returns and the beginning of a cycle of improvement to help lift them out of poverty. IPS farmers could earn about $1 000 per hectare in sales after the deduction of the cost of seeds and fertiliser, and even after the government has taken $380 in taxes, levies and the transporters' fees for delivering the produce to the markets. For each hectare of tobacco farmed, the IPS package also provides seeds and fertiliser for half a hectare of maize for food security, and for legumes, such as soya or groundnuts, thus providing a source of additional income.

For the farmer, the difference can be seen in the plight of Kamzawa, who was getting, outside the IPS system, 'seven to eight bales of tobacco,' he said in his native Chichewa or 'ten oxcarts of maize' per hectare. This compares with his near neighbour Gabriel Kumandakuyitana (a name that literally means 'the grave is calling'), 33, who was on an IPS contract and had increased his yield from 10 bales of tobacco (each around 90 kilograms) per hectare to 23 bales. When combined with the crop rejections on grounds of quality suffered by those outside the IPS and the lower price (in 2015 non-IPS farmers received $1.45 per kilo compared to $1.71 per kilo for the IPS contract farmers), the difference in income is stark.

The problem is that there are just too many farmers – or, put differently, too few other opportunities in Malawi, and too little demand for tobacco globally. This is why Kamzawa and most of his fellow villagers are not on the scheme. With demand small and finite, and quality essential, such as for burley tobacco, regulation has a critical role in providing stability in the market and a decent return for farmers.

To compound these challenges, Malawi faces a stupendous population increase over the next 35 years. Its population at independence in 1964 was just 3.8 million. Fifty years later it crossed the 16 million mark, and it is projected to rise to 50 million by 2050. Such growth will place considerable pressure on land. In the central region, the average farm plot is around 1 hectare. In the richer farming areas of the south, it is half this size, where population growth is, in the words of one commercial farmer, '15 years ahead of the central region'.

The effect of this population growth will be to reduce plot sizes still further as land is passed down the family line. While Malawi's farmers usually want more land, as Kumandakuyitana put it, 'The chiefs have no land any more' to distribute. And compounding this vicious and seemingly never-ending cycle is the fact that yields have remained low. A doubling of yields would have a dramatic effect.

Malawi is vying with Burundi, Niger, the DRC and the Central African Republic to be officially the world's poorest country in terms of per capita income, which was just $381 (in current terms) in 2015. Malawians are more than three times poorer, statistically, than Zambians. Yet Zambians, who in 2015 earned $1 300 per person,[33] are already very poor by global standards, where the average income was over $10 000.

Still, statistics aside, the difference between the two countries is stark. The journey from Lilongwe along the M12 to the border post at Mchinji illustrates a country operating at a low ebb. Throngs of walkers line the narrow 120-kilometre road, along with suicidal cyclists, their bikes loaded with heaving, tottering stacks of firewood, beams, sugar cane, charcoal, woven mats and the occasional goat. They are coming from a myriad of small towns: Mphandula, Kamwendo and Kahona, among others. Tired-looking maize grows by the edge of the road, the villages a scruffy collection of stalls and shops, rubbish and the occasional burley barn, small wooden structures where tobacco is hung for drying.

The chaos increases as the road approaches Mchinji. The border town, a relative excitement of trucks, piles of bricks, notices for international NGOs, several petrol stations, an insurance agency and armies of touts, has as its centrepiece a 1970s-style brick structure where passports are stamped with a surly *thunk* and where giant ledgers apparently keep control over vehicle movements. The road condition worsens, the verges become cratered with potholes appearing with staccato frequency – not for nothing are Malawian drivers referred to as 'PhDs': pothole dodgers.

Through the creaky boom and the chaos of the Mwami border control, and along the road to Chipata, the difference on the Zambian side is stark, with its Shoprites, Spars, fast-food joints, and smart new petrol stations. It's like Switzerland by comparison, the difference between endemic poverty and having some money.

It's not just Zambia. New competitors have emerged, including in next-door Mozambique, once also the world's poorest nation, with a per capita income of just $160 in 1996. Yet Malawi's per capita GDP as a share of Mozambique's has fallen from 150 per cent in the mid-1980s to less than half today. Much of that is down to the success of Mozambique's outgrower tobacco scheme in Tete Province, which started in the early 2000s.

But Malawi's plight today is not the result of what others have done, but fundamentally rather what Malawians have done – or more precisely, not done. The answer to its jobs and income crisis does not lie in more aid. The donors already provide an equivalent to a stunning quarter of Malawi's GDP. It lies in what Malawi can do for itself.

The solution to Michael Kamzawa's challenge of survival lies in the de-politicisation and liberalisation of the maize market. Until now, with maize, where regional demand is huge, government intervention to keep the price low has had far-reaching negative consequences.

In the 1980s, a World Bank-supported partial privatisation of the Agricultural Development and Marketing Corporation (ADMARC) left it with limited funds to supply fertiliser and seed to smallholders, and led to the closure of many of its depots. However, the private sector lacked the capacity to provide competitive marketing services across the country. The sector was also unable to store enough maize to cover for lean periods, and traders were restricted in their ability to import maize to maintain prices during shortfalls. As a result, subsidies reappeared and the government-controlled ADMARC again played an increasing role, thus reversing liberalisation.

The challenge relates in part to an absence of land tenure and the inability therefore to raise finance, but principally it is in the pricing structure and the role of ADMARC, whose routine dumping of maize is not only costly for the fiscus, but drives the price down. This trend is exacerbated by export bans. 'Cheap food undermines the economy, the beneficiaries of which are the three to four million urban Malawians at the cost of four million farming households,' says Jimmy Giannakis of *Farmer's World*,[34] echoing a widespread opinion.

Instead, there is a need to increase market pressure 'to take supply and demand closer to the edge' by liberalising the maize price. Government's role would be to ensure a safety net for the most vulnerable through accurate forecasting and monitoring, thus avoiding the sort of policy changes that have characterised Malawian maize policy. An example of such policy swings would be the politically attractive farm input subsidy scheme introduced by the late President Bingu wa Mutharika and hailed as a major contribution by many donors to food security, even though it was unsustainable and depressed the price through non-market-related production. Until now, political interests have been in supplying cheap maize, even though the economic interests of the farmers – and thus Malawi per se – lie in producing a more expensive staple.

Get the pricing right, and quantities and yields will rise, say the experts, as the farmer responds. There is always likely to be regional demand, given the vagaries of weather and politics. 'There is always someone,' says a Malawian farmer assessing the market opportunity, 'misfiring on maize in the region.' To gain access to regional markets, however, greater effort will have to go into reducing transport costs, which are $4 400 for a 40-foot container from Lilongwe to Beira, just 950 kilometres away, whereas shipping from Beira to the United Arab Emirates is just $1 450. Fixing this means, too, addressing the stupefying inefficiencies of the border posts, Mwami and Mchinji included.

There is a deeper issue with which Malawi's leadership has to deal if it wishes to expand the economy. The private sector remains crowded out, the incentives skewed to reward those in government, or acting as trading middlemen, the licensing or customs official, the handler of agricultural goods between the seller and purchaser, the politician who relies on access and preferences to safeguard business interests. It is a malaise that results in vested interests trumping national development needs, ensuring the poverty of the likes of Michael Kamzawa.

Conclusion: Some jobs, greater mechanisation

Realising Africa's agriculture potential will demand more than just capable, meticulous farmers – though this will undoubtedly help. It will also need a range of integrated actions. As Gideon Schreuder notes, 'to get farming right, you need not just better farming, but also a full back-up system of companies doing seed, chemicals, fertilisers, equipment and logistics, among other things, along with government policy that makes it sufficiently attractive'.

There will be bitter policy and political pills to swallow along the way, especially for government. Notably, these will concern the limits of small-scale farming in cereal production, not least given the costs of the type of machinery and practices that will be needed to offer the productivity gains that Africa's growing urban populations will necessitate. For South Africa, to take one example, the minimum benchmark size, says Schreuder, for a profitable farm growing cereals and capable of affording second-hand capital equipment 'is at least 400 hectares'. In the Western Cape's Overberg region, it is at least 1 000 hectares.

The future is not just about staples, improving outputs to enable Africa to feed itself, exporting the surplus to the cities, enabling a division of labour away from agriculture into other, higher-value occupations in industry and services. For a continent seeking jobs, there are also opportunities in those crops whose production cannot yet be totally mechanised. In South Africa such crops are oranges, a market in which the country has become the world's second largest exporter,[35] as well as various new farming areas, such as avocados, nuts, berries, fruit and flowers. 'Such crops,' says wine and apple farmer Paul Cluver, 'are higher value and more labour-intensive, and could employ a lot more people.'[36]

In all this, the bottom line, says Schreuder, 'is that farmers need to feel safe enough to put their life's investments on the line'. It is a comment that applies across all business sectors, but particularly to those involving fixed, immovable investments, like agriculture and mining.

Chapter 5
Mining

Five steps for success:
- Improve policy and investor certainty. Stable, efficient and transparent regulatory and administrative processes are vital investment determinants for mining companies.
- Develop a compelling, forward-looking, realistic narrative with the mining sector about the role it will play in national development, and stick to it.
- Further beneficiation is dependent on cheap electricity and domestic manufacturing opportunities.
- Appreciate the logistics systems needed for investment in bulk minerals (especially iron and coal) and the immense costs involved.
- Government policy has to reflect the realities of fluctuations in commodity prices and the long-term needs of investors.

Challenges and opportunities: As large parts of the world expand their infrastructure grids and manufacturing sectors, there will be demand for minerals. This offers some African countries opportunities for upskilling their workforce, industrialisation, and international investment and trade. Yet mining is a cyclical business and the prospects of the sector are subject to the changing balance of supply and demand. In Africa mining projects have also been characterised by a lack of trust between mining companies, governments and the nations they lead. Mining is a complex, long-term and capital-intensive undertaking, where risk and reward need to be carefully balanced, and can be easily thrown out by policy change and instability.

Key statistics: Africa is well endowed with minerals. The continent has 20 per cent of known global gold reserves, 23 per cent of titanium, 28 per cent of vanadium, a quarter of all manganese, more than half of the world's cobalt, over 60 per cent of gem diamond reserves, 80 per cent of phosphates, 90 per cent of chromite and 95 per cent of platinum. Large areas of Africa are also underexplored for mineral deposits. Even though taking advantage of the commercial opportunity presented by minerals has proven problematic, dependency on commodities has risen in key producers over the past 15 years. In Botswana the mineral export contribution to GDP (principally diamonds) has gone from 58.7 per cent to 83.7 per cent; in Zambia dependence has increased from 79.4 per cent to 83.6 per cent; and in the DRC, from 72.4 per cent to 78.3 per cent.[1] Despite an increase in average income during the commodity-price boom of the 2000s, over half the population of those African countries that are dependent on extractives live on less than $2 a day.[2]

James, 29, is from Maseru.[3] He works as an illegal miner, or *zama zama* (literally, those willing 'to have a go', 'try your luck', or 'take a chance'), in the Durban Deep area, 20 kilometres south-west of Johannesburg. He mines with four of his countrymen, standing in ankle-deep freezing water, washing diggings in a plastic bucket. Drawing water in buckets from an old mine dam, the solution is dropped through perforations in the bucket onto a ribbed carpet which picks up the dense gold-laden concentrate. Later it is milled before being mixed with mercury to pick up the gold content, and then heated with oxyacetylene torches to finally leave the prized yellow shine of pure gold.

James sells his bounty to a local dealer, for which he receives, he says, $21 a gram, less than half the international market rate. He and his friends make $3.50 each a day, he claims, for their labours, hardly enough to eat and pay rent.

The Durban Deep area was mined actively until 2001 when, following a failed merger with Johannesburg Consolidated Investments, the mill was shut and the shafts plugged, leaving an estimated 12 million ounces of unmined gold. At the time of writing, a new Australian-led venture, West Wits Mining, was endeavouring to reopen the mine, working together with a property developer to construct affordable housing for 75 000 people on the prospecting area's 4 000 hectares, making inroads into the 800 000 housing backlog in Gauteng.

South Africa produced 144.5 tonnes of gold in 2015, valued at $6.6 billion. *Zama zamas* mined another estimated eight tonnes, $400 million worth. They are at the bottom of the employment pile. An estimated three-quarters of them are desperate illegal immigrants from Lesotho, Mozambique, Malawi and Zimbabwe. With South African unemployment touching 40 per cent, it's always going to be a struggle for migrants to find jobs. And it's hardly a bonanza – more like their last, or only, chance.

Mine officials and security personnel estimate that, overall, there may now be as many as 15 000 *zama zamas*, compared to 120 000 miners working in South Africa's formal gold-mining operations. In 2015 there were more than 65 *zama zama* deaths. To put the risk into context, South African gold mines lost 33 workers in accidents in 2015. With the pillars supporting the mine roofs containing some of the richest, unmined material, some *zama zamas*, literally, undermine themselves.

In a highly organised, syndicated system, with crime bosses at the top running the gangs and, in the words of one Australian miner, 'shit-kickers at the bottom', many are murdered by rivals. In 2014 one gang trapped 200 *zama zamas* by blocking the exits from an illegal mine. Untold numbers died, with no official consequences. Four years earlier, more than 100 'illegal miners' died in a single incident in Welkom.

There should be empathy with the plight of the individual *zama zama*, who works in tough, threatening conditions for meagre returns. However, there are considerable costs incurred by their activities – beyond the loss of tax revenue, investor returns and confidence. The *zamas zamas* are part of a shadowy network of ruthless criminality, with little or no concern for property, the environment or the safety of others, all the while breeding and nourishing corruption within the public and private sectors alike.

Of course, South Africa is not alone. From Colombia to Zimbabwe, there are an estimated 25 million artisanal miners, defined as those as effectively subsisting through mining rather than being employed by a mining company, and using rudimentary and dangerous techniques and technologies of extraction. A further estimated 150 million people in more than 50 developing countries are estimated to be indirectly reliant on these miners.[4] Artisanal mining usually takes place in remote areas, largely free from government interference, and from environmental and other controls.

The rise of the *zama zamas* reflects the dramatic decline of South Africa's mining industry. In the late 1980s, South Africa's share of formal global mining overall was 40 per cent, with employment peaking at 880 000.

Then, gold mining alone accounted for 540 000 jobs. By 2016 South Africa's share was less than 5 per cent of total global mining and the industry employed 473 000, even though it still accounted for 8 per cent of the country's GDP and more than half of its foreign-exchange earnings.

Lack of investor confidence combined with a restive labour force and increasingly difficult, deep and expensive ore extraction have resulted in South Africa producing 87 per cent less gold in January 2015 compared with the same month in 1980.[5] Its gold output has fallen from first place in the world in 2006 (when it mined 300 tonnes – small compared to its all-time peak of 1 000 tonnes in 1970) to, 10 years later, seventh behind China, Australia, Russia, the US, Canada and Peru.

This decline reflects a lack of investment and, behind that, lack of confidence in the future. By 2011 South Africa's global share of greenfield mining projects was just 5 per cent; Australia's, by comparison, was 38 per cent. Such a drop in investment is consistent with trends in other parts of Africa (such as Zambia, for example) and serves to undermine growth.

Mining does not have to be a sunset industry, though. A 2010 Citibank survey put South Africa as the world's richest mining country in terms of non-oil reserves, worth an estimated $2.5 trillion at then current prices. This is greater than the value of reserves in Russia and Australia, at around $1.6 trillion apiece.[6] At the time of the report, experts estimated that, with the right regulatory environment, South Africa could at least double its coal, platinum, iron and manganese outputs within five years, adding 200 000 direct and indirect jobs.[7]

But a new South African gold mine, given the depths involved, takes five years of investment, requiring at least $140 million just to get past the feasibility phase. A further $2 billion to $3 billion is then required (at 2016 prices) to get to 'medium depth', to the reef itself, which entails another 10 years of work. Only then does the mine start to recoup the capital investment and, ultimately, after another decade or more, to return a profit.[8]

Yet arresting the decline in Africa's mining industry does not require major new investment, but rather just collaboration – and improved trust – between business and government.

The reason for the shutdown of Durban Deep and the subsequent emergence of the *zama zamas* is lack of investor confidence that things in South Africa will turn around. It is also linked to questions about the rule of law and bureaucratic responsiveness to commercial concerns and needs, a lack of basic security in the mining areas, the continually changing policy landscape, especially around black economic empowerment. In short, there is a lack of government vision for the long-term future for mining and of sensitivity to commercial realities and commodity-price volatility.

Durban Deep's Australian owners believe that, with security, a quick response on mining permits, and planning permissions issued for the housing development, they can 'sterilise' the surface area and resuscitate the mine. They calculate there are 500 000 ounces of gold available near the surface, to be excavated and back-filled. This gold will provide the funding for the next stage, which will enable the mining of another 1.5 million ounces located above 270 metres. If things go to plan, the mine could employ 2 500 workers in its new incarnation, who would be supporting 10 times that number, not least because 'the Wits reef,' say geologists, 'does not lend itself to mechanisation'.[9] Employment and government revenue are not the only drivers, however. There are environmental, health and other safety considerations, a special concern for those at risk from mining detritus and *zama zama* activities in surrounding communities.

Without improved levels of confidence in mining policy, political stability, and the resultant fresh capital, South Africa's formal mining sector can only continue to decline, just as the number of *zama zamas* will rise as workers struggle to find other employment. Without the commitment of fresh capital, such informalisation indicates a dead end for the industry, and is a clear sign of policy failure.

The African challenge

African economies are heavily dependent on the extractives sector, which made up 28 per cent of the continent's combined GDP in 2012, 77 per cent of total exports and 42 per cent of all government revenues.[10] Studies by the International Council on Mining and Metals (ICMM), for example, demonstrate that for every $1 generated by mining, at least an additional $3 are generated elsewhere in the local economy, and that for every direct mining employee, as many as 15 more jobs are created elsewhere in that economy.[11]

The total value of global mineral production grew sixfold from 1992 to

2012. During this boom, lower-income countries came to depend more heavily on mineral exports, especially in sub-Saharan Africa.[12] Hence, the fall in Africa's mineral exports, as depicted in Figure 5.1, has led to a downturn in economic growth across sub-Saharan Africa, especially among countries reliant on commodities for export and government revenue. For example, the continent's growth expanded by only 3 per cent in 2015, well below the 6.8 per cent average between 2003 and 2008. The World Bank has attributed the weaker performance largely to the plunge in commodity prices.[13]

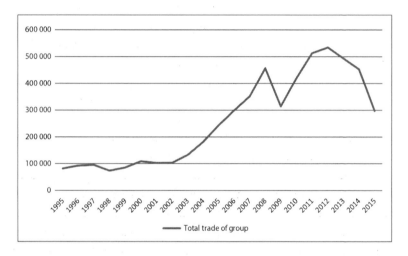

Figure 5.1: African trade of primary commodities, precious stones and non-monetary gold (in current $), 1995–2015

Source: UN Conference on Trade and Development, http://unctadstat.unctad.org/wds/ReportFolders/reportFolders.aspx

Despite the boom years, the relationship between the industry and government in many countries in Africa has been characterised by abiding levels of mistrust on both sides, fuelled by misperception. Legend persists that mines equate with massive wealth and, at an extreme, mining companies deliberately steal ore or withhold tax through under-declaration or 'transfer pricing'. Meanwhile, the mining companies complain that the long-term nature of their business, through good and bad times, and the levels of risk they have to shoulder are not understood by those who set the rules.

Such tensions are compounded by increasing capital intensity and mining mechanisation, the effect of which is felt particularly in those countries where mining is the mainstay of the economy.

Perceptions as to the value and role of mining are amplified in environments where there are few other opportunities. The predominant narrative on mining has been about huge profits made at the expense of the population – a 'win-lose' scenario. Paradoxically, the communities around mines are heavily dependent, frequently from cradle to grave, on the mining companies, to whom the state often abrogates its responsibility. Yet, often, the very companies bringing in this development have to deal with considerable interference, corruption and rent-seeking, reflecting the difficulty of managing a fixed, immovable asset where there is little else going on in the economy.

Rather than engaging the industry as a long-term developmental partner, some governments, playing to popular public pressures and desperate for revenue, follow a short-term approach, seeking to target the sector with high-tax regimes and other redistributive mechanisms, including calls for beneficiation and value addition.

But calls for increased value addition seldom take into consideration the extent to which ore is already beneficiated. It's hardly as if the companies are exporting rocks. Far from it. In the case of the extraction of copper, to take one example, after geological surveying and drilling (to create a three-dimensional model of the deposit), followed by blasting, digging and hauling, the oxide beneficiation process involves crushing, milling, flotation, leaching, solvent extraction and electrowinning to create cathodes. Meanwhile, the sulphides are beneficiated with flotation to create copper concentrates. Producing copper anode from the latter involves an equally elaborate, high-temperature smelting process. The largest mine in Zambia, Kansanshi, uses, daily, a quarter of a million litres of diesel to mine 80 000 tonnes of ore feed, from which 700 tonnes of copper are extracted. It produces upward of 270 000 tonnes of copper annually. The calls for further beneficiation seem to reside in a belief that the companies are pulling pure copper wire out of the ground.

Similar value-addition processes apply to other minerals, for example platinum. The complexity is defined by the process of extracting the mineral. The relentless regime of 'drill-blast-clean-support' extracts the platinum ore, which is scraped by means of winches and shovels from the mining face to a centre gulley. From there it is moved to the stope box, where it is emptied into trains that proceed from a cross-cut to a station tip. Then, it is tipped down at an ore pass and hoisted to the surface in 7-tonne skips, which run at speed every two minutes, sending it to the crusher. From there, the ore, containing around 6 grams per tonne of minerals, is moved to a concentrator. This improves the purity to 140 grams per tonne, sending tailings of 0.6 grams per tonne to the dam. The concentrate is smelted, which removes silica, and the resultant smelter 'matte' is processed further in a convertor to remove iron and sulphur, the latter then made into sulphuric acid for sale. The slow-cooled convertor matte is crushed and fed to a magnetic concentrator plant, which splits up the 'magnetics' (the platinum group of metals) for the precious-metal refinery, which extracts platinum, palladium, rhodium, iridium, ruthenium, gold and silver, and the 'non-magnetics' for the base-metal refinery for copper, nickel and cobalt. The platinum is then transported by helicopter to a secure facility.

Downstream beneficiation is increasingly concentrated in bigger businesses, since smaller-scale projects do not have the same economies of scale.

Despite (or perhaps because of) the calls for greater value addition, the overall health of the mining sector is intrinsically in the interests of government, not just for reasons of long-term revenue, jobs and the prospects of industrialisation, but because many governments hold a direct stake in mining operations.[14]

Although the success of mining requires a partnership of common interest, and although Africa's fast-growing young population need jobs, policy instability has planted the seeds for a vicious downward cycle in mining.

Policy uncertainty leads to investor uncertainty and limits the pool of capital available. Undercapitalising the mining sector inevitably results, in turn, in higher-cost mines and, within the general global competition for funds, a shift of interest away from mining in riskier countries. Thus, decisions on many major mining investments are consequently put on hold. As large mining companies continually rebalance portfolios and seek out the most cost-competitive mines, policy uncertainty continues to fuel the cycle from reputable to less reputable, and ultimately to small-scale mining companies, leading to the eventual 'de-evolution' of the mining sector. As smaller mining companies tend to have less-developed governance systems, this increases the burden of regulatory oversight in an environment in which many governments already possess only limited capacity.

There is therefore a need for a fresh start in these relationships, given clear common interest. The vicious cycle needs to be broken, trust needs to be re-established, a shared narrative developed and a fair deal agreed. To start this process afresh, which will not be easy, new avenues for dialogue need to be found, and common interests identified. First, however, governments need to be aware of the constraints investors face.

What investors look for

A number of factors drive investments in commodities: the type of mineral, geography, ore grade, the stage of the project (e.g. exploration versus early or late production), the complexity and cost of the engineering and the infrastructure required, the political and policy environment, and the duration of investment from entrance to exit.

This is an industry with very long-term horizons. For some mineral deposits, the exploration phase alone can last for up to 15 years. Fewer than one in 10 exploration projects make it through to the construction phase, which may last between three and seven years, inclusive of the feasibility work. It will take a further five years or so to recoup the capital investment, presuming there are strong enough cash flows, and most mines are based on a 20-year life cycle. This requires an act of investor faith beyond the immediate government and policy regime, since there could be as many as three or four presidents during the life of the mine.

There is also a fundamental difference between precious minerals (gold, diamonds, platinum, silver) and base minerals (coal, copper, iron, manganese, bauxite, tin, zinc, nickel, etc) in terms of the volumes and therefore the transport logistics required, where proximity to road, rail and port infrastructure is key. Power and water are essential for all mining operations. The nature of a commodity and a mining prospect can be further divided into 'bulk' and 'non-bulk' – essentially the difference between coal and iron ore (bulk), on the one hand, and the rest on the other. Bulk minerals, which are relatively low in value but high in volume, require additional capital for haulage, handling and technical skills, demanding a strong balance sheet to both enable and sustain their operations.

Miners search, like any stakeholder, for the greatest certainty in calculating where to invest. 'The problem is,' notes one London-based fund manager, 'that the assets are seldom in countries with sound and stable policy. Where they are – in North America, for example – they are very picked over. It's thus usually then been a question of going to the "least worst" environment.'[15]

There are two fundamental approaches that mining companies use to assess risk. The first, a so called 'scientific method', attempts to boil risk factors down to numbers. These figures go beyond the technical issues of grade, volumes and cost of extraction to encompass other issues, such as the probability of increased tax, changes in currency values, likelihood of appropriation, environmental concerns and the possibility of the prevention of the repatriation of royalties. The other is the 'art approach': essentially a visceral 'binary decision' where top management make a judgement based on their instinct and experience. Underlying either are the prime assumptions about price, inflation, foreign exchange and political risk over the life cycle of the project.

Sometimes the judgements made can go expensively wrong. Anglo American's Brazilian Minas-Rio iron-ore mine exemplifies the dangers inherent in buying into a market where miners – and governments (especially in Africa) – are price takers, vulnerable to exogenous factors, but where sometimes raw emotion can also dictate events.

Minas-Rio was bought as a development project for $5.5 billion at the peak of the price cycle in 2008. The purchase was apparently motivated by both a belief that the super-cycle was a new norm and by the fear of Anglo American being left out of the boom. The development of Minas-Rio was supposed to cost $2.7 billion, including the construction of a 525-kilometre ore slurry pipeline to a dedicated port.[16] Six years and at least $8 billion later, by which time iron-ore prices had tumbled from $145 at the time of the purchase to $55 per tonne, Anglo finally started to ship from the mine. Costs and the development schedule were driven up by delays and the demands of seeking permits, especially those concerning land use and access, even though Anglo had a team of 400 lawyers behind it. Such difficulties were, in the opinion of some, complicated by the decision to buy out the Brazilian partner, which left Anglo operating on its own in the backyard of Vale, the Brazilian mining giant and one of the world's most prodigious iron-ore producers.[17]

Anglo is not alone in losing out from bad timing and poor strategic management. Vale also spent a similar amount of money developing its Moatize coalfield in Mozambique's Tete Province. The Moatize coal basin contains coking coal, used in the manufacture of steel. The project included building a 900-kilometre railway, crossing Malawi, to the Mozambican port of Nacala. The cost of the investment, combined with a drop in coal prices (from $150 a tonne in 2011 to below $80 at the start of 2016) and the disappointing quality of Moatize's coal, resulted in a reported loss of $500 million a year for the Vale group, including writing off $2.4 billion on the investment in 2016.[18]

While the 'art form' highlighted above suggests a certain reliance on prejudice and gut instinct, which is true if conversations with some mining investors are anything to go by, there are more systemic conditions and concerns regularly articulated by miners.

For those looking over the long term in Africa, especially when it comes to mining base metals, their appetite is shaped by the levels of uncertainty around the frequency of policy changes, exchange-control regimes, general arbitrariness of the politics and levels of corruption. The challenges on policy and politics are summed up by the conundrum around requiring a local partner. 'First, this opens us up to questions about exposure to PEPs [politically exposed persons],' says one business development manager for a major multinational. 'But it's a double whammy. It also tells you that you cannot rely on the legal framework to protect you, but rather you need a local partner to do so.' Not only does such corporate behaviour run against the instinctive attitude of some miners towards avoiding 'capture by the state', but it can also contravene laws based on the 2003 Financial Action Task Force standards on money laundering, including the UK Bribery Act and the US Foreign Corrupt Practices Act.

Mining companies are also concerned, especially in Africa, about control over physical access. Frequent challenges in this regard explain why successful mining operations in Africa are usually, with few exceptions, in diamonds and gold, which don't require large sums of infrastructure investment (and in the case of gold are usually counter-cyclical in price to industrial minerals), compared to iron ore and coal, which have a significant logistics component. African governments also usually lack the resources to invest in such infrastructure, even though they sometimes have majority ownership. This inevitably leads either to delays or free financial carry by government on the investment – or both. With rail priced at '\$5 million to \$15 million a kilometre,' notes one mining-infrastructure specialist, 'you want to be certain that you have priority on the line if you are paying for it. But the problem,' he says, 'is that African countries see such infrastructure as a national asset, involving rights, too, for passengers and other freight, which complicates matters.'

Finally, the attempted application of the 2010 Australian mining super-profits tax – and the repeal of the subsequent Minerals Resource Rent Tax in 2014 – should provide a further salutary warning to African governments. At a stroke, the tax relegated Australia from having the 'best' iron ore mines in the world. 'Best,' explains one miner, 'is defined by an economic-policy perspective, not geography or the nature of the asset.'

Mining investment is like other sectors, in that it is a balance between risk and reward. The willingness to accept the risk is, however, influenced by the size of the bet taken and the likely life cycle of the mine. The greater the confidence in government and in continuity of policy – in essence, that the regulatory regime will not change with changes in the political regime – the increased likelihood of investment. This also has to be considered along with, as one miner puts it, 'all sorts of technical discontinuities around price, exchange rates, grade and volumes. We are used to surprises on the upside; but even more on the downside.'[19]

Guinea is a case in point where the risks have so far outweighed the possible rewards – and where the expectations of government and citizens don't seem to be aligned to those of mining companies.

Missed opportunity

Guinea is enormously wealthy on paper. Not only is it blessed with one-third (or 16 billion tonnes) of the world's known bauxite reserves, but it also has abundant stores of uranium, diamonds, gold and other metals, including an estimated 6 billion tonnes in iron ore reserves, reputedly a quarter of the world's store. The Simandou mountain range in Faranah Province, near the border with Sierra Leone and Liberia, is said to be a giant iron lump. The same applies to Nimba Mountain in the neighbouring Forestiere Province, to the south.[20]

Yet more than half a century since independence, Guinea ranks in the bottom 20 poorest places on earth. With an average annual per capita income of just over $500, half of the country live below the poverty line. Agriculture employs 80 per cent of the workforce. There is very limited light industry – just soft drinks, beer, palm oil and other minor agro-processing. Bauxite and alumina make up more than half of all export earnings. While it has enormous hydropower potential, given that it is one of the wettest and most mountainous countries in West Africa, Guinea produced just 220 megawatts of electricity in 2013. The capital, Conakry, is subject to frequent stoppages, and the rural areas, where two-thirds of the population live, have permanent outages.

Indeed, by 2013, Guinea was 'top of the bill', as one European diplomat described it, in every one of the 'bad' metrics: incompetence, government capacity, skills, education, corruption, organisation and destruction of infrastructure. In each of these measures it was a failed state. Even though it has not been at war with itself, it was nonetheless one of the six countries that has been the focus of the UN's peace-building commission.[21]

Alpha Condé's government, in power since 2010, stated its development vision: for Guinea to be an 'emerging country' by 2030, in which mining would be, unsurprisingly, the key sector. The government aimed for $20 billion worth of investment by the time Condé came up for (successful) re-election in 2015. That was the year a giant Rio Tinto project was supposed to start exporting iron ore by means of a $12 billion, 650-kilometre new railway and port facility. This single project was expected to create 10 000 direct jobs in the construction phase alone, and to increase GDP threefold to $15 billion.

Since 2010, however, various mining projects have sunk into virtual limbo. This stalemate occurred against the backdrop of declining world ore prices and an original (though subsequently reworked) mining code that posited a tax and royalty regime pegged to the more lucrative era. The cost of developing the Trans-Guinean Railways, a long-mooted government ambition to connect the country north to south, provided a further hurdle. The government initially demanded majority ownership of the line and the inclusion of passengers along with non-iron freight. The reality is that the shortest way to the export markets for the miners is via Liberia. Moreover, Guinea's government lacked its $6 billion share to put into the railway project, and adding passenger and other cargo into the mix has only served to further complicate matters, adding to already significant project costs.

Yet the failure to develop the mines was not all the government's doing. The rights to the Simandou deposit were given to Rio Tinto in 1997. After the Guinean government declared that the Anglo-Australian company was developing the mine too slowly, in July 2008, Rio Tinto was stripped of its licence by the then president, Lansana Conté. Rights to exploit half of the deposit were then granted to Beny Steinmetz Group Resources (BSGR), a company that had, until then, been focused on diamonds. Despite Rio's protests, the government deal with BSGR was ratified in April 2009. Steinmetz then sold a 51 per cent stake in its Simandou operation to the Brazilian mining giant Vale for $2.5 billion, for what was reportedly at that stage a $160 million investment by BSGR. At the time, the government budget in Guinea was less than half of this figure.[22] Paul Collier, an adviser to the Condé government, had a less than sanguine view of such operators: 'Their technical competence is a social-network map. They know how to get a contract – *that* is their skill,' said the Oxford-based economist.[23] When Condé was elected in 2010, following a review of all mine contracts the BSGR and Vale venture lost its title after the government found BSGR had obtained it through bribery – something the company denies.

In 2011 Rio renegotiated its deal, paying the government $700 million in up-front taxes. The government, however, insisted that its vision of finally completing the Trans-Guinean Railways be realised as part of the deal. The trust between government and business hit rock bottom as a result. The president's adviser asked whether it was ever the intention of the mining companies to invest in their operations: 'How else do you explain that Rio Tinto has been here for fifteen years and not exported even a tonne of ore?' he enquired.[24] The mining companies, however, feared that attempts to operate in isolation from other general improvements in the country would lead to 'rising expectations and … predatory behaviour,' as one executive put it.[25] These quite different expectations have added much friction and resulted in delay. Of course, companies wish to guard against flooding the market with cheap commodities.[26] But, while they should be given time to develop their assets, around 10 years, failing progress it is reasonable to expect that these should be released to others.

In October 2016, it was announced that Rio Tinto had signed an agreement to sell its stake in Simandou to Chinese company Chinalco. Rio would receive payment of up to $1.3 billion for a project that has an ore reserve of over 2 billion tonnes, annual production potential of 100 million tonnes, and a mine life of over 40 years.[27] The same month, the International Finance Corporation also announced that it would sell its 4.6 per cent stake in the same project.

Whatever the long-term potential rewards, the price of iron, the challenges of financing, and the costs and complexities of the infrastructure required appear to have tipped the balance from 'develop' to 'sell'. Firms are unwilling to invest where there is a high risk of uncertainty: political, policy and price. Zambia is another case in point.

Zambia's tax somersaults

Zambia illustrates the cost of having an industry at loggerheads with government on policy, despite the poor track record of nationalisation of the industry.

Zambia's copper production in 1973 was 720 000 tonnes, or 15 per cent of the global total, and the industry employed 48 000 people. Following nationalisation that year, production went into a long decline, with copper production dipping to 257 000 tonnes by 2000, the year of privatisation, when 21 000 where employed (see Figure 5.2). As a result, real GDP per capita fell from $1 455 in 1976 to $1 037 by 1987, or −3.6 per cent per year, and then to $892 by 2000, by which time the state incurred a cost of $1 million per day to run its mines.[28]

Nationalisation of the mines is calculated to have cost Zambia $45 billion in production losses, more than the total in aid received over the period.[29] Put differently, if Zambia had maintained its 1970 share of global copper production, it would now be generating 2.7 million tonnes.

Following fresh investment post-privatisation, by 2014 production had risen again to over 700 000 tonnes, with some 65 000 employed by the industry. But, given progress elsewhere, this tonnage amounted to less than 4 per cent of the global total. The mine at Kansanshi, a post-privatisation investment, is Zambia's biggest copper producer, at around 250 000 tonnes annually, from which over $3 billion has been paid in taxes and nearly the same amount again invested. More than 8 000 workers are employed, with wage

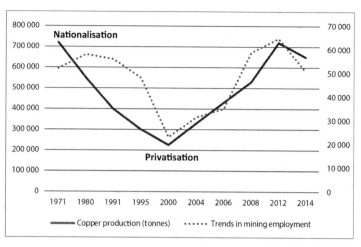

Figure 5.2: Trends in Zambian copper production and mining employment, 1971–2014

Source: Author's calculations[30]

and electricity payments inserting a further $50 million into the Zambian economy monthly. The mine's contribution to Zambia is huge: there have been a number of years when Kansanshi alone has been responsible for as much as 90 per cent of the corporate income tax paid in Zambia.

Yet mining remains a beleaguered industry in Zambia. The giant $2.1 billion Kalumbila mine in Zambia's north-west, which is beset with challenges of power provision and land-title rights, was the country's last major new mining investment. New investments and mine life extensions are being deterred by government changes to the mining tax regime and abrogation of development agreements that assured investors of a 15-year stability period on fiscal policy. Since 2008, no fewer than 797 statutory instruments (essentially, ministerial directives to amend, update or enforce existing primary legislation) affecting the mining industry, both directly and indirectly, have been issued by the Zambian government, of which the majority (501) have been passed since 2011.

In 2011 the Zambian government implemented a 6 per cent turnover tax and 30 per cent corporate tax for the mines. In January 2015, it switched to a flat 8 per cent turnover tax on underground mines and a 20 per cent mining royalty tax[31] for open-pit operations. As the IMF concluded in June 2015, 'at

50 per cent, the AETR [average effective tax rate] for Zambia was second-highest among major copper producing countries'.[32] This came on the back of an earlier change to VAT arrangements, resulting in government prevarication on repaying around $1 billion to mining companies.

After much heated debate, in 2016 the government proposed a 30 per cent corporate tax and a sliding royalty scale of 4–6 per cent.[33] Yet the consensus globally is for a 30 per cent corporate tax and a three per cent royalty.[34] As the Minister of Finance noted to Parliament in April 2016, such policy instability damages Zambia's investor credibility, which 'is anchored on two themes: predictability and consistency. If somersaults are going to be our recipe, such will reduce investor confidence in our country.'[35]

The failure to adopt better or more consistent mining policy is not because there is a lack of publicity around best (and bad) practice, or that these practices are all outside Africa. For example, the Chilean experience, discussed below, is widely known, not least since southern African miners have operated successfully there.

What success looks like – Chile and Mauritania

Chile's economic growth since the 1980s has been nothing short of remarkable, particularly during the 1990s, when it averaged an annual rate of over 7 per cent. It is easily forgotten, however, that in 1972 it was classified as the second worst economy in Latin America, when, under conditions of state economic dominance, inflation had reached 500 per cent, there were frequent strikes and 'nationalisation, price controls and high tariffs were the order of the day'.[36]

From a low of $4 000 per capita in 1975, real income per person more than tripled over the next 30 years. By 2011 foreign capital totalling almost $82 billion had been invested in the mining industry, equivalent to more than half of all foreign capital invested in Chile since 1974.[37]

The country's transformation has been built on two pillars.[38] The first was the institution of free-market economic reforms in the late 1970s and early 1980s led by a team of bright young economists. The second was a massive increase in domestic copper production. Copper, of which Chile supplies nearly a third of the world's annual consumption, accounts for some two-thirds of the country's export revenue.

The changes in this sector over of a quarter century have been spectacular. In 1990 the private sector accounted for less than a quarter of Chilean copper-mining output. By the end of the 2000s, the state mining company, CODELCO, was producing more than twice as much copper as it had done 20 years before, yet the private sector was producing two-thirds of the annual national output of 6 million tonnes. In 1970 Chile produced the same amount of copper as Zambia; four decades later, it produced eight times more.

Foreign investment was facilitated by a low and stable tax regime and non-discriminatory treatment of foreign and local companies. Chilean tax laws were agreed upon by the state and investors, mostly under Decree Law 600 of 1974. This law provided for a 'contract' between the investor and the state of Chile, the establishment of free trade zones, the introduction of policies guaranteeing the remittance of profits and capital, free choice as to the percentage of foreign ownership, non-discrimination with local investors and tariff liberalisation.

Byzantine labour policies were unwound through a series of measures aimed at decentralising collective bargaining, improving transparency in union voting and allowing greater choice in union membership. Reform of the pension system in 1980 also allowed workers to opt out of the government-run pension system and instead put the formerly mandatory payroll tax (10 per cent of wages) into privately managed personal retirement accounts.

During this transformative period, Chile kept corruption down. It has consistently ranked in the top-20 (i.e. better performing) countries in Transparency International's Corruption Perception Index, ahead of many developed countries.

If the Chilean example is deemed too distant by African policymakers, there are other illustrations closer to home.

The road from Mauritania's capital, Nouakchott, to the mine at Akjoujt strikes out for 250 kilometres north-east, in the direction of the border with Western Sahara. It is tough territory, more Mars, it seems, than Mauritania.[39]

A short stretch at the start is built to link the new international airport with the capital, the four lanes lit by solar-powered lamps. On the city limits the route is a dodgem of donkey carts, petrol tankers, trucks, camels and suicidal Mauritanians. It is lined with a scruffy salad of plastic rubbish, old tyres, desert shrubs, vehicle detritus, the occasional mosque and the ubiquitous *khaimas* – tents around which goats scuffle and out of which occasionally a shepherd appears in a colourful boubou and veiled in an equally bright *cheche* headdress. Red sand from rolling dunes spills onto the road at various points, whipping across it at others in a ghostly mist, adding to the challenge.

And then, suddenly, there is virtually nothing. Just a black strip, a string through the endless sand, punctuated by an occasional tent, solar-powered cellphone towers, grazing camels and busy goats, sedentary police road-blocks, and the odd roadside water bladder. One of the 10 most sparsely populated countries in the world, Mauritania has a human density of 3.5 people per square kilometre across its million or so square kilometres – putting it alongside Botswana (3.48), Iceland (3.24), Namibia (2.56) and neighbouring Western Sahara (2.25).[40] The per capita cost of delivering infrastructure over this vast territory is high.

Once on the economic margins of the world – confused even by courier companies with tropical Mauritius on the other side of the continent – Mauritania has benefited from the global mining boom, given its large stores of iron ore and copper. Annual foreign direct investment (FDI) leapt from $100 million in 2006 to $1.5 billion in 2012, 90 per cent of which was in mining. The country enjoyed five years of annual growth of 5.4 per cent from 2010.

Nevertheless, Mauritania remains one of the poorest countries in the world, with a per capita GDP of $1 300, placing it 156th among the 188 countries on the UN Human Development Index. Although its population is growing slowly by regional standards, 60 per cent are under the age of 25; literacy is just 52 per cent. Its infrastructure is fragile – just one-fifth of the population have access to electricity, and there is a chronic national water shortage. Mauritania imports as much as 90 per cent of its domestic food requirements.[41]

And macroeconomic troubles have surfaced as the commodity super-cycle has cooled. With a 10 per cent drop in mining production in 2015, GDP growth fell to 3 per cent from 6.4 per cent the previous year. And government debt rose to over 90 per cent of GDP, forcing the devaluation of the ouguiya.

However, continued partnership with the mines offers some relief. Mauritania is the second largest iron-ore producer in Africa, and aspires to be in the top five global exporters of iron ore by 2025, with an annual production of 40 million tonnes. There are also investors operating copper and gold mines, including Mauritanian Copper Mines at Akjoujt. With an injection of finance and technology by owners First Quantum, this mine, originally started by Anglo American in the 1960s, produces around 40 000 tonnes of copper and 60 000 ounces of gold annually.

The road from Nouakchott to Akjoujt was rebuilt in 2012 by Mauritanian Copper Mines at a cost of $25 million. It was in the company's self-interest to do so, as it needs to move an average of six 30-tonne fuel tankers and fifteen 50-tonne copper-concentrate trucks down the route each day. Mauritanian Copper Mines has a wider role, pumping water 120 kilometres away from an aquifer at Benn'chahab. In the heat of summer, with temperatures reaching over 50 degrees, the mine gets less than 75 per cent of the water that originally entered the pipe, the rest being diverted to the local town, and various communities and camels en route. In the town of Akjoujt, 360 houses are owned by the mine, which has also set up training programmes for youth, women, farmers and schoolchildren.

This adds a premium, of expectation as much as expense, to the mine's activities, already burdened by distance and the cost of services. The cost of transport, for example, to the port at Nouakchott is $16 per tonne, plus $10 in handling charges and $35 in shipping to China. To this have to be added processing costs, which explains why plans to extract iron ore from the discarded copper-gold concentrate at the mine had to be put on hold when iron prices slipped below $60 per tonne.

Reducing inequalities and tackling wealth redistribution, notes the World Bank, 'are key challenges that Mauritania can overcome, provided that it continues its commitment to good governance, particularly in the mining sector and in the supervision of state enterprises'.[42] Indeed, the government–private partnership epitomised by the mine at Akjoujt answers some of the development questions posed by Mauritania – and the Sahel as a whole.

Conclusion: Developing a 'win-win' deal

Getting more value and securing revenue streams from mining in Africa will require moving from a series of tactical actions to a more cohesive, inclusive and strategic approach. Countries have to shift to a positive, constructive cycle, which offers a win-win deal for all. Such a strategy will need to build on a number of existing domestic and international initiatives, but to do so with much greater cohesion, commitment and urgency.

For this to occur, all parties need to recognise the inevitable outcomes of the current cycle – the gradual deflation and downsizing of the industry – and the losers: current and future workers, governments, communities and, ultimately too, the mining companies.

The difficult issues that have underwritten the current crisis in many sub-Saharan African countries will need to be addressed in an honest and open fashion: how should the historical legacy be dealt with? How much profit is reasonable? What is a mining company's responsibility to its employees and communities?

Equally importantly, agreement will have to be reached on what a successful mining industry looks like. There must also be recognition that mining is an inherently risky and long-term endeavour. For success and the mutual benefit that ensues from mining, risk needs to be reduced as far as possible by all parties. Much more than an enlightened business case is needed: mining also needs to understand the problems that government has to address and in so doing make a strategic contribution to wider issues, including enterprise development, water, land, education and so on.

Although there is broad consensus on the lack of a common narrative across the mining industry, a lack of unity has prevented its development. Such a cohesive narrative needs to make a case for the maintenance and development of the mining industry for each audience (government, the nation, lobbying organisations). It needs to address the status of the industry in society and issues of historical legacy, the need for policy stability, balancing revenue generation with the need for beneficiation, the need for the minimum essential but fair constraints and the need for a fair settlement for all parties. Failure to address these aspects will ultimately lead to further decline in the industry.

Government, for its part, has to realise that mining demands capital and long-term partnerships that are patiently managed over time and underpinned by consistent regulations and transparent rule of law. Establishing and maintaining trust through communication with the mining industry are at the core of this process. And setting, and adhering to, sound, agreed industry standards is an essential part of the trust equation. Competitiveness is not just for mining companies, but for the country as a whole.

Some minerals are very scarce and are mined whatever the risk. Think rare earths in the Congo. Most minerals are, however, not that scarce, such as iron ore, coal, bauxite and even copper. Because of the relative lack of scarcity, mining investments are driven, to a large extent, by commodity price and the cost of their extraction.

To compete, Africa needs to ensure it's an attractive investment destination. With prices low, now is the time to reform and put the right frameworks in place. These can help countries realise the full value of an upswing in prices if and when this happens.

Chapter 6
Manufacturing

Five steps for success:
* Attract manufacturing businesses migrating from China, understanding exactly what these businesses require to 'move to Africa'.
* Recruiting manufacturing business will depend on being more competitive than one's worldwide rivals.
* Government should tackle bureaucratic delays and reduce opportunities for corruption, as these are essential elements of setting the business environment for success.
* Use trade policy, preferences and agreements to drive industrial development rather than 'industrial strategy'.
* Higher-value 'mindfacturing' depends on developing basic manufacturing skills and complementing them with relevant education, research and training institutions.

Challenges and opportunities: A substantial increase in manufacturing will help provide jobs for Africa's quickly growing urban populations; Africa's own growing population will provide an increasing domestic market. Billions of dollars in investment will leave China in the next few years as rising wages make that country less competitive at the low end of the manufacturing supply chain. Manufacturers can locate anywhere in the world, but to survive and prosper they need investment and to be competitive. Africa can compete on skills, the cost of labour and location, but it is often poor policy frameworks that cause African countries to fail to attract much needed investment. Manufacturing companies need consistent, competitive, economic conditions, an infrastructure where power is guaranteed and the transport links to facilitate competitively priced exports.

Key statistics: In sub-Saharan Africa, manufacturing accounts for only 14 per cent of GDP.[1] This is lower than every part of the world, except for the Middle East and North Africa.[2] Overall, the African manufacturing sector accounts for just 1.5 per cent of world manufacturing.[3] Sub-Saharan Africa's population with access to electricity is 35.3 per cent, whereas the average for South Asia (the next-lowest region in terms of access to power) is 78 per cent, and East Asia 96.1 per cent.[4] The time it takes to start a business in sub-Saharan Africa is 25.8 days (the 2015 figure), compared to the global average of 20.4.[5] Commodities account for more than 60 per cent of merchandise exports in 28 of 38 African countries. An index of export diversification for sub-Saharan Africa increased by 1 per cent from 1995 to 2013, while the share of the region's manufacturing sector in terms of contribution to GDP has fallen since 2000 from 14 to 10 per cent.

Exceptionally poor and challenged countries can become industrial power-houses in a generation. Vietnam and Mexico both illustrate this prospect for Africa.

Vietnam[6] has managed an extraordinary development turnaround within a generation, from a (real) per capita GDP of $97 in 1989 to $2 052 in 2015.[7] This performance reflects a dynamic growth record, averaging over 6 per cent since 1997, though this has been higher in the cities. With more than 6 million people, Ho Chi Minh City (previously called Saigon) delivered 9.6 per cent growth between 2010 and 2015.

'We envision Vietnam to become a country of industry and modernity by 2025,' says Le Thanh Liem, the vice-chairman of the city, his seniority denoted by a gold party lapel badge.

'To achieve this,' he explains, 'we use our internal strengths and mobilise external reserves through investment. The negotiation of the Trans-Pacific Partnership is,' he notes, 'part of it, but we aim to try to make investors feel welcome here. Capital is key, as is the development of human resources, and, increasingly total factor productivity (TFP)' (meaning the improvements in outputs not accounted for by labour and capital improvements, including technology and governance). 'Although the city is growing at 9.6 per cent per annum,' he observes, 'our year-on-year increase in TFP has grown from 20 per cent in 2014 to 32 per cent in 2015.'

This sophisticated analysis, however desirable, is not expected from a city official anywhere, let alone in a country that hesitatingly started its market reforms just 30 years ago, and only after its attempts at a command economy had collapsed in the midst of famine.

For all of the drawbacks of a single-party state, including widespread corruption, and the rhetorical adherence to the ubiquitous hammer and sickle, and socialist banners, the Vietnamese thinking is both liberal and pragmatic enough to realise the need for the state to lessen its hold on the economy.

The extent of Vietnam's transformation can be seen in the role of its state-owned enterprises (SOEs). With privatisation – referred to more palatably as 'equitisation' – the number of SOEs halved between 1990 and 2000 to 5 800, and to 3 135 by 2013. This divestment has paralleled a transformation in the economic contribution of SOEs, which, in 2001, employed 60 per cent of total capital to generate 38 per cent of GDP. By 2012, these figures had fallen to 38 per cent and 33 per cent, respectively.

By 2015, SOEs officially contributed 31.5 per cent of GDP and employed just 1.7 million jobs, or 3.2 per cent of a total workforce of 52.2 million, falling from 1.8 million the previous year. By comparison, two-thirds of the country's jobs came from the private sector, and 26 per cent were from foreign investment enterprises.[8]

Public listings are another measure of this transition. The Ho Chi Minh stock exchange was launched in 2000 with two companies. Fifteen years later, it listed 303 stocks with a $50 billion market capitalisation and another 370 on the Hanoi Bourse. A further 400 SOEs were expected to be listed by 2017.

A number of businesses have successfully made the leap from state-owned to commercial private enterprise.

Started by a Soviet-trained engineer in 1976, Vinamilk is based north of Ho Chi Minh City at My Phuoc. Its $120-million state-of-the-art hyper-automated milk factory is capable of producing 400 million litres annually. Vietnam's annual milk consumption has risen from just 10 litres per person in 2010 to 17 litres five years later, due to a combination of improved wealth and greater awareness of the health benefits. This consumption level is still some way behind that of China (26 litres), Thailand (35 litres) and Malaysia (58 litres) – hence plans to double the capacity of the factory, which was built by Tetra Pak, by 2018. Vinamilk attracted a number of foreign investors to its initial public offering (IPO) in 2003.

The same is true of Vinatex, a textiles firm, which moved to become a joint stock company through its $57 million IPO in September 2014.

Similarly, Tân Són Nhát International Airport is scarcely recognisable from when it was the principal American air facility during its war in Vietnam. Then it was one of the busiest military airbases in the world. In the early 1990s, the American-built military aircraft facilities were still discernible, daubed with peace signs and slogans. Today the airport has been transformed – a busy hub, handling 26 million passengers in 2015.

Vietnam Airlines is among the big SOEs that remain to be 'equitised'. This divestiture is being driven, in part, by the Trans-Pacific Partnership, its provision including a condition to end subsidies. In this way, just as with Mexico and the North American Free Trade Agreement (NAFTA), trade policy drives industrial policy, not the other way around.

Of course, there are problems and setbacks. Businesses are hampered by corruption and the requirement for endless paperwork, for lots of what are referred to as 'baby permits' to comply with by-laws and regulations. To tackle this issue, Vietnam has established some 300 industrial parks, where the operation of one-stop shops and special customs facilities largely circumvents greedy officialdom. This initiative has encouraged foreigners to invest.

Vietnam's ability to rapidly expand manufacturing despite its challenging legacy is hardly unique. Other countries have been able to achieve similar goals.

The African challenge

Can Africa be the next China? This is the question on the lips of those contemplating the development opportunities made possible by rising labour unit costs in the People's Republic and as its industries move into higher-tech, capital-intensive production. An estimated 85 million jobs will be up for grabs in the next decade as China moves up the industrial ladder. Can Africa take advantage of this, in the process employing the continent's preferential trade agreements with the US and Europe?[9]

Answering this depends largely on putting the right conditions in place, from economic policy to infrastructure and political stability. And it means doing things better than one's rivals. Others will compete for the space potentially being vacated by China; they are unlikely to just sit back and watch.

This question is not just appropriate for low-cost labour markets. It is also relevant for richer African economies, including South Africa, given especially the temptation of trying to deal with development policy dilemmas through state-owned enterprises.

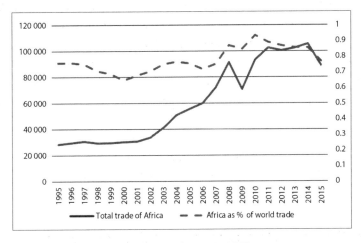

Figure 6.1: Trade of manufactured goods, 1995–2015

Source: UN Conference on Trade and Development, http://unctadstat.unctad.org/wds/ReportFolders/reportFolders.aspx

African policymakers are routinely keen to point out that they are doing all the things that are expected of them to build a manufacturing base. For instance, many are establishing special economic zones to offer duty- and tax-free terms to export manufacturers, along with a range of other incentives. These zones can be useful, in that they offer reliable supplies of power and water, good road links and land that may prove otherwise difficult to access, with assured availability of power especially important to value-addition of mineral endowments. The problem is that, because most other countries across the world are already undertaking similar reforms, these measures, although essential to keep up, do not offer a special advantage. The same applies to 'one-stop shops'. African labour costs are no differentiator either, being generally no cheaper (and mostly more expensive) than those of their Asian competitors, while the cost of corresponding services in Africa can be higher and less reliable.

Of course, at the bottom end of the production chain, such as in textiles and clothing manufacture, price and productivity do matter. Still, the key overall differences between success and failure appear to be a combination of governance and attitude.

According to the World Bank's Doing Business indicators – the authoritative database that is often referred to by business – in 2016 only a handful of African countries had business environments that were better than awful. Mauritius is ranked an impressive 32nd, but after that only Rwanda (62nd), Botswana (72nd), South Africa (73rd), Seychelles (95th) and Zambia (97th) are within the top 100 countries in the world.[10] Certainly, African countries have made some progress in the last decade, but the rest of the world has not stood still either. As a result, sub-Saharan Africa, with the exception of a few small countries, has not managed to systematically move up the rankings in the manufacturing business environment.

It remains exceptionally hard to do manufacturing in Africa, as Lesotho and South Africa illustrate.

Lesotho: Failing to ascend the manufacturing ladder

Lesotho, a small country, is an excellent example of the possibilities offered by, and the disappointments in, the manufacturing sector. While the focus has often been on much larger countries in Africa, Lesotho has actually had more real opportunities and, being a small nation, would not have had to attract that much manufacturing to make a fundamental difference. Yet its Doing Business Indicator ranking in 2016 was an unimpressive 114th.

The road south from Maseru to Moshoeshoe Airport tells its own story of Lesotho's development travails. The route is lined with tin kiosks and junk yards, less small businesses than survival strategies for a nation with 40 per cent unemployment, where the population has grown 25 per cent since 1985 to over 2 million. Nearly half the population live in poverty; HIV prevalence is 23 per cent, the second highest in the world; and half a million people are dependent on food aid.[11]

Despite being totally enveloped geographically by South Africa, Lesotho has enjoyed a number of development advantages. In 2000 it was granted duty- and quota-free access to the US market through the African Growth and Opportunity Act (AGOA). Chinese clothing manufacturers were quick to take advantage of this, and by 2005 the number of clothing and textile companies had mushroomed to 38, employing 55 000 Basotho.

Lesotho also receives a regular share of the customs proceeds from the Southern African Customs Union, and has a comparatively rich prospective market all around it in South Africa. (South Africa has an average per capita income more than six times that of Lesotho's $980.) It benefits from its giant neighbour's relatively sophisticated road and port infrastructure. The mountain kingdom is also blessed with abundant water resources, which it is able to sell to thirsty South Africa.

Nevertheless, Lesotho-based companies have, unlike their Asian or Mexican counterparts, been unable to move up the manufacturing ladder into higher-value production. The principal reasons for this failure are a legacy of political instability and poor governance.

In January 1986, Lesotho experienced the first in a series of military coups, when Major General Justin Metsing Lekhanya evicted Chief Leabua Jonathan. Jonathan had ruled with steadily increasing authoritarianism since independence in October 1966, including staging his own palace coup after the 1970 election, which had been won by the opposition Basotho Congress Party.[12]

Fast-forward three decades and the country's problems, like its population, only seem to have got bigger. The military are now serial political offenders. The change of government in February 2015 had its origins in a failed coup in August 2014. Before then, there has been a steady stream of attempted coups and assassinations. Lekhanya was removed in May 1991 in a coup staged by Colonel Elias Ramaema. Democracy ensued in 1993, but following the 1998 elections there were protests and rioting over the results, and a SADC force led by South Africa was deployed to restore democracy and the rule of law. Operation Boleas, the code name for the deployment, quickly became controversial, and in September 1998 the South African National Defence Force lost 11 members while attempting to quell a mutiny in Maseru. By the time the force left in May 1999 large sections of the city were destroyed.

Underlying the political musical chairs and the muscle flexing of the military in politics is a history of corruption and rent-seeking. As former minister of development and planning (as well as Lesotho's delegate to the IMF) Moeketsi Majoro commented: 'While the legacy of incomplete political reform is the accelerant in this present conflict, corruption and crime are the root causes. During the life of the previous government, instances of public funds being laundered through tenders for both party and personal gain have been investigated and are a matter of public record.'[13]

International assistance and interest has dried up. By 2016 there were just five full-time, foreign diplomatic missions (China, EU, Libya, US and South Africa) resident in the kingdom. Even the UK, the former colonial power, has closed shop. Today it is represented by an honorary consul. It's a far cry from the anti-apartheid heyday, when 'every European country, among others,' said one minister, 'had an embassy here'.

The country still receives $300 million annually in aid, or over 11 per cent of its gross national income. But all aid seems to have achieved over time is to mitigate some of the downsides rather than making Lesotho more prosperous and more stable, though, gauging from the tempo of the violence, even that strategy seems flawed.

By 2015 the number of clothing and textile companies had declined to 18, employing 35 000 personnel. The decline was the result of the volatile rand (to which the local loti is pegged), high costs of inputs (notably electricity and transport), and lack of confidence in the political situation. The termination of the global Multifibre Agreement in 2005 favoured those with greater 'cost efficiencies – essentially Asia over Africa', explains one Chinese producer. 'Asian salary costs,' he notes, 'are lower, and their governments offer greater incentives, including tax-free imports and local sales.' In Lesotho, although labour costs are low (R1 212 minimum, or $80 a week) competition is tough within the region: in Kenya labour is $76 and in Ethiopia $50. Bangladesh's is around half of this figure ($43), Vietnam's is $52, India's $49 and Cambodia's $50. The decline in Lesotho's textile industry is exacerbated by payment on a 'piece-by-piece' basis in Asia, not permitted in Lesotho, and by the African country's high absenteeism rate of 8–10 per cent. Comparing productivity between Vietnam and Lesotho tells its own story: in Vietnam 28 operators produce 1 000 pieces a day; in Lesotho 36 workers produce 600 of the same item.

Local shipping times are also longer and freight costs higher than in Asia. For example, in 2011 the cost of sending a 40-foot container from Lesotho to the US was $4 620. This compares with $2 600 for freighting the same from Vietnam, $2 800 (Cambodia) and $3 100 (Bangladesh). The costs of utilities have steadily risen, too, with electricity prices tracking those of Eskom in neighbouring South Africa.

The country also has an energy shortage. Lesotho's Muela Dam produces just 72 megawatts, while the country's electricity requirement in 2016 was in excess of 120 megawatts, and demand is rising. To fill the gap, the country is at the mercy of Eskom, as it were. There are plans afoot for another dam, Polihali, with linked power-generation capacity, but whether this comes to fruition or not hinges on stability and investor confidence. Water costs also rose by 13 per cent in 2016.

Without AGOA, it would be difficult for Lesotho to compete. The agreement with the US offers as much as a 33 per cent discount on products from Lesotho thanks to its duty-free, quota-free status. Accordingly, a number of the larger producers have moved into manufacturing fabrics that normally attract higher duty (nylons, notably) to take full advantage of the access to the US market.

These are challenges that Lesotho should be able to overcome. Some Asian countries have already exited from textile and apparel manufacture as their living standards and workers' salary expectations have risen. Despite its textile boom, Lesotho has failed to improve its competitiveness and ascend the industrialisation ladder into higher-value-added goods. Its attempts to do so, and efforts to create Basotho (rather than Chinese) industrialists, have generally failed to deliver.

Lesotho's minister of small business, Thabiso Lits'iba, a former university professor, says that this dearth of progress is due to the relative absence of competent people among the country's 44 000 civil servants; it is also because of 'a lack of leadership in establishing a clear strategic direction and goals'. In other words, part of this malaise is down to government not listening, and part of it is due to its unwillingness to take tough decisions. Or, as another former senior official put it, 'Instead of looking at the long-term benefits of the textile agreement, we look to see who has benefited in the short-term.' Rather than thinking generationally, politicians are too busy, as per Majoro's argument, fighting over the scraps.

In 2008 at the invitation of His Majesty King Letsie, the Brenthurst Foundation brought together a group of experts from high-growth economies – Singapore, Costa Rica, Colombia, El Salvador, Chile and Vietnam – to share lessons and identify a high-growth path for the kingdom. This visit was coupled with work commissioned specifically on the business climate in Lesotho and on the tourism sector. Noting Lesotho's progress in manufacturing by taking best advantage of AGOA's opportunities and its record in carrying out complex, large infrastructure schemes, like the Lesotho Highlands Water Project, the final report focused its recommendations on job creation and export-led growth as the only route to a more prosperous future for the country.

Yet none of the reforms suggested – such as removing business constraints and establishing a forum to forge consensus on domestic growth – were implemented, despite the full attention of government at our meetings, and nodding agreement to our recommendations.

Tim Thahane was our principal government interlocutor. Before taking up his job as Minister of Finance, he had served with distinction as deputy governor in the South African Reserve Bank. He reflects that our initiative died, as did the subsequent World Bank growth project, owing to what he describes as the 'short-termism of government'. In other words, senior people were unwilling to expend political will to make it happen. Or, as another senior Basotho participant put it, 'It was a great initiative. It was ahead of its time. We were doing the same work five years later. But you,' he smiled, 'left with it.'

South Africa's challenge

The case of Lesotho demonstrates many of the attitudes towards manufacturing across Africa. Many of the same issues can be seen in South Africa, one of Africa's largest economies, and a country that should, by all of the usual indicators, possess a thriving manufacturing sector.

Manufacturing contributed 13.4 per cent of South Africa's GDP in 2014, making it the fourth largest component of economic activity, behind finance, real estate and business services (20.3 per cent); general government services (17 per cent); and wholesale, retail and motor trade, and catering and accommodation (14.4 per cent). However, manufacturing's contribution to real annual GDP growth has declined steadily, from 0.7 per cent in 2010 to 0.1 per cent in 2013. Moreover, the sector has shed more than 300 000 jobs since the 2008/09 global recession, losing 100 000 alone between 2015 and 2016.[14]

The record shows how difficult the environment is for manufacturers, particularly in the small and medium-sized business sector, where the bulk of manufacturing jobs, the government hopes, will be created in the future.

Take the example of Newcastle. Originally a post halt between Durban and Johannesburg, Newcastle in South Africa was founded in 1864 as the fourth settlement in the colony of Natal. Today, it is a city of nearly 400 000, the province's third largest, behind Durban and Pietermaritzburg. It is in the throes of adjusting to new realities.

Even as recently as 1969, Newcastle could be described as a one-horse town. Then came the announcement of the creation of the Iscor steel mill, envisaged as a three-phase development that would employ 25 000 by 2000. Investment followed in the town's infrastructure, including housing. By the time the cancellation of the second and third phases was announced in 1983, the plant employed 13 000 people. Privatisation in 1989 brought employment down to 9 000, leaving 750 empty houses in the town.

Cancellation of the development of the steel plant spurred the municipality to pursue an aggressive industrial policy. In 1983 the city got its first foreign investment in the form of a Hong Kong-based company, ramping up quickly to a rate of one factory opening per month. New businesses were attracted by generous decentralisation incentives. At its peak, the Riverside and Madadeni industrial zones housed 65 textile and apparel factories. The shift in South Africa's diplomatic relations from Taiwan to China in 1997 caused some businesses from the former to close down and the latter to open up. By 2015 the textile and clothing sector employed 6 500 workers, or one-third of the industrial workforce of the town, down from its peak of 35 000.

But, today, it is tough-going in Newcastle, reflecting the changing fortunes of an industry that has seen a decline since the 1980s, and one that employs only about a fifth of the number of people 25 years later. The ending of incentives, fluctuations in the value of the rand, competition from cheap imports from Bangladesh, India and China in particular, and the establishment of AGOA all undermined the competitiveness of South African-manufactured yarns and clothing. Under AGOA, South Africa was classified as a developed country and, therefore, unlike its neighbours Lesotho and Swaziland, not eligible to convert cheaper third-country textiles into clothes for the US market. As a result, a number of the larger clothing manufacturers left in the mid-2000s. Then, in 2011, the National

Bargaining Council attempted to shut down several Chinese-owned factories to enforce compliance with the council's minimum wage. When they did so, the workers marched on the Bargaining Council and threatened to burn down its premises.

The city's economic situation is more complicated than the sum of the external shocks or the payment of a minimum wage. As the chair of Newcastle's Chinese Chamber of Commerce and Industry, Alex Liu, explained, 'While price is a big issue in garment manufacture, the problem with the Bargaining Council's wage is about the way in which our business runs. While the Council says you cannot reward productivity, but rather years of service, this takes away the power of the factory owner to manage our factories and to reward those who are more productive. You simply cannot pay everyone the same, as you will kill off the morale of the factory, and it would become unmanageable. It is not so much a question of affordability,' he adds, 'as business logic.'[15]

The municipality has attempted, by the business owners' own admission, to 'look after them as best as possible', troubleshooting with central government to resolve matters such as work permits, labour relations, environmental management and other issues, acting as 'a mother and father' to this group. Part of the frustration felt by factory owners and the local municipality, however, 'is that Pretoria is not listening. We have no direct channels to government departments', they say, 'or even government in the province.'

Business may be Eveready, but government must be too

Manufacturing businesses in South Africa face similar challenges – even further up the value chain.

Octagonal zinc blanks are pressed into tubular cans at one end of the production line, creating a cathode. The cans march along the conveyors where they are filled with manganese dioxide in a cardboard sealant and a graphite stick to form the anode. At various points along the conveyors they are moved to large bins, waiting for their turn to be covered with caps, seals and wraparound exterior decals.[16]

In South Africa, Eveready makes 50 million batteries a year, supplying around half the country's demand. The company has been based in Port

Elizabeth since 1937 when British Eveready established its factory in Harrower Road. It moved to its current facility in the city's industrial area in 1972, as the brass plaque in the foyer testifies: 'Officially opened by Dr The Hon N Diederichs, Minister of Finance.' In the 1970s Eveready was bought out by Hanson and then, in 1996, Gillette. In 2003, when Gillette divested of all battery types aside from Duracell, the South African operation was bought by management.

The team has had to work hard to position the company in a new market, under pressure from cheap, mainly Chinese, competitors. In seeking new opportunities for the business, and to keep opportunities alive for its 220 employees, Eveready has diversified into household wood products and, recently, wind generators. The facade of the building now exhibits a line of its locally developed 3.5-kilowatt Kestrel turbines above the blue-and-white E-V-E-R-E-A-D-Y sign, their fibreglass blades and vanes angling, jockeying and whirring away in the Windy City.

Though Eveready has sold 3 500 Kestrels, most of these have been into an export market. 'The problem, fundamentally,' says CEO Avijit Das, 'is that government does not believe that business is positive for the country. This shapes it perceptions and its policies.' More than that, he adds, 'we need to decide whether we are a developed or a developing country. A decision on this will shape what policies we push for, including those relating to labour and product standards, and will also shape expectations.'

The turbine offers a practical and turn-key power solution to off-grid communities. 'Government could,' Das says, 'make it happen if it chose to.' In contrast, in competing with imported products, Eveready has asked the authorities to implement environmental and safety standards, apparently to no avail. 'The role of the government should be to create policies that enable jobs, not simply to create them for themselves. They should be trying to make investing simple and easy.'

But government has not, says Das, helped in any way. 'We are the only manufacturers of micro-turbines in South Africa, and our products are certified in the US and the UK. But we have never had an engagement with anyone in government to ask, "What can we do to help?" This,' he observes, 'is quite unlike India, my home country, where, despite the frustrations with bureaucracy, the authorities routinely ask: "What can we do to help you manufacture here?".'

The experience of Volkswagen, 25 kilometres north of Port Elizabeth in Uitenhage, is higher tech, and dependence on more interventionist government policy to make up for inefficiencies elsewhere in the South African system.

In 2013 a R500-million, fully automated, state-of-the-art metal-pressing system was installed in the VW factory, capable of churning out several hundred body panels an hour. The new line, set in sterile conditions more akin to an operating theatre than a machine shop, is the first in the world to combine wave-motion pressing technology with Cobra robotics to move parts quickly through the process. New technology helps to explain why employment at VW is at 4 000, down from a peak of 10 000 in the 1980s.

The company has invested more than R5 billion in the modernisation of the Uitenhage facility, which will see it nearly double annual production to 170 000 units, and be the sole producer of the new Polo sedan.

It's a far cry from 1946, when South African Motor Assemblers and Distributors was launched with share capital of R1 million to assemble Studebakers on the same 20-hectare site, bought then for R2 500.

Despite winning regular awards as the best VW factory out of 119 worldwide, the survival of the plant depends entirely on the South African government's subsidy programme for vehicle production, the Automotive Production and Development Programme (APDP), by which the price of locally assembled vehicles is rebated against the duty on imported components in their manufacture. 'The minute the APDP ends,' says Thomas Schäfer, the head of VW South Africa, 'the plug will be pulled. We have a slight advantage with labour costs, but no more compared to Portugal or the Czech Republic. And we have a big cost challenge with logistics. Whatever we save via the APDP is cancelled out by the €500 extra per unit we spend on South African shipping costs.'

VW is not alone in this regard. Ford, based near Pretoria, has staged something of a remarkable turnaround in its fortunes since the production of its new Ranger pickup started in 2015. Within a year, it had a dominant slice of the South African market, with 36 000 sales, exporting another 60 000, primarily to the UK and Germany. 'Geography is a challenge in South Africa,' says CEO Jeff Nemeth, 'whether manufacturing or otherwise, exporting or importing, the country being 10 000 kilometres from the major sources of supply and markets.'

Although Ford South Africa's productivity is 30 per cent better than a similar Ford plant in Thailand, like VW, the company is hammered by logistics costs. Studies show that the cost of transporting cars by rail should be, for the great distances involved in South Africa, 60 per cent lower than by road. In South Africa, however, the cost works out the same, illustrating high levels of inefficiency in South Africa's rail network. The export costs of shipping a car from Thailand to Saudi Arabia are $800 cheaper than sending the same vehicle from South Africa to Saudi Arabia.

In the centre of Port Elizabeth is the General Motors plant. Opened in 1948 at a staggering cost then of £1 million, some six decades on it produces 40 000 units of two models.

The industry, says the GM CEO, Ian Nicholls, is bedevilled by the high cost of skills and the distance from the export markets. Efforts to improve the pool of talent, however, through government schemes deliver little. The extent of unionisation compounds the costs and challenges, with the negotiation of 10 per cent annual increases when there is just 6 per cent inflation, reducing competitiveness. 'Never in this environment,' he says, 'where I know how difficult it is to get rid of people, would I take on a single person without absolute knowledge that I need them.' His logistics component amounts to 8 per cent of unit costs, with just a 5 per cent profit margin. With GM's four largest plants, now in China, producing 500 000 units annually, only a combination of the APDP, the desire to maintain a strategic foothold in Africa, and 'inertia' keeps the firm making cars in South Africa.

The APDP puts South Africa, according to Schäfer, in 'the lower half of subsidy countries, below South Korea, Mexico, China and Turkey', for example. Although the subsidy scheme remains important, he says, what will ensure the success of the industry in South Africa, is policy stability 'for a decade at least', driving down the cost of logistical inefficiencies and keeping inflation under control. All of this hinges, however, on an attitude whereby 'government helps rather than burdens industry'.

The South African government did aim to double local vehicle production to 1.2 million units by 2020 since the advent of the APDP in 2013. However, this won't happen unless logistics costs come down and, related to this, local content volumes increase. In a vicious cycle, however, the ability to generate local content is shaped by economies of scale, along with electricity, labour and other cost variables. Dealing with these factors demands business and government collaboration. And that, in turn, would require a government that is willing to accept that business is there to make reasonable money, and to help it to do so.

Mexico's story highlights a different path, showing that, despite challenges, sustained development from a low base is possible with strong government leadership.

Mexico's race to the top

Mexico[17] once had the profile of many African states: a country highly dependent on oil, with a reputation for corruption and with one political party that had long governed despite its economic failures. The profile was so entrenched that in the mid-1990s, the Mexican ambassador to South Africa was distraught about a television advert for a brand of corn chips, which portrayed an indolent *campesino* wearing a sombrero and speaking in an accent that would make even Eli Wallach's character in *The Good, the Bad and the Ugly* blush.

The erstwhile diplomat had a point. By the time the advert was flighted, things in Mexico had changed. More than 30 years earlier, in 1965, his government had launched a border industrialisation programme, better known as *maquiladoras*,[18] which transformed the country's job market and export profile by exploiting the comparative advantage of abundant cheap labour through 'quick and dirty' assembly and export.

To give one example of the success of the programme, by 2016 Monterrey had become Mexico's wealthiest and most industrialised city. No fewer than 46 000 trucks leave each day carrying manufactured goods bound for the US market, where Mexico's share has grown fourfold to 20 per cent in the 21 years since NAFTA came into force. These are no longer cheap *maquila* goods, however, but high-value exports. Mexico's rise up the value chain is epitomised by public-private research and innovation incubators such as the Parque de Investigación e Innovación Tecnológica, near Monterrey's international airport.

Mexico's experience illustrates that it is impossible to start higher-value 'mindfacturing' without first developing basic manufacturing skills and complementing them with relevant education, research and training institutions. The *maquilas* were, in this way, an essential antecedent to today's more sophisticated operations.

Guanajuato, in the heart of Mexico, and once the centre of the global silver-mining industry, is developing a modern-day Silverado in the form of the auto industry. A giant General Motors plant there produces 370 000 pickup trucks a year. And GM is not alone. Mazda, Honda, Hino Motors, Toyota and VW have followed suit. Guanajuato State produced 550 000 vehicles in 2015, the same number that the entire South African auto industry produces.

Mexico has moved quickly from assembler to manufacturer to innovator in the auto industry, and is now the world's seventh largest producer. South Africa, which has the largest auto industry in Africa, ranks just 24th.

Although, with its huge population, 125 million, Mexico still experiences many social problems, manufacturing provides direct employment for more than 2 million. As Jaime Serra Puche, trade economist and Mexico's lead negotiator on NAFTA, puts it, 'Today we are exporting $1 billion per day, about 80 per cent of which is manufacturing. At the start of NAFTA, we were exporting about $100 million per day, and a big chunk of that was oil.'

Despite the country's challenges of drug-fuelled crime, Luis de la Calle, the former Deputy Minister for International Trade Negotiations, insists three factors make Mexico's rise 'unstoppable'. The first relates to demographics. There is a clear increase in Mexicans of a working age, along with a declining dependency ratio between those working and those not. These young people are providing heavy demand for the consumer manufactured goods that Mexico is now well positioned to produce.

The second is the reduction in energy costs in North America, making it the cheapest region in the world for energy. This drop is driven by an increase in US gas production from 64 billion cubic feet per day in 2006 to 90 billion cubic feet in 2015, along with a doubling in US oil production to 10 million barrels per day during the last five years. Mexico's energy reforms and targeted investments as part of an integrated North American gas network will pipe Texan gas to remote Mexican locations that never had industry before, while also driving down costs for existing industries. At the same time, deregulation in the electricity sector has brought the commercial price of electricity down by 25 per cent.

The third reason concerns the real appreciation of the US dollar. This has bolstered existing Mexican exports, like cars and appliances.

As a result of these drivers, Mexico is today the only large developing economy that competes with China in manufacturing. In terms of the value of exports per capita, Mexico is almost twice as large as China.

Most importantly, however, Mexico's progress has relied on trade agreements rather than summitry. Being open and connected with tangible transfers has proven crucial to Mexico's progress as both a value-added exporter and a modernising industrial nation. In this regard, Mexico focuses on agreements like NAFTA, which has allowed it to capitalise on its natural advantages in the US market for over 20 years, whatever the sentiment of some US politicians as to the agreement's future.

Mexico's clearly defined trade strategy not only forms the backbone of the country's foreign policy, but also determines its competitive output, avoiding an industrial policy that many economists and technocrats in Mexico believe to be overly cumbersome and rent-seeking.

For all of its problems of security and corruption, Mexico's political environment has moved this century from institutionalised cronyism to increasing competiveness. At the tip of the democratic revolution this century was Vicente Fox, president from 2000 to 2006. Fox was the first opposition leader to hold the office in more than 70 years.

Back in 1810 Guanajuato was the site of the rebels' first military victory during Mexico's War of Independence from Spain. Fast-forward 180 years, and the state was again the epicentre of political change. It prospered under the governorship of Vicente Fox and the Partido Acción Nacional (PAN – National Action Party), whose combined efforts led to the state's lowest unemployment rate, offering the continuity and policy conservatism which, as the auto industry acknowledges, was key to encouraging investment.

Fox was chosen as the PAN candidate for the 2000 national election. His victory broke the hold that the PRI (Partido Revolucionario Institucional – Institutional Revolutionary Party) had enjoyed on Mexican politics. The PRI had started with a radical social policy agenda but, as the 20th century progressed, had become more corrupt and populist. As the predominant, or even hegemonic party, the PRI had enjoyed three major sources of electoral support, says one Monterrey businessman. The party appealed to the poor *campesinos*, who were looking for redistribution, the bureaucrats, who wanted to keep their jobs, and the unions, who wanted political favours. To stay in power, the party used the tactics of redistribution from Mexico's oil boom – repression, rent-seeking, distribution of contracts, corruption and election fiddling. For a long time, such vested interests overcame any desire for reform. As the saying (attributed to Fidel Velázquez, leader of the Confederation of Mexican Workers trade union) goes, '*El que se mueve no sale en la foto*'. ('The guy that moves does not come out in the photo.')[19]

Such political cynicism may have reached a nadir with the 1988 election of Carlos Salinas after a computer malady conveniently halted vote counting. Salinas attempted sweeping reforms, which included the conclusion of NAFTA – viewed as the most significant step towards an open and modern Mexico – and independence for the Central Bank. Yet these moves were at the time overshadowed by a spate of corruption scandals, the Zapatista insurgency in the southern state of Chiapas, a rise in drug trafficking, and a debt crisis that his successor, Ernesto Zedillo, was left to deal with. As president, Zedillo also instituted a new transparent electoral system, which helped to ensure Fox's election.

With NAFTA came greater openness and accountability. 'The more closed you are,' says Joy Langston, a political scientist at the Centro de Investigación y Docendia Económicas, a research organisation in Mexico City, 'the greater the opportunities for rent-seeking. This has been,' she says, 'exacerbated by a judicial system that is semi-dysfunctional at best, from the courts to the police, from protecting contracts to protecting lives.'

Fox runs a foundation focused on leadership from his family's original hacienda in his home town of San Cristobel, an hour's drive from Guanajuato. He acknowledges that the PRI set the stage for their own downfall. 'They had become corrupt and inefficient, and their lack of functionality was against development. They had to collapse. We took advantage of that. Our planning centred on clear-cut communications, in convincing Mexicans that they would be better off without the PRI.'

With a minority in Congress, it was not an easy reform ride for Fox, though he achieved limited improvements in education and healthcare, and particularly in social welfare by expanding the Oportunidades system of welfare cash payments. 'Our brand of democracy, freedoms, respect for human rights and openness met with lots of resistance from the old, dark and violent parts of Mexican society. Moving from one paradigm to the other required a very big effort,' he says.

Though the PRI was returned to power in 2012 (ironically, with Fox's support), the PAN victories in the 2000 and 2006 presidential elections have helped to transform Mexico's politics and to change the image of the PRI from a party that never lost power whatever its failings and excesses, to one that can and does. Decentralisation between the federal government, the 32 states and the 2 500 municipalities, as well as increasing competition at these levels, has further reduced the chances of a reversion to political business as in days gone by.

For a long time, Mexicans were fleeing their own country to pursue the so-called 'American dream' north of the border. But, as one businessman says, 'Most are now chasing the Mexican dream. A life where you work for dollars, but live in pesos, in Mexico.' The rapid conversion of the *maquilas* offers opportunity to achieve this new dream.

Mexico's journey over the last quarter century shows that getting the politics right, domestically and regionally, is crucial. It shows that trade agreements can be used to drive industrialisation and, in so doing, that manufacturing does not have to be a race to the wage bottom – rather one to the top.

Conclusion: 'Move to Africa'?

These case studies (see also the Ethiopian case study in Chapter 11), illustrate that the creation of low-wage, light-industrialisation jobs is highly sensitive to infrastructure, logistics and wage costs, as well as to negotiated trade preferences. It is difficult to progress up the wage and technology ladder without improved skills and other efficiencies.

During the research for this book, we met no one who said that Africa could not compete in the international economy. Instead, we found many entrepreneurs who were willing to devote their lives and their capital to exporting from Africa. No one said that the geographic challenges were too daunting. Even in landlocked Lesotho, there is active interest in developing industry. And no one said that the governments did not know what to do to promote manufacturing. Rather, time and time again, the issue came down to how well governments enabled businesses to operate in a way that investors can make a profit that justifies their time and capital. Both Lesotho and South Africa have repeatedly failed to set the right conditions, with the result that numerous manufacturing opportunities were missed.

When faced with the same challenges, Vietnam and Mexico did not miss those opportunities. The result is that those countries are much richer today, their people live longer and their children are better educated. They show that, with a government focus on creating the right trading and employment environment for business, light manufacturing offers considerable rewards. These countries also illustrate that the manufacturing sector does not have to be a race to the bottom of the wage pile.

Chapter 7
Services

Five steps for success:

- The service sector needs to be actively nurtured by governments, with a focus on providing the required infrastructure and regulatory environment.
- Keep government costs (and overheads) low, and match ambition with pragmatism, and growth will follow, as has been shown in the case of airlines like Ethiopian and Emirates.
- Assist the development of a domestic tourism industry by making access easier than that of competitors. This includes making it easy to acquire visas and reducing the costs and hassle of running hotels, through single-permit processes.
- Establish conditions to encourage foreign banks to assist the rapid acceleration in the development and sophistication of local banking systems.
- Actively support the development of the insurance industry and recognise its regional nature by removing protectionism and providing effective regulation.

Challenges and opportunities: The service sector offers the potential for large-scale job creation in return for fairly modest capital investment. By the mid-1990s, services – economic activities like tourism, banking and insurance that do not produce a tangible commodity – accounted for almost two-thirds of world GDP, up from about half in the 1980s. Even in countries that are still industrialising, the service sector is growing relative to the rest of the economy.[1] The service sector offers Africa a significant opportunity to leapfrog stages of development and radically increase employment. For example, in 2012 McKinsey estimated that retail and hospitality alone could add 9 million out of 54 million potential jobs in Africa by 2020.[2] Unlike raw materials, services can be produced anywhere. While a few African countries have unique advantages in some aspect of tourism, they compete against all other countries in the market for services. Robust service offerings require complex commercial operations and often take advantage of the benefits of technology.

Key statistics: The market for services is massive. For instance, in 2014, there were more than 1.1 billion international tourist arrivals worldwide, of which Africa (including North Africa) accounted for less than 5 per cent. Just two African countries, Morocco and South Africa (with around 10 million apiece), received 40 per cent of the continent's total tourists. One job is created for approximately every 10 tourists who visit a country. Kenya tops the list of the banked population in Africa, with 25.4 million mobile-money subscribers in 2015. Of the adult population in Africa, 339 million, or 80 per cent, are unbanked – that is, they do not have access to formal financial services.[3]

The before-and-after image of Dubai is similar to that of Singapore. The before is that of a lot of sand, a creek and little else; the after, countless skyrise buildings, including the world's tallest, the 830-metre Burj Khalifa, as well as numerous malls and a world-class air-and sea port.

This transformation has occurred in just two generations. Fifty years ago, most homes in Dubai did not possess running water, and the advantages of Dubai seemed few and far between, certainly when compared to its regional Emirati competitors.

The story of Emirates Airline illustrates this transition. Started in 1985 with just two aircraft (a leased Boeing 737 and an Airbus A300) the airline is, today, a global connector. In 2016, despite the tough trading times sparked by the Chinese economic downturn, and the stripping out of fuel surcharges, Emirates was anticipating over 10 per cent growth. At the same time, the airline is working to improve the Dubai airport concourse, including the ground transport to aircraft, ensuring its status as the global air 'super connector'.

The success of Emirates reflects the country's style of leadership. The oil boom only started in 1966, well after Sheikh Saeed bin Maktoum bin Hasher Al Maktoum's had begun his drive in the 1920s for diversification, growth and development. Historically, Dubai had been a relatively insignificant port. To develop the emirate, Dubai's leadership has taken responsibility for growth, closely monitoring projects and the overall health of the economy.

Dubai also used its oil dividend to diversify. During the mid-1970s, oil accounted for half of Dubai's GDP; by the end of the 2000s, the figure was just over 2 per cent. By then, trade and repair and maintenance were Dubai's largest industries, accounting for 39 per cent of GDP.[4] Critical to Dubai's growth has been its relative openness to other cultures and to foreign expertise. By 2016, 80 per cent of Dubai's population of 2.5 million were expatriates, principally South Asians. Put simply, Dubai created an environment where other people could succeed, unlike in much of Africa, which remains fraught with envy and suspicions about the motives of outsiders.

Nevertheless, along the way, Dubai has faced considerable challenges. Regional insecurity is endemic. The 2008 global financial crisis dealt a cruel blow to the economy, temporarily as it has turned out. But Dubai still remains vulnerable to commodity price fluctuations.

Its record of rapid diversification is both impressive and startling when one compares it with Africa. Whereas Dubai is built on trade openness, and financial liberalisation, African countries have lagged behind and, for example, have been variously unable or unwilling to implement the Yamoussoukro Declaration of 1988 to open African skies. To take another example, South Africa has made it harder for tourists to visit by introducing overly complicated visa requirements and procedures, whereas Dubai has continually made it easier for them to visit and spend their money.

The African challenge

Historically, agriculture has been developing economies' most important sector. But, as countries develop and their people get richer, the service sector becomes more prominent. In most developed countries, the service sector is now the dominant sector, in part due to tourism. But, as Figure 7.1 shows,[5] the service sector makes an important contribution to growth in all countries.

The comparatively high labour intensity of services ensures that, as a country develops, jobs created in this sector compensate for those lost in agriculture and industry as increasing capital investment provides for mechanisation and other labour-saving technological progress.

By the mid-1990s, services accounted for almost two-thirds of world

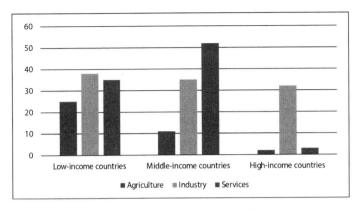

Figure 7.1: Structure of world economy, 1995 (% GDP)

Source: World Bank, www.worldbank.org/depweb/beyond/beyondco/beg_09.pdf World Bank Data

GDP, up from about half in the 1980s. Even in countries that are still industrialising, the service sector is growing relative to the rest of the economy.[6]

African countries have often placed unnecessary barriers to growth in the service sector, making it difficult to take full advantage of the potential for employment. However, the good news is that things can be done to change current policy stances and thus generate many new jobs.

Tourism and the challenges of airlines

Tourism is one of the most – perhaps *the* most – promising sector for many African countries, because it offers a possibility for the creation of a large number of jobs, especially for new entrants to the labour market. However, for tourism to be successful, African countries must be served by airlines that are viable and focused on delivering as many visitors as possible.

Most African tourism markets remain difficult to access, and are fraught with concerns about security. Getting airlines to operate effectively has proved particularly challenging. The trajectory of South African Airways (SAA), rated regularly as the top African airline, is a good example.[7] Unfortunately, poor management has led it deep into debt. By 2016 government bailouts to the ailing national carrier had totalled $2 billion,[8] including a $350 million guarantee provided in October 2012 on condition that SAA's board develop a turnaround strategy, and again in January 2014, when the government announced that SAA would receive another $460 million bailout.

Zambia has experienced a similarly troubled airline history and there has been a surprising ambivalence towards the tourism industry. The names and bones of old aircraft littering Lusaka's Kenneth Kaunda International Airport are a graveyard of failed dreams. Since the liquidation of the state-owned Zambia Airlines in 1994, Zambia Express, Aero Zambia, Zambia Skyways, Zambian Airways, Mahogany Airlines, Airwaves and Zambezi Airlines have all come and gone. Most were killed by unrestrained ambition, too rapid expansion, high overheads and low load.

Tony Irwin, a former Zambian Airways pilot, started Proflight with a five-seater Beechcraft Baron, focusing on the tourism sector. Six years later, he added another, a nine-seater Piper Chieftain, running tourists to Mfuwe in South Luangwa Park and to the Victoria Falls resort in Livingstone, synching with the British Airways flight to London. In 2003, with funding from Barclays, Proflight purchased its first Jetstream, an 18-seater British-built aircraft. 'It was what we could afford,' says Irwin. 'It is pretty fuel efficient, has low engine overheads, and its low capital cost enabled us to get into the game.' Even so, he says, 'we were pretty mad to do it then, looking back now. We needed more work for the aircraft, so we went up against Zambian Airways, which had been created from Roan Air, the old ZCCM [Zambian Consolidated Copper Mines] airline, to break into the Copperbelt.'

By 2016 Proflight was operating six Jetstreams and one CRJ regional jet, with 70 per cent of its passengers travelling for business, not pleasure. Irwin says: 'It's a small market, for which airlines need real economies of scale.' Proflight averaged 136 000 passengers a year between 2012 and 2015. 'Good management is key, including a low staff turnover and high technical skills.'

Fuel costs, which are nearly twice as high as in South Africa, are a symptom of a 'terribly inefficient local refinery' and the cost of being landlocked. More importantly, while the tourism industry could create a tremendous number of jobs (the industry ratio in Zambia is 1.3 direct jobs per bed), the seasonality of the tourism industry is an impediment to growth. The rainy season is compounded by limited infrastructure, which restricts access to Zambia's national parks. 'During our worst week to Mfuwe, we move 80 passengers; during the best, 880,' Irwin says, 'and six months of the year, during the rainy season, very little happens.'

Access to the country has also been complicated by the 2004 EU ban on Zambian Airlines, which was finally lifted, after much delay, in June 2016. Such problems have also been compounded by the role of the airports company, 'one of the last bastions of government monopoly, which at least needs proper management and a separation of the handling functions from those of running the airport'. Its poor operational performance results in higher aircraft turnaround fees, thus adding to the cost of flights.

More generally, in Zambia the number of international-quality beds countrywide is around 5 000, and there are just 850 in Lusaka. This lack of quality accommodation reflects the challenges of Zambia's so-called 'permit culture'. Nearly 40 permits are required to open a hotel and, although the rate of corporate tax has remained level, hotel prices have increased dramatically, adding considerably to the costs of doing business and providing numerous opportunities for corruption.

However, some African airlines have been successful. Ethiopian Airlines (ET) – a firm with a great history, but one that certainly could have gone the way of so many other state enterprises in Africa – is perhaps the best example of how good governance can promote a vibrant service company.[9] The modest headquarters of Ethiopian Airlines, just a stone's throw from the main terminal at Addis Ababa's Bole Airport, is true to the government's mantra about keeping overheads low. Its CEO, Tewolde GebreMariam, speaks with the same disarming frankness about the airline's trajectory, which, unlike many other African national carriers, has been up, not down.

According to Mr Tewolde, the airline's 70-year history can be divided into two phases: the first 60 years, when there was steady, if unspectacular, growth; and the next decade, when, following the first posted loss after the end of the war with Eritrea, the company enjoyed a strategic turnaround.

Tewolde returned from New York in 2004, where he had headed up Ethiopian Airline's operations. As a result of a 'strategic analysis' undertaken with the help of Ernst & Young, the airline developed its Vision 2010, 'which repositioned the airline,' says Tewolde. The goal was to increase turnover from $400 million in 2005 to $1 billion within five years. This was to be achieved by a 'revamped network', with a 'morning bank' of some 52 flights to African destinations and an 'evening bank' when these, apart from those west of Togo, would return and go out again to the Middle East, Europe, Asia and the Americas.

By 2010 the airline's turnover was $1.3 billion, exceeding initial projections, as did the passenger and cargo numbers. Vision 2025 was then put in place. 'The new technology of aircraft,' explains Tewolde, 'like the 787 and A350 demanded a longer-term horizon.' By that date, ET plans to have 120 aircraft flying to 90 destinations internationally and 20 within Ethiopia, turning over $10 billion. The planning cycle is broken up into three five-year phases, short-, medium- and long-term. Tewolde admits that such a long-term cycle 'is controversial in an industry where it is difficult to plan for one year, let alone 15'. The planning is complicated by 'the need to be self-sufficient in Africa because there are not enough private-sector contractors. This means we have to provide catering, support and technical services ourselves.'

The airline's strategy, says its CEO, is broken up into a number of different pillars. The first concerns affordability and sustainability. 'We have to remain creditworthy,' he says, 'since we have no other means of funding growth, and we don't expect a cent from government.' Maintaining the fleets to global standards at the lowest possible costs is also necessary. 'Our competitive advantage is cost,' he admits, 'but to achieve this we have to adjust our operating model.' Although it remains a 'hub-and-spoke' carrier out of Addis, ET's establishment of regional hubs in Togo, West Africa (through its investment in Asky), in southern Africa (through Air Malawi) and, it is planned, in Central Africa offers further possibilities for competitive growth.

Another pillar is infrastructure. 'Our mission drives our fleet, which means we need long range and high capacity. Diversity,' he says, 'is a necessary evil.' Given the absence of alternatives in Africa, the airline is self-sufficient in training, with its Academy (which includes technicians, pilots, sales, marketing and crew) capable of training 4 000 students at a time. Ethiopian Airlines also possesses the largest cargo terminal in Africa and the largest technical maintenance and repair operation, and it will expand its catering facility to produce 80 000 meals a day, again making it the largest in Africa. 'Outsourcing is not big in Africa outside South Africa,' he observes, 'hence this approach.'

The final pillar is the integration of the airline's people, process and technology, including information and communications technology, into a fully automated system 'from cargo to payroll,' he says, 'and finance to the manifests'. It also applies to airline personnel. 'All staff members swipe their card on entry and exit, and this is directly linked to payroll. They don't come, they don't get paid.'

Ethiopian Airlines has been a notable story of success during a period when the aviation business has been seen, in the words of Warren Buffet, as a 'great way to make a small fortune from a large one'. Perhaps its success is not in spite of the absence of deep pockets, but because of scarcity. There are plenty of competitors capable of outspending ET. 'Turkish Airlines now has 40 destinations in Africa,' Tewolde acknowledges, 'and Kenya remains a rival. He signals Emirates out, however, as their biggest competitor, 'given its depth, already handling five million African passengers each year.'

But what of the lessons for others?

'First, you need to take a long-term view, and this has to come from government,' says Tewolde, 'and not just the airline, since you need clear policy. The government has to answer the question about whether it sees the airline as a strategic asset or simply business,' he says, since that will shape its role and investment. 'And then you need sound and consistent management, especially in a business where even a small mistake can completely drain you. You have to be frugal,' he warns, 'with a low managerial overhead, with careful cost control.' People, he says, including himself, 'work here not for the pay cheque, but for a sense of national contribution, of national duty.' Although there is an international market in pilots' salaries, and the airline has been reluctantly forced to adjust upward its offer to retain its more experienced crew, employees are a key driver of costs. 'You cannot,' he warns, 'be as lavish as South African Airways, and expect to survive.'

In all this, he says, 'governments need to make flying easy, affordable and safe for the public if these countries want to trade with each other. One example is the fuel price. Although, in 2016, the international oil price has come down, it has not come down as much as it should in Africa. Whereas we are paying $1.25 a litre in Europe, in some places in Africa it's still $3.50. Most governments do not have an understanding of the value of aviation,' he adds, 'but rather see it as a cash cow to pay for other things – so they tax it too high, and constrain growth and service.'

Better banking

The usual complaint from African countries is that there is not enough external funding to meet development needs. There have now been two generations of calls for more aid to Africa and much celebration when the amount of aid increases, and debt relief is obtained. In fact, there are an enormous number of funds available to African countries from Western aid, Chinese aid, foreign investment and international credit markets. The problem is that governance in most African countries is not good enough for these funds to be used in a productive way. To a very real extent, the world is awash with funds chasing the relatively few African projects that are both viable and operate in an environment relatively free of onerous government regulation and concerns about corruption.

Aid and foreign investment are usually thought of as the primary funding sources for African development because poor countries, by definition, do not usually have free-floating domestic resources. However, there is money even in poor African countries that could be channelled towards development if the right banking and insurance systems were in place. Furthermore, substantive efforts to improve domestic banking and insurance would send a powerful signal to foreigner investors and serve to attract both their attention and capital.

The advent of mobile telephony has served to radically improve access to money in key African markets.

As will be seen in Chapter 8, through M-Pesa, Kenya has the largest banked population in Africa, with 25.4 million mobile-money subscribers by 2015. Uganda had 18 million subscribers, and Tanzania just under 10 million. By 2014, eight out of every 10 Kenyan adults were banked, which is more than in South Africa, with 70 per cent, Nigeria with 44 per cent and Ghana with 40 per cent. This also puts Kenya above the global average of 62 per cent.[10] But, overall, in Africa, by 2016, just 20 per cent of the overall population was banked. Banking is connected to wealth and wealth creation, and to technology. Between 2011 and 2014, some 700 million more people became 'banked' worldwide, and the global total of the unbanked dropped 20 per cent to 2 billion. Much of this progress has been attributed to the spread of mobile phones and access to the internet.

Yet, for all of this technological progress, which has enabled Africa's banking breakthrough, there is a difference between transactional and traditional banking, between paying electronically and borrowing money. Moreover, credit, as opposed to debit cards and transactional banking, is limited. According to MasterCard, in 2014, just 2 per cent of retail transactions in Africa were electronic.[11] Therefore, although technology has helped Africans make some major steps forward, it has not yet solved some of the fundamental issues needed to increase the spread of traditional banking.

Banking is both 'derived development', in that it follows increased income, and a 'driver of development', in that access to finance encourages entrepreneurship. Therefore, the small proportion of people across Africa who are banked both reflects and has a negative impact on the state of development.

In a nutshell, a well-developed, functioning banking system is a key ingredient for a developing country's growth prospects, prosperity, infrastructure investment, job creation and general advancement. As Laurie Dippenaar, chairman of the $90 billion South African-based FirstRand financial services group, says, 'Governments of developing countries often wish to "protect" their local banks. It is a mistake for African countries not to encourage both the presence of and investment by foreign banks. The presence of foreign banks rapidly accelerates the development and sophistication of the banking systems of African countries, with generally beneficial consequences.'[12]

Standard Bank has more than 150 years of history in South Africa, and started building its franchise in the rest of Africa in the early 1900s.[13] By 2016 it operated in 20 countries on the continent, including South Africa, along with some other emerging markets. In Africa it has, until now, found that the margins to be made on transaction banking are very small, which in part explains why electronic money transfer works better than traditional banking. Standard Bank has also found it difficult to break into the lower, micro-loan end of the market, given that 'poor people are less worried about debt and credit ratings, and have little or no collateral'. The notion that 'the poor will pay you back because they will want to borrow again' is 'only true, it seems, if there is one lender'. The result is the 'more money lent, the more money is taken'. Despite high capital requirements imposed by the South African Reserve Bank, Standard Bank has managed impressive rates of return on its businesses: around 15 per cent in South Africa and over 18 per cent in the rest of Africa.

Digital banking offers a new frontier for Africa, but, again, in mostly a transactional context. Standard Bank found, by 2016, that the traffic through their branches was down some 20 per cent over the previous two years, but that the use of the banking app had increased over the same period by 300 per cent. It believes that two other bits of 'software' can help to spur banking growth. The first is regional integration, in the form of freer movement of capital, goods and people, just as the East African Community has managed to achieve. The second is regular, peaceful elections, given that 'the only cure for bad governance is political competition'.[14]

It is unsurprising that the micro-loan business in Africa has thrived where the traditional commercial banking sector has faltered. The potential of the micro-loan banking sector is estimated to be as large as 25 per cent of Africa's GDP. Micro-finance loans are usually given to those who are informally employed and on incomes of one-third of the national average. The loans, therefore, have to rely on collateral not traditionally used by the banking sector.

This also helps to explain why the African mortgage market is the world's smallest, at just 3.7 per cent of the urban potential in 2011. As one illustration, the value of Nigeria's mortgages, which more than quadrupled between 2006 and 2011, is still equivalent to no more than 0.5 per cent of GDP, compared with more than 25 per cent in South Africa.[15] The spread of mortgages is also hindered by high housing costs. A 100-square-metre state-subsidised apartment in Ethiopia sells, for example, for 35 times the average Ethiopian's earnings whereas, by comparison, in Britain, the ratio is around five times. Improved, transparent and simplified bureaucratic processes might assist, cutting the time to register ownership, but the gap is vast.[16]

Moving money around cheaply and safely is an important part of any development story. Being able to borrow and leverage assets is for much of Africa still a missing piece of the financial puzzle. A number of steps to improving access to banking services stand out.

For the lowest-income countries, access to banking could be improved by developing national ID systems that are 'good enough' to permit banks with international links to process remittances without the risk of falling foul of US and EU laws on money laundering. Middle-income countries could encourage the development of private-sector credit registries (without succumbing to political pressure to enforce credit information amnesties), and strive to avoid unorthodox bank regulation, such as interest-rate floors and caps, and ad hoc increases in reserve requirements (such as has happened with the former in Kenya, and the latter in Mozambique). Then, for the most sophisticated financial countries (for instance, South Africa, Namibia, Mauritius and Morocco), while maintaining reputations for good regulation, there is a need to become more active in international regulation-making, so that global rules are more sensitive to financial needs of developing countries. Put bluntly, the rules are currently made in Basel and Washington to address US and European risks. In the developing world, these rules make borrowing more expensive while curing a disease (the result of too much leverage by the banks) that Africa does not yet have.

Overall, Africa should seek to use concessional finance (for development banks) to crowd in private finance, and not to replace it. Taxpayers (whether in rich countries or Africa) are generally willing to take riskier and longer-tenor tranches of debt or equity. This makes private-sector money able to lend to the same projects, ensuring more power generation, or whatever the need, sooner.

Little wonder, then, that the head of Standard Bank, Sim Tshabalala, sees 'a lot of room for expansion' in banking in Africa. 'We think that bank assets will have more than doubled between 2010 and 2020. Roughly speaking, demand for financial services expands at 1.5 times GDP, so if the continent's GDP growth averages about 4.5 per cent over the decade, that's probably about correct. Certainly,' he adds, 'there's a lot of room for expansion. Africa remains very underbanked (as measured by assets/GDP and formal bank accounts per capita). We also think – based on what happened in other regions – that insurance grows first. The first product people buy after a transactional account is funeral, life or car insurance.'

Insuring Africa

Insurance is also a key aspect of modern economies, and an important one for underpinning infrastructure and financial services. But it is an industry that needs to be fostered.

Africa is, by international standards, under-insured. The continent's non-life insurance penetration rate – excluding South Africa – measured as a percentage of GDP is just 0.73 per cent, and the penetration of life insurance is just 0.4 per cent, about one-fifth of the world average. Yet the availability of insurance improves economic sustainability, reduces public liabilities and enables consumer purchases, most notably home ownership.

South African companies have been quick to seize on this wider African opportunity. However, this success has not been without its challenges.

Founded in 1980, Hollard is the largest South African independent and privately owned insurer, known for the emphasis it places on innovation and informality. Since 2000 the company has branched out across Africa, with investments in Mozambique, Namibia, Botswana, Zambia and, in 2015, Ghana. So far, its business is dominated by non-life commercial cover, essentially insuring big corporates. This approach has parallels with the African banking environment. In fact, the ratio of corporate to individual insurance in Africa for Hollard is 70:30 – the opposite of the global average.

For the six years since 2010, its African regional operations have enjoyed 30 per cent year-on-year growth, representing 28 per cent of the company's profits by 2015, up from just 3 per cent in 2011. The company has focused on leveraging its brand and establishing local rather than expatriate teams, accessing technical expertise and the balance sheet of the South African mother ship as a backup.

Much more is possible, however. Insurance penetration across Africa is constrained by a combination of culture, regulation and relative wealth/poverty. Hollard has found that insurance regulations are seldom aligned to the interests of small business, being 'very old school and inflexible'. The company supports attempts to require some local retention of premiums. However, in some markets – for example, Nigeria, at 80 per cent – the desired retention is considered too high, and reflects a lack of openness in markets. 'Without freer markets,' says one Hollard African expert, 'it is difficult to share risk, expertise and products, demanding layers of commitment to small economies, which raises costs.' These difficulties are compounded by attempts to retain premiums in state companies, and by increasing compliance demands globally. The latter serves to undermine regional and national companies, and strengthens the multinationals, which have the necessary enabling skills. 'Local regulators have throttled the industry,' says a specialist with 35 years of experience, 'killing the intermediaries and driving up the costs.'

With less protectionism and regulation to match the market, there is plenty of scope for product innovation and expansion. Products that enable protection for farmers against drought or floods, driven by digital weather surveillance and intelligence, are one such example, with payments being made by cellphone transactions.[17]

Finally, currency volatility makes it a lot more difficult to determine insured values, where these values continue to fluctuate. For this reason, clients wish to insure in 'hard currency', but this may often be not allowed in a country, as the premium would have to be paid in the same currency in which the policy is issued.

As a result, the African insurance market has, until now, underperformed, realising merely an estimated quarter of its potential value.[18] Improving this situation demands, in sum, better governance and increased openness – traits that have seen the growth of one of Africa's greatest exports – SABMiller.

Getting complex logistics right: The story of SABMiller

In November 2015, the two biggest brewers in the world, Anheuser-Busch InBev (AB InBev) and SABMiller, agreed to the terms of a $107 billion merger, which would create one of the largest global corporate entities. The deal was revised in July 2016 after the fall in the value of the pound following Brexit, which made the original terms less attractive. The new firm would produce about 30 per cent of the world's beer. AB InBev, whose brands include Budweiser, Corona and Stella Artois, had a workforce of 155 000 and revenues of $47 billion. SABMiller had 70 000 employees in 80 countries, including 18 directly (and a further 21 indirectly through a 20 per cent share in the Castel Group) in Africa.

This story illustrates what it takes to succeed in a complex business. SABMiller is, at its core, all of a services (i.e. distribution and entertainment), manufacturing and agriculture business, while its health reflects the quality of government policy and infrastructure provision. In the case of SABMiller, its distribution and entertainment operations mean the company has a strong service element.

South African Breweries' expansion into Africa coincided with a series of privatisations in African countries, including in Mozambique, Tanzania and Zambia in the early 1990s. (SABMiller was later created in 2002 with the takeover of Miller Brewing.)

'At the beginning,' says Jon Kirby, the General Manager of SABMiller's Africa operation, 'there was a great deal of mistrust of South Africa and of its corporate sector. At the beginning, our board meetings with the Tanzanians would last several days. Now they are just a few hours.'

'It did not involve huge amounts of money in global terms,' reflects Keith Doig, who finished his 20-year career at SABMiller in 2012 as the Director of Corporate Finance and Development for Africa, South Africa and Asia-Pacific. 'We believed that we could bring business and management acumen to existing businesses, and add value. We also had a share of businesses in Botswana, Lesotho and Swaziland, and had a previous position in Zimbabwe, where we had been left with a 20 per cent shareholding, and had some experience in operating in less sophisticated markets. As Meyer Kahn [the SAB chairman at the time] always said, "Africa is our backyard". We believed we knew how to deal with it.'

In 1993, in the first of these transactions, SAB paid $22.5 million for 50 per cent of Tanzania Breweries. 'Rather than just take the money,' recalls Kirby, 'the government in Dar put the proceeds of the sale back into the business. That was impressive.' In 2016 the market capitalisation was $1 billion, and the company's earnings before interest, taxes, depreciation and amortisation was $250 million. The ensuing 23 years have seen Tanzania Breweries increase its market share from 35 per cent to 95 per cent.

On the surface, the logic of the growth seems faultless. Formal alcohol sales make up just 40 per cent of the overall alcohol market in Africa, the remainder being unlicensed 'homebrew' of various types, from maize beer to banana wine. Yet the African consumer is as ambitious on brand and quality as any other. Or, as Doig puts it, 'The aim was to double the price of beer and halve the price of beer – offer a better product for the premium end of the market and improve affordability at the other.'

And given that per capita beer consumption across Africa is around only 15 per cent of that in South Africa (9 litres per person per year versus 58), the 'opportunity today is still obvious,' states Kirby.

The secret of its success, he says, is that SAB got in early, and 'got back to basics into beverages'. Its African expansion was matched by 'an Eastern European beachhead' and a joint venture in China.[19] Success relied on the building of regional scale and efficiencies in production, logistics, marketing and finance. As Doig recalls, 'We would go in, fix up the plant, clean up the brands, improve the quality, and get the marketing right. In fact, getting the basics right was the core of it.'

Mistakes were made and lessons learnt along the way, notably with the failure to break into the Kenyan market, a 'classic case of watch out for the Excel spreadsheet' rather than understanding the competition, remembers Kirby. 'It was a pretty big market, around 3 to 4 million hectolitres [100-litre measures], and we thought that a 12 to 15 per cent share would be easy. We eventually got to 15 per cent, but we never made any money. For five and a half years, we were losing $10 million a year. It was a war with East African Breweries. In the end, no stockist was willing to put a Castle fridge and our products at the front of their outlet.' The Kenyans were not going to give up easily and, says Kirby, 'we should not have expected that they would. Eventually we came to a deal by which we took 20 per cent of East African Breweries in Kenya and they took 20 per cent of SAB in Tanzania. In the end,' he sighs, 'we all made money.'

Over time, mergers and acquisitions became increasingly sophisticated, such as in Ethiopia, where government had a keener sense of the potential worth of the businesses. 'Still, there were never any major issues,' remembers Doig, 'in terms of getting authority approvals.'

And the experience was carried over to other markets, such as Nigeria. SABMiller bought into its first brewery in Nigeria in 2009, when it acquired 75 per cent of Pabod Breweries in Port Harcourt. In 2011, it effectively swapped International Breweries in another Nigerian city, Ibadan, with its Castel operation in Angola. And in September 2012, SABMiller invested in a greenfield site in Onitsha, in Anambra State. The investments quickly proved to be a big success, with the new brewery 'hitting capacity in its second month', and the other two almost immediately going through expansion plans.

SABMiller has successfully developed two new local brands in Nigeria: Hero and Trophy. 'Rather than fighting for customers from other brands, as we had done in Kenya, we fought on price, in the process growing our market share from nothing to 23 per cent in five years,' says Kirby. The same experience was true for Ghana, where market share increased from 30 per cent to 50 per cent over the same period, and similarly in Uganda.

Although the cost of building breweries in Africa is between 40 and 50 per cent greater than in Latin America or Europe, the standard of African breweries is rising. 'Today,' said Kirby in March 2016, 'three of our top 10 brewery operations globally are in Africa.' The reason for this, and why the Latin American breweries constantly perform well, 'is down to people'.

In the foyer of the South African SABMiller headquarters in Jan Smuts Avenue, Johannesburg, is a painting of the various company heads in the first hundred years of the company, starting with William Hackblock in 1897, progressing through the years of Anglo-American involvement notable in the appointment of Gordon Waddell in 1984, and ending with Meyer Kahn in 1990. 'Graham McKay [who succeeded Kahn as managing director] always allocated half his time to new projects, and backed his managers. He always had a saying,' remembers Kirby: "If there was more of Africa, I would invest in it."'

More than anything else, SABMiller's success has been built on excellence in people and leadership. As one measure, for those researching in Africa or Latin America, a stop at a SABMiller brewery usually offers a most incisive insight into the local political and economic scene. The company, notes Kirby, 'developed an outstanding relationship with the government in most places'. In part, this was due to the size of the company: 'We are a big fish in a small pond in many African environments. Our taxes are critical to meeting the civil-service salary bill, for example.'

Africa has been a big part of this success story. 'In 1995,' Kirby says, 'we did a high five when we made $7 million operating profit in Africa. Twenty years on, this figure is $140 million.' In this way, the company's success is 'the biggest, fattest compliment to SAB, to corporate South Africa and to government in allowing the company to expand outside and to list in London. This should spur us on.'

In terms of its overall strategy, says Doig, 'we had quality management. Malcolm Wyman [the financial director] and Graham McKay were the architects with Meyer's backing.' From a strategic perspective, 'the decision to move the primary listing was a definitive statement of SAB becoming a global player. An emerging-market player did not otherwise require tapping the global equity markets for which we required a war chest. This was not easy. Investor relations in London faced a lot of hostility from the city's analysts, who did not like a FTSE company without operations in London. But it worked out in the end.'

It certainly did, and in doing so, it showed that Africans are as aspirational for quality as any other group, and that making money in Africa involves in the same necessary mix of good policy, the right people and efficient logistics as anywhere else. Fundamentally, the government has to loosen its grip to allow the private sector the space in which to operate.

Conclusion: A wealth of opportunity

The service sector offers a wealth of opportunities for African countries if governance can be improved. For example, Kenyans currently spend $140 million every year on medical tourism to India.[20] Not only would a functioning healthcare system employing public-private partnerships and telemedicine (which is described in Chapter 8) reduce this outflow, but it could actually reverse the current position and lead to revenue inflows, particularly from those in the region seeking high-end healthcare.

Similarly, an ageing Western population offers the prospect of establishing old-age villages in Africa for wealthy Europeans, as Namibia has piloted, utilising Africa's advantages of good weather and available labour. The potential of analytical data acquired via transactional banking opens another range of exciting and reinforcing possibilities, from improved selling of consumer goods and better targeted financial products, to healthcare services that meet national and, possibly, international needs. Making these and other opportunities happen requires the integration of good policy, appropriate legislation, technology, infrastructure and political will.

Indeed, services are an ideal sector for Africa because they do not require massive capital investment, as do, for example, the mining and manufacturing sectors.

Half-hearted government engagement can produce badly stunted service sectors that will not realise anything like their full potential to create jobs and vibrant economic activity. Critical in this is tailoring regulations to suit the market in banking and insurance. It is also crucial to keep costs (and overheads) low, and match ambition with pragmatism, as airlines like Ethiopian and Emirates have shown.

Chapter 8
Technology

Five steps for success:
- Openness to the international economy is a requirement if African business is to benefit from new technologies and for the development of such technologies locally.
- Efficient government depends on its integration with technology to improve service delivery from healthcare to education.
- Regulatory and political barriers must be eliminated to extend broadband access to more citizens.
- Investment in research and development should be encouraged through tax breaks.
- Government should accept the reality of job losses from technology in some sectors, while seeking to maximise gains in others.

Challenges and opportunities: To gain the benefits of the free flow of information, and of capital and goods, governments will have to agree to allow their citizens full participation in the world economy, including information and trade. In particular, the benefits of the internet will not be achieved unless women and other marginalised groups who have not enjoyed access are provided with connectivity. Ensuring that productivity and efficiency increases are matched with the spread of new technologies will help to ensure jobs are created, rather than lost. This will involve dealing positively with Africans' mistrust of and discomfort with 'outsiders', and instead encouraging the inflow of new technology, and the companies, finance and skilled individuals that come with it.

Key statistics: African mobile-phone penetration rates are at 70 per cent[1]; internet penetration is much lower, however, at 29 per cent, most of which by far is accounted for by mobile technology. Africans can pay 30 to 40 times more for internet access than Europeans.[2] But things are changing quickly: in 2005, internet penetration in Europe was 20 times higher than the African level; by 2014, the figure was only four times higher.[3] There is an educational and research dimension to using technologies well. This challenge is most acute in sub-Saharan Africa, where just two-thirds of learners complete junior school.

Mark Zuckerberg paid a flying visit to Kenya in September 2016. The 32-year-old internet entrepreneur, philanthropist and founder of Facebook announced his arrival on his Facebook page: 'Just landed in Nairobi! I'm here to meet with entrepreneurs and developers, and to learn about mobile money – where Kenya is the world leader.' In a brief but slickly organised and well-promoted visit, Zuckerberg popped in at iHub, a leading continental innovation hub.

Founded in 2010, iHub has generated 30 start-up companies in its first six years. At any one time, seven companies use the incubator space in addition to up to 80 tech entrepreneurs, who sit on blue chairs tinkering behind their screens in the mellow green-and-white workspace.

There Zuckerberg met with techies behind BRCK, an internet connectivity device, PayGo Energy, which enables mobile payments to buy cooking gas, and Gearbox, a hardware manufacturing 'space'.[4] The Facebook CEO also met entrepreneurs from Twiga Foods, a mobile-based business-to-business supplier of fresh fruits and vegetables, Mookh, a digital-payments start-up, and Vivo Active Wear, an online women's clothes store.

Kenya's reputation for high-tech innovation has its origins in the success of M-Pesa, a mobile cash-transfer service launched by Kenyan mobile operator Safaricom in 2007, enabled by the smart cellphone revolution. From little over 2 200 in 1995, by 2015 more than 80 per cent of Kenyan adults had a mobile phone, and there were 25.4 million M-Pesa subscribers. As a result, eight out of every 10 Kenyan adults is now banked – more than the number in South Africa, and the highest figure on the continent.

M-Pesa is not the only standout Kenyan technology. M-Kopa sells solar power systems to the very poor. Its $200 power system comprises a solar panel, two LED bulbs, an LED flashlight, a rechargeable radio and adaptors for charging a phone. Customers pay $35 upfront and make daily payments of 45 cents for a year, after which they own the system. By the end of 2015, M-Kopa had sold 250 000 systems, and aimed to top a million units by the end of 2017.[5] In the process, it has established a credit system for poor consumers.

Little wonder that Nairobi has been hyped as the tech hub of Africa, branded as the 'Silicon Savannah'. The government hopes the Kenyan technology industry will provide 180 000 jobs, $1 billion in exports, $500 million in venture-capital start-ups and up to 8 per cent of the country's GDP by 2020.[6] The expectations are high. In praising Kenya's tech entrepreneurs, President Barack Obama said, 'This continent needs to be a future hub of global growth, not just African growth.'[7]

It is estimated that about 40 per cent of Kenya's GDP passes through M-Pesa, equivalent to about $30 million each day. M-Pesa (*pesa* is Swahili for 'money') has undoubtedly transformed banking in Kenya, and farther afield, enabling secure and efficient cash transfers. There is however a big difference between transactional banking (paying electronically) and traditional banking (borrowing money to start a business or buy a home). This is why, by extending credit to the poor, M-Kopa is less an energy firm than a finance company. (*Kopa* means 'to borrow' in Swahili.) Most of its customers earn less than $2 a day. The loan officer is the SIM card in the device that can turn the power off remotely. Its 600 new customers a day are equivalent to $100 000 made in fresh loans.

Given levels of risk, it is hard to loan money to poor people at accessible rates. Finding the means to service 'a huge target market' in a way to get one's money back 'is a huge challenge and a huge opportunity,' says Tim Carson, the CEO of the Premier Group, an East African micro-loan business headquartered in Nairobi.

Premier does this in three ways, mixing old-school footwork with high-tech processing. Personal loans, which are usually in the $400–500 region, 'are carefully vetted by careful interviewing, checking of credit histories, and the use of technology'. Market stalls and homes are geo-located, references assiduously checked, and cash flow carefully calculated. The loan tracking system is cloud-based. Most disbursements and repayments are done by mobile money. All loans and documents are scanned and archived, and reconciliations automated.

Despite the use of technology, this system still places a premium on loan officers in the field: Premier has 400 in Kenya to manage 24 000 customers, 250 in Uganda for 14 000, and 100 for its 5 000 Tanzanian debtors. But such micro-loans are never more than 12 months in duration.[8] They might help with cash to tide matters over, but they do not provide a stream of resources for longer-term investments, such as housing loans.

Even with M-Pesa, financial-transaction costs remain as high as 44 per cent per payment. Despite the spread of cellphones, access is still bound by poverty. Since Kenya got its undersea fibre-optic cable in 2009, the number of internet users has gone up sevenfold to over 21 million. Yet 80 per cent of Kenyan mobile subscribers spend just $1 per month on data bundles.

Just under half of Kenya's 44 million people live below the poverty line, an estimated 3.9 million of them in slums.[9] Official Kenyan projections suggest the numbers of citizens living in urban settlements will increase from 32 per cent to 54 per cent by 2030.[10]

The contemporary Kenyan workforce is over 20 million, with just 5 million in wage-earning jobs; the remainder work in farming or are self-employed. Only 1.3 million work in the private sector. In 1990 the share of the informal sector in the job market was just 20 per cent.

This situation especially affects Kenya's young people under 35, or two-thirds of the population. Some 800 000 Kenyans join the labour force each year. Most are unemployed and poorly educated. More than 40 per cent have never attended or completed primary school, and less than a fifth have completed secondary school, partly because they are sent out to work and fend for themselves at a very early age.[11] It is a shocking statistic that more than 50 per cent of workers under the age of 15, some 1.9 million Kenyans, work 66 hours a week or longer. Something will have to change or things will change for the worse in Kenya, where the underclass grows faster than the middle class.

The question is, then, can technology – including mobile broadband – play a role in reducing this deficit of education and the divisions in wealth and access? And, by creating new jobs, can technology allow African countries like Kenya to leapfrog development stages? The answer largely depends on what government does or doesn't do.

The technology bind

The pace of technological change appears to be relentless. According to Moore's law, computing power doubles every 18 to 24 months. Not only is it impossible to escape, but on the face of it, technological modernisation has much to offer Africa.[12]

There are three big potential advantages to be gained for Africa from digital technology. The first is its ability to improve the efficiency and effectiveness of government. It could help expedite regulation and administration, including licence and permit applications, as well as tax returns, for example.

There are already positive examples of such efficiencies emerging in the area of government. One is the payment of welfare through smart cards, a system that is used in South Africa. Nearly half of South African households receive a form of social-welfare grant. Since 1996, the number of social-welfare recipients has grown from 2.4 million to over 16 million.[13] This has dramatically reduced poverty levels. By 2015, about 21.5 million people, or about 41 per cent of the population, lived in poverty. This figure had decreased from 27.8 million, or 56.8 per cent, just five years before.[14] Corruption in the social-grant system has been substantially reduced by introducing biometric technology that stores fingerprint and voice records for authentication when cash is disbursed.[15]

In another area, big improvements in infrastructure provision are possible by utilising predictive data techniques to understand the impact of decisions, as well as new construction techniques.

The second major advantage of technology is seen in the flow of information. In agriculture, for example, information on weather patterns, seed and fertiliser use or market information could radically ramp up production, perhaps even ensuring the continent could feed itself. High-speed internet could also bypass inefficiencies in government and the challenge of geography in the distribution of education, electricity and healthcare. As Bob Collymore, CEO of Safaricom, observes, 'There is no way you can teach a classroom of 100 kids in rural Kenya properly. Tablets offer the means to deliver a new standard of education that teaches skills rather than teaching people to regurgitate.'[16]

Africa remains well behind international rates of enrolment in basic education (as seen in Figure 8.1), and especially tertiary education (see Figure 8.2). As a result, the ratio of scientists and researchers in sub-Saharan Africa stands at just 79 per million population, compared to a world average of 1 081 per million. And it's not just the numbers, but also the

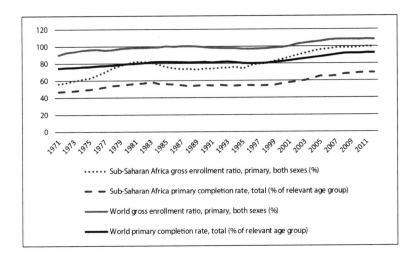

Figure 8.1: Primary-school enrolment and completion rates, 1971–2011

Source: UNESCO Institute for Statistics, http://databank.worldbank.org/data/reports.
aspx?source=world-development-indicators&preview=on#

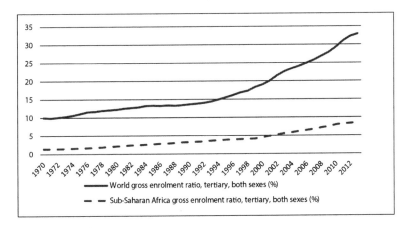

Figure 8.2: Tertiary enrolment rates, 1970–2012

Source: UNESCO Institute for Statistics, http://databank.worldbank.org/data/reports.
aspx?source=world-development-indicators&preview=on#

disciplines that are significant. Only 22 per cent of African university graduates are emerging with degrees in science, technology, engineering and mathematics, compared with 40 per cent in China.[17]

Technology has already revolutionised university access by offering cheap (or free) courses online. The largest open online course database (MOOC – Massive Open Online Courses) has, since 2009, tracked more than 400 000 enrolments, with participants from more than 150 countries. It now records 4 200 courses offered by more than 500 universities worldwide, reaching over 35 million students.[18]

Cape Town-based GetSmarter, which offers career-focused short online courses, provides an online residential campus experience, focusing on industry-relevant skills to professionals in areas such as fintech and big data. Two brothers, Rob and Sam Paddock, started the business in 2007 with short courses before the MOOC boom. GetSmarter has since enrolled thousands of students in partnerships with the universities of Cape Town and the Witwatersrand, and have extended this internationally with the University of London, MIT and Cambridge University. In the process, they have built a company with over 350 employees, the vast majority of them part-time, which operates a 19-hour day across time zones, arbitraging low-cost but world-class South African skills. The courses are designed in modules using a combination of tutorials, videos, applied learning, written individual and collaborative projects, and grading. In 2016 it had 1 000 students enrolled on its MIT fintech course, and 900 on MIT's big data and social analytics courses, with students from 77 countries. There were also 3 000 students on courses at UCT and Wits.[19]

In terms of technology's role in connecting smallholder farmers to the markets, to each other and to sources of crucial information, Bill Gates, no less, has noted that the enabling effect of technology should help farmers to get a slice of the $40 billion market in annual African food imports. 'Something is not functioning properly,' says Gates, 'when half of the continent's labour produces food, and the continent still buys its food from somewhere else!' There is, he says, an 'information disconnect', which 'stems from the fact that agricultural markets, like banks, exist on a formal plane, whereas smallholders exist on an informal one. So farmers and markets cannot communicate effectively. Smallholders don't know what the market will pay. They can't grow crops according to the market's specifications because they don't know the specifications. They have no way to learn the farm-management practices that would let them double or even triple their yields. Instead, they grow mostly what they can eat or trade locally, the way they've always grown it.'[20]

This is why M-Farm, which operates from Nairobi's iHub, is aimed at allowing farmers to get wholesale market information and sell their products using mobile technology.

The third advantage of technology is the potential to create a slew of new jobs. This could be realised through improving competitiveness by better connecting Africa to global markets, capital and knowledge. It can also be achieved through the types of innovation on exhibition at Nairobi's iHub or the 90-odd similar tech hubs across more than half of Africa's countries.[21]

For example, there are immediate opportunities to be had by using Africa's 80 million mobile 'wallets' for payments across sectors, from health to insurance, electricity and education. The majority of the African consumer market – some 330 million adults, no less – are unserved by financial and many other related services. By integrating such services, the opportunity goes beyond banking to point-of-sale technologies, and the ability to work across borders, networks and sectors, including energy, education and health. There is also, in this regard, a need to build up information on African consumers, where technology can play a role.[22]

Michael Macharia got into the technology business 16 years ago by helping to integrate banking services in Rwanda. Today he runs Seven Seas Technologies from upmarket premises Nairobi. His 200 employees focus on three major technology areas: healthcare provision, social services and national security.

From experience, Macharia sees a big future for technology in providing health and education solutions. To do this, he says, 'you need five things: public-private partnerships, innovative financial models, skills, supply chains and technology'. Working with General Electric, and with a commitment of government funding over seven years, starting in May 2015 Seven Seas introduced radiology equipment to 98 Kenyan hospitals, reaching 400 000 patients in the first 14 months. Telemedicine connects the outlying hospitals with experts around the country. Macharia plans to go into primary healthcare with container-based clinics, again connected to experts elsewhere.

Seven Seas has also embarked on its Huduma Centres, a programme to convert Kenya's 300 post offices into government service centres, enabling the payment of rates, and applications for ID documents and passports. In the first three years, 47 centres have gone live, says Macharia, 'reducing congestion and corruption'. The biggest challenge in all this is 'to get government to accept the solution. The middle class,' he notes, 'are very cynical about such schemes since they can bribe their way through it. But this is about the people at the bottom of the pyramid, the same people whose lives were transformed by M-Pesa since they could not get to cash a cheque at a bank before.'[23]

This digital promise is evident in the impact of mobile-phone connectivity in Africa. In the mid-1990s, sub-Saharan Africa's connectivity rate was estimated to be just 0.5 lines per 100 inhabitants (compared to a global average of 15 per 100), with a waiting list of 3.6 million for fixed lines.[24] Half of African countries had no connection at all to the internet in 1995.[25]

Spurred by greater openness to foreign capital through privatisations and regulatory changes, this situation has been transformed. By 2019 it is predicted that voice-call traffic in sub-Saharan Africa will increase to 930 million subscriptions from 653 million in 2015. Similarly, mobile-data usage will increase an estimated 20 times between 2013 and 2019, twice the anticipated global expansion, when three in four mobile subscriptions will be internet inclusive. This increase is in line with the global growth in mobile usage, from just 11.1 million users in 1990 to around 4 billion in 2015, half of whom are using smart phones.[26]

And there will be other effects that emanate from this expansion in communication technology. It will help improve transparency. There is a generational dimension here – and a political one – in that young people are the ones most likely to be early adopters of technology.[27] Indeed, mobile technology helped to both trigger and spread the Arab Spring protests.

This phenomenon is not lost on some governments in Africa, which have clamped down on the use of online media promoting good governance and expressing dissent, and have shut down social media during elections and disrupted mobile communications in order to stifle protests.[28]

There are also challenges inherent in the adoption of new technologies. The experience of the developed world suggests that technology is likely to place pressure on existing jobs while creating few new ones.

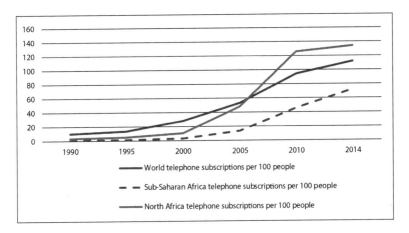

Figure 8.3: Mobile cellular subscriptions per 100 people, 1990–2014

Source: International Telecommunication Union, World Telecommunication/ICT Development Report and database, http://databank.worldbank.org/data/reports. aspx?source=world-development-indicators

Disruptor or helper?

There is very little doubt about the disruptive power of technology on the workforce, and the way the world works. Take Instagram and Kodak, for instance.

Instagram, a photo-sharing platform, was created by 14 highly skilled people who employed the power of the digital network. After 18 months, they sold the company for nearly three-quarters of a billion dollars, just months after the bankruptcy of Kodak, another photography company, which had, at its peak, employed 145 000 people and held billions of dollars in assets.[29]

Blockbuster video stores is another example of a victim of disruptive technology.

In its heyday, it was a ubiquitous part of American shopping malls. The company filed for bankruptcy in 2010, devastated by competing streaming video services, such as Netflix. At its peak, Blockbuster employed 60 000 employees in 9 000 stores in the US alone.[30]

These are not the only examples of the disruptive effect of technology on traditional business models. Online trading has had a major impact on traditional retail stores, changing the way they operate, and even the fast-food business, through touch-screen ordering and automated food preparation. Dispensing kiosks no longer only provide chocolate bars and snacks, but also sell high-value electronics goods and can rent out the movies that Blockbuster once did. Increasingly, consumers are familiar with robotics in retail stores, not just at the unmanned checkouts and information kiosks, but through a reliance on phones as a way of paying and obtaining information.

Automation, coupled with outsourcing, has inevitably exerted a downward pressure on labour earnings. At the same time, income inequality in the developed world has reached levels not seen since the Great Depression. Over the past quarter of a century, for example, real incomes and wealth have stagnated for the vast majority of Americans.[31] Inflation-adjusted median household income in the US was $56 516 in 2015; in 1999 it was $57 909.[32] This has paralleled the decline in the manufacturing sector. In Ohio, for example, in 1960, more than half of the state's employment was in manufacturing; now the figure is barely a tenth.[33]

The US is not alone in terms of intergenerational inequality. Pensioners have experienced higher disposable-income growth than young people in almost every wealthy country over the last few decades. In seven major economies (UK, Canada, Germany, France, US, Spain and Italy), growth in income of the average young couple and families in their 20s has lagged dramatically behind national averages over the past 30 years.[34] In many cases, this is because property inflation has outstripped wage inflation and property, as a result is much more costly to own, and in part because the millennials are being paid less, in real terms, than their parents were at the same age.

This has occurred while wealth among the elite has skyrocketed. The median salaries paid to the CEOs of Fortune 500 companies trebled to over $10 million between 1992 and 2013.[35] Hence the popularity of the argument made by French economist Thomas Piketty of the inherent inequalities of capitalism. Piketty argues that economic and political power are concentrated in the hands of an oligarchy. This has led some to conclude that '[t]oday the conflict is no longer between the working class and the middle class; it is between a tiny elite and the great majority of citizens'.[36] This has led to calls for greater wealth redistribution to maintain social stability.

Yet, for much of Africa, these levels of inequality have long been the reality, with a small middle class, a large underclass and a tiny politically connected elite, as the example provided of Kenya at the start of this chapter illustrates. More generally, Africa is less focused on inequality so much as just generating more resources.

Even so, technology can, in a fiendishly vicious cycle, given Africa's needs, take away some jobs. To illustrate this, in the mining industry the increasingly preferred process is robotic.

In underground kimberlite diamond mining, this future involves driverless, gyro-guided dump trucks, requiring about 30 per cent less labour compared with a conventional underground mine. Although labour costs are likely to remain the same, with higher salaries for better-qualified workers, 'the maintenance costs,' says one mining veteran, 'will come sharply down. There's no testosterone, so no sudden braking or accelerating, or crashing into the side. And there are no lunch breaks and absenteeism. The vehicles run smoothly between regular maintenance cycles.' The sinking of the shafts is also becoming increasingly mechanised – driven by technology.[37]

Technology is making itself felt across other mineral types, where the future is also likely to be increasingly mechanised. In South Africa's platinum and gold mines, the nature of the depth, thickness and grades of the ore bodies determines the mix of technology and labour that can be used, whether the mining is labour-intensive, employing conventional hand-held pneumatic-drill methods, or whether it uses more mechanised techniques, such as remote-controlled, low-profile equipment both to cut and move the ore around.[38]

This is not the only South African industry where greater efficiency and new technology have an impact on jobs. Yet, although technology is indubitably a great disruptor, this does not mean it always has to result in job losses.

More than an apple a day

South Africa accounts for 1.2 per cent of world apple production. Apples are produced by some 700 commercial farmers working 23 625 hectares.[39] Because China, which accounts for half of the world's apple production of 64 million tonnes, exports very little,[40] South Africa enjoys a disproportionate importance in the global apple-export market. It accounts for over 5 per cent of the total export market of 7.5 million tonnes, at just under 375 000 tonnes. This market is worth nearly $400 million. And the deciduous fruit industry overall is of even greater domestic importance in terms of jobs, directly supporting, as it does, about 108 000 workers and four times as many dependants. In the case of apples alone, the figures are about 27 000 and 107 000, respectively (the figures are for 2015).

Based in Grabouw, near Cape Town, Kromco processes 53 000 tonnes of apples annually. Two-thirds are destined for export, where prices are twice as high as in the domestic market.[41]

Technology is having an impact on Kromco's business, doing away with some old jobs, but creating new ones at the same time. Previously, much of the sorting was done when the fruit was picked. This was a slow process with high wastage but, now, with new processing technology, there is as much as a 15 per cent increase in fresh fruit for packing. Previously, this fruit would have been rejected and sent for juicing. The return on fresh fruit can be three times higher than that sent for juicing.

Now all apples are loaded from the tree, without being sorted, into large bins, each containing approximately 3 000 apples. From there, they go directly to the high-tech processing and sorting line or to the cold store. At the sorting plant, which can process 24 tonnes of apples an hour, an automated system submerges the bins in water and the apples float to a bay, where six workers check the fruit for visible cuts or bruises. These are removed for juicing.

From there, they are moved to a conveyor line where they are automatically sorted by weight and quality, each apple being photographed more than 30 times in the process. They are then graded according to 57 categories and loaded again into the bins, which have, by this time, been automatically washed. A bar code is applied, denoting size, origin and quality. From there, the apples are taken back to the cold store or to the packing facility alongside, where (mostly) women busily pack the fruit into garishly coloured boxes. Every carton can be traced electronically to the farm, orchard, line and even the packer.

While Kromco's number of sorting workers has fallen from 70 to under 25 today, the number employed on the packing line, conversely, is increasing. Apples are now packaged at the facility for the end supermarket and consumer, a system that reduces the number of intermediaries in the export markets. Kromco employs 300 permanent staff and as many as another 700 seasonally.

With increased production capacity and quality control – enabled through technology – Kromco anticipates 30 per cent growth by 2022. This is also driven by a detailed understanding of the preferences of the export markets. More than 30 per cent of South African apple exports were to the rest of Africa in 2015, which is its largest market (the UK accounts for 25 per cent and East Asia 24 per cent). 'We have to understand the particular preferences of African markets,' says Willem Coetzee, Kromco's managing director. 'Whereas Nigeria might prefer a particular quality of apple, it might be different in Angola. These markets are more sensitive, given that vendors often sell the fruit individually.'

These are not the only applications of innovative technology in South Africa's apple farming. Paul Cluver, one of the 13 farmers who supply to Kromco, has taken to picking his fruit at night. This has doubled output, given that temperatures are lower and the focus of the workers more intense given the lighting. His 40 tractors are now fitted with GPS, which has reduced speeds, maintenance and diesel costs.

None of this technology is revolutionary. Far from it. Kromco's French robotic sorting line can be bought off the shelf for $4 million. The tractor's GPS is similarly commonly available. The trick is in the application, the integration of systems and technology.

Morocco offers another example of how to manage the technology bind – the use of technology to create new jobs – so far, to good effect.

Morocco's use of technology for development

Some 10 kilometres outside Rabat, on the Tangier–Casablanca highway, is Technopolis, an incubator campus for start-up companies.[42] Inside the glass-and-concrete buildings, adjacent to the International University of Rabat, congregate 50 fledgling businesses, attracted by low rents, good connectivity, the availability of finance to scale up their activities, and mentoring. There is a cluster of another 260 IT start-ups 90 kilometres way at the Casablanca Technopark, opened in 2001. A third similar park, in Tangier, opened in 2015.

For Morocco, job creation is not primarily about new technology, but about policy, process and people.

The Aéropole aviation free zone, 30 kilometres from Casablanca, is home to 100 companies, including subcontractors Matis, Aircelle, Snecma, Sagem and Teuchos, as well as big names such as Boeing, Bombardier and Airbus. Combined, these companies employ 11 500 people, and turn over $1 billion, or 5 per cent of Morocco's exports.

Morocco aims to get a bigger manufacturing slice of the 35 000 aircraft to be constructed worldwide over the next two decades. Its aviation industry is aiming to double its employment and output by 2020, in part by increasing the proportion of locally produced components in its assemblies to 35 per cent.

Morocco's car industry is also on a roll. In 2005 Renault acquired a manufacturing plant in Casablanca from Fiat, which, by 2015, was producing 62 000 cars. In 2011 it opened a new $1-billion factory near Tangier, which made 229 000 cars in 2015. The bulk of its market is a short ferry ride away to Spain, and thereon to France and Germany.

The factory's aim is to make 330 000 units by 2020, bringing Renault's production in Morocco to around 400 000 units. In 2016 Renault signed a second $1-billion investment to increase local content to 65 per cent. PSA Peugeot Citroën is slated to open a $620-million plant in Kenitra in 2019, aiming at an output of 200 000 cars in three years. And there are plans for a third manufacturer, which will further increase production and add to the 150 automotive subcontractors already based in Morocco.

Morocco's total automotive exports reached $5.3 billion in 2015, making it the country's top foreign-exchange earner after remittances from the 5 million Moroccans living abroad (a figure of some $7 billion), and ahead of the country's other big 'export' sectors of tourism, agriculture and phosphates. Providing 100 000 jobs now, and potentially a further 90 000 by 2020, when Morocco aims to export $10 billion in parts and cars, the automotive sector is a big success story.

This triumph is no fluke or quirk of geographic fortune. Industrial growth has been built on a number of factors – the country's proximity to the European markets; relatively cheap labour (Moroccan car workers earn about half of their European counterparts when productivity is factored in); trade agreements worth $1.5 billion with the US, the EU, Turkey and several North African countries; its efficient logistic systems; and tax and other incentives.

But at the root of its success are both policy changes and government action. Ahmed Chami worked for Microsoft for 11 years before becoming Morocco's Minister of Industry, Commerce and New Technologies. 'The major challenge,' he clarifies, 'is that we have to create 200 000 jobs in Morocco each year to absorb our graduates.'[43]

When he came into government in 2007, Chami said that he had two things to work on. The first was 'to secure the macroeconomic foundation. This included reducing government debt, inflation, and fiscal and balance-of-payment deficits, and improving our foreign-exchange reserves. Once we had that in place, we had to think about the drivers of development. In the 1990s, we had one and a half engines of growth: one was tourism and half was agribusiness.'

This situation, he stresses, had to change. To achieve diversification, and provide for its 33 million citizens, the government had to focus on improving infrastructure. 'As a sector by itself', this would both increase growth and act as an enabler, says Chami. The result is that Morocco's highways, ports and rail system are much improved, even compared with 10 years ago. Meanwhile it has just switched on the first phase of a $9-billion, 580-megawatt solar-electricity plant, the world's largest, at Ouarzazate.

Other plans were initiated too. Government embarked on complementary schemes to grow tourism numbers. Morocco had 10 million annual visitors in 2015, four times more than 20 years earlier, and a 'Green Morocco' strategy was launched to boost agriculture.

Nevertheless, more was required. Since no country can become developed without industry, Morocco scrutinised, with the help of consultants, 80 manufacturing sectors. It came up with six priorities: aeronautics, automotive, offshoring, textiles and clothing, electronics and agro-industry. 'We had to think of Morocco as a company, identifying things at which we could be good and where we could be profitable,' says Chami.

While there was already an emergent industrial strategy in place by the time he arrived, Chami's role was to turn this strategy into practice, 'from PowerPoint to Word, or perhaps into Microsoft Project,' he laughs, given his background. A road map of 111 actions, known as *Le Pacte National pour l'Emergence Industrielle* (a strategy for industrial development), involving nine ministries, was signed in February 2009.

'What made it possible,' he reflects, 'was not only that it had an owner in our ministry, but that it involved the private sector along with a team of "super-heroes" in my ministerial cabinet.'

The budget for the project was linked directly to delivery on its target of 220 000 jobs per annum. This did not guarantee success, however. 'In general, the administration is terrible,' Chami muses, 'with people used to working in a strict hierarchy and in silos. To get things done, we had sometimes to do things personally, to cut through protocol.'

A similar approach was taken to the application of technology, for which the government envisioned four roles. The first was social transformation, an example being the 80 per cent subsidy of laptops for students. So far, these have reached 140 000 beneficiaries. This was financed by a telecom fund to ensure universal access in rural areas.

A second role for technology was in e-government – for example, paying taxes, making appointments and registering permits. A third was through the use of IT to improve the competitiveness of small and medium-sized companies (i.e. with less than $10 million in turnover).

And, finally, to create the conditions to enable there to be one day 'a Moroccan Microsoft or Google', the government came up with the Maroc Numerique ('Moroccan Digital') Fund to finance start-ups at the technoparks, and to promote IT, business processing and knowledge processing outsourcing at five offshoring facilities in Casablanca, Fes, Rabat, Oujda and Tétouan.

To make this idea a reality, the government established a range of incentives. The free zones in Tangier, Kenitra, Oujda, and around Casablanca's aeronautics park, have cheaper rents, zero income tax for the first five years and 8.75 per cent for the next 20. In the technoparks and offshoring facilities, rent is also cheap, telecom costs are lower, bandwidth bigger and speeds faster, and personal income tax is less than half (20 per cent) the rate outside (44 per cent). Training costs are also reimbursed. Up to 20 per cent of capital investment in the auto sector could also be met by government's Hassan II Fund.

All this required a champion – 'the king himself,' says Chami. Morocco's king, Mohammed VI, has been central in driving change across Morocco's economy and politics since his accession in 1999. The country's early moves towards liberalisation and privatisation were, however, given sharp impetus by the 2011 Arab Spring, which prompted the drafting of a new constitution with devolved powers across the 1 503 municipalities, 78 provinces and 12 regions. Morocco faced a crisis, and so far it has used it well.

Of course, the situation is far from perfect. Job creation for graduates has tapered off to around 60 000 annually, from a peak of 130 000 in 2011, shortly before Chami left the ministry.

Much more will have to change to ensure Morocco can continue to address its considerable social pressures. 'All these things have to work with the right people,' Chami explains, 'otherwise it's all just theory.' Morocco's education system suffered from political interference in the 1980s when 'government tried to fix a system that was working' by introducing Arabic at the centre, moving away from French. This is linked to a wider concern about social inclusion. Migrants from the rural areas can become marginalised at the periphery of the cities, have large families, underachieve educationally and drift into menial jobs, and sometimes crime.

Still, while many countries face the same pressures of social and economic change, and have laid out a vision, and even plans, to diversify and modernise their economies, far fewer ever do it.

So far, Morocco's tech story is about applying existing technology to create business opportunities, and improve governance and service delivery. No futuristic 'back to the future' flux capacitors or continuum transfunctioners are essential for this new future. Rather, what is needed is dollops of political will, good policy and capable, high-energy leaders.

Conclusion: Back to basics?

Zuckerberg has proposed Free Basics, an initiative to provide free internet access to cellphone users in under-served countries, including Zambia, Tanzania and Kenya. This has met with resistance, being derided as free access to only parts of the internet. His move would allow him to tap into Africa's big data, enabling consumer analytics, thereby tailoring responses and changing people's lives. It is also consistent with taking the world off telecoms and onto the internet with products such as WhatsApp and Messenger, with their identification and authentication ability.

The world of the millennials is predicted to be increasingly hopping from one Wi-Fi hotspot to another. This is bad news for telecoms companies, but enables faster and cheaper transactions. Deloitte forecast that some 300 million customers worldwide would be using voice over Wi-Fi and/or voice over LTE (Long-Term Evolution – 4G) by the end of 2016, double the number at the start of the year and five times higher than at the beginning of 2015.[44] This can only continue to grow, simply because it's cheap.

Indeed, Kenya's M-Pesa is, in this way, a reflection as much of failure as of success. 'It works because the payment system is broken in the country,' says one banking executive based in Kenya. 'The reason why it has not been adopted worldwide after eight years,' he notes, 'is that other people already have systems that work better and at less cost.'

Incubators can deliver implementable ideas. But turning them into businesses, as the experience of iHub shows, is much more difficult. Overall, policy around technology has to be geared to encouraging small and medium-sized businesses, which represent the vast majority of jobs in low-income countries.[45] Ensuring that these entities prosper necessitates, as Morocco illustrates, finance for start-ups, including ensuring the right ecosystem for collaborative endeavour.[46]

Caution is also necessary in the application of new technology. Using drones to send blood samples for testing in Malawi or for distributing medicine in Rwanda is not going to solve the problem of HIV infection, the state of those countries' hospitals or cure unemployment. And, anyway, as others have pointed out,[47] it would be a lot cheaper, and probably more reliable, to send samples by motorbike. But not as sexy, of course, and probably not as attractive for funding by a Silicon Valley high-tech firm or a media-savvy donor.

Neither can technology leapfrog the need for sound policy, well-drafted regulations, rule of law, clean toilets and potable water. The presence of these conditions will, more than a new app or start-up, enable the funding gap – between the list of infrastructure projects on paper versus those that are banked – to be 'leapfrogged'.

If Africa is to benefit from the free flow of information, its governments will have to allow their citizens to participate in the world information economy through improved connectivity. This requires taking action on five realities.

The first is for governments to accept the power of credit. For credit to be issued widely and without onerous conditions, there is a need for transactional information. Making these transactions cheaper, in turn, helps this process, though the opposite also holds true. As Safaricom's Bob Collymore acknowledges, 'Technology can also deepen inequality. Access to a smartphone can accelerate the user away from those who don't have this access – the difference between being connected to the world and being stuck as a pastoralist in Turkana.'[48]

Secondly, governments have to accept the role of global production chains in manufacturing. Getting to produce a small part of something many times over – being one of the dozens of component suppliers to Apple's iPhone, for example – is the way of the world, and desirable.

Thirdly, the need for openness means encouraging the inward migration of skills. The fast-tracking of visas for skills and entrepreneurs is essential, among other steps. By 2016 a dozen countries had start-up visa programmes, including Australia, New Zealand, Singapore, the UK, Ireland, France, Spain, Italy, the Netherlands, Denmark, Canada and Chile. One of the few established start-up visa programmes in a developing economy, Start-up Chile, was launched in 2010. It provides seed capital to entrepreneurs, ranging from $15 000 to $90 000, depending on the stage of the start-up. It has attracted more than 2 000 entrepreneurs since its inception, and the resulting businesses have raised more than $100 million in private capital. This initiative has positioned Chile as an innovation hub in Latin America.[49]

This will require a fair bit of political capital in environments where foreigners are viewed with suspicion, and as taking jobs away from locals. It will also mean allowing foreign companies, and individuals, to openly and easily repatriate their dividends and capital. And it will also require a hefty dollop of political leadership in another way – to change the local mindset from job seekers to job creators, as Namibia's president, Hage Geingob, argues in Chapter 11.

Fourth, these basics include getting education right and investing in research and development, a spur for innovation. Sub-Saharan Africa's R&D expenditure is less than a quarter of the global average of 2.1 per cent of GDP. Even in the continent's most advanced country, South Africa, it was just 0.73 per cent in 2012.[50] A system of corporate-tax breaks and government support for tech incubators and universities would also help.

Finally, governments have to appreciate the costs of regulatory variation between countries and their overburden on business. While India is a market of 1.2 billion people, it has only one regulator per sector. Africa also has a population of 1.2 billion, but 54 regulatory bodies. To drive down the price of telecoms, government needs to ensure the conditions for competitive practices.

Technology will offer Africa answers and can reduce barriers to entry. Alone, however, just like aid, technology cannot provide an instant and single solution. It will bring fresh challenges. And its usefulness will rely on African governments getting other aspects of the necessary package of reforms in place, including allowing the space in which the private sector can operate. For example, digital solutions may help the plight of Zimbabwean farmers by connecting them with the market, by timing their planting better, providing them with insurance and improved yields. But technology is never likely to mitigate the disaster wreaked across the agriculture sector by President Robert Mugabe's land policies.

The immediate, big advantage for Africa in technology lies in integrating it within a package to solve 'process problems', just as M-Pesa did with financial transactions, or Seven Seas is doing with healthcare and its Huduma Centres. A related longer-term big advantage of such integrated solutions lies in the potential to gather information and analytics on the population, especially in providing a credit rating for those at the bottom of the (income) pyramid.

If Africa fails to take bold steps to promote not just digital access, but also access to the flow of goods, skills, services and technology, its countries risk falling even further behind in a world economy that is increasingly integrated.

Part 3

Making Africa Work

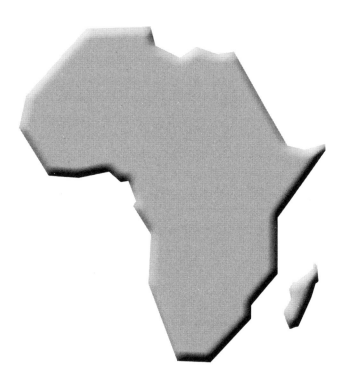

Chapter 9
Mobilising resources, de-risking investment

Five steps for success:

- Foreign aid can help, but investment will come from the private sector; it is therefore critical to adopt a business-friendly mindset.
- Creating stability and certainty in the policy, legal and regulatory spheres is key to a successful investor strategy.
- Aid will not overcome weak governance. Improved state performance and delivery have to be locally generated and owned.
- Chinese engagement should be embraced but care should be taken to ensure value for African people rather the enrichment of elites.
- Aid must be aligned to national plans and tailored to reducing the costs of doing business.

Challenges and opportunities: Given Africa's relatively poor FDI performance to date, the upside is considerable. Yet the barriers to entry for private capital into much of Africa remain formidable. African countries have not, until now, usually possessed a regulatory and policy environment suitable for attracting the type and scale of investment that creates jobs. Neither has aid answered the funding challenge of African development and may, instead, have provided the wrong incentives to African governments by weakening the link between leaders and their electorate. While China has provided a new model of financing support to African countries, this additional assistance will not, by itself, solve Africa's development challenges.

Key statistics: Global FDI inflows were $1.23 trillion in 2014, with developed countries accounting for $499 billion, Asia (excluding China) $465 billion, and China $129 billion. Africa received $54 billion of this FDI, of which sub-Saharan Africa obtained $42 billion. Out of sub-Saharan Africa, West Africa received $12.8 billion, East Africa $6.8 billion, Central Africa $12.1 billion and southern Africa $10.8 billion. South Africa was the largest single recipient, at $5.7 billion. Some 48 per cent of African FDI stock was in services, 31 per cent in primary goods and 21 per cent in manufacturing.[1] Global aid flows increased from $60 billion in 2000 to $160 billion in 2014.[2] Since 2000, Western aid to Africa has doubled to over $50 billion annually. Chinese assistance, not included in this figure, has totalled nearly $100 billion over the same period. Remittances from Africans living abroad are estimated to be at least $40 billion annually, but may be as high as four times that amount.

The manufacturer's plate on the giant turbine casing hints at the vintage of the hydroelectric station: 'English Electric Company Ltd, Queen's House, Kingsway, London'.[3] The once-great British manufacturer of railway locomotives, guided missiles, computers, and Lightning and Canberra aircraft, among other iconic engineering contributions, no longer exists. It was subsumed into the General Electric Corporation in 1968.

However, there are still some remnants today of the old English Electric Company in Africa. Zambia's Mulungushi hydroelectric facility, at the bottom of a 355-metre ravine, 60 kilometres south-east of Kabwe, was constructed by the Broken Hill Development Company and opened in 1925 by HRH the Prince of Wales, the future Edward VIII. It was built to provide power to the Broken Hill Mine; a second, sister facility was built 60 kilometres away at Mita Hills.

Even today, the road from Kabwe to Mulungushi takes a back-breaking two hours in a truck as it wends its way through remote villages. The tenacity, foresight, engineering skill and dedication required to build the Mulungushi plant all those years ago is breathtaking, all the more so given how steep the gradient is, its inaccessibility, the prevalence of disease and much else besides.

The engineers not only had to construct the hydro plant, but also its series of sluice gates, the winch house, 5 kilometres of canals and diversion dams, and the Mulungushi Dam itself to pool the feed for the turbines. And then they had to lay a kilometre of large steel pipes in bulky concrete encasements down into the valley to provide the speed of flow needed to drive the generators.

The trip down the Mulungushi ravine is exhilarating. The trolley goes down a narrow track at a 45-degree angle connected to the winch at the top by a single cable and some rudimentary engineering. (The winch bears the name Allen West & Co, Brighton, England.) At the bottom, 15 minutes later, the giant silver pipes from the top turn at right angles to feed the turbines via a complicated series of inlet valves and pressure nozzles. Inside the corrugated-iron building, the four turbines are laid out side by side, the two English Electric machines flanked by two newer Chinese turbines from the Chongqing Huayuan Hydroelectric Technical Engineering Co. Ltd, to give its full title.

In 1925 there was just one 2.5 megawatt turbine. Two more 6.2 megawatt units were added two years later, and a fourth, 8-megawatt turbine in 1941, by which time the Broken Hill Mine – producing zinc, lead and silver – was in full production.

With the nationalisation of Zambia's mines in 1972, there began a long, slow process of decline. Broken Hill (renamed Kabwe Mine) was closed in 1990. Twelve years later, the two hydro plants feeding the mine were privatised and sold to the Lunsemfwa Hydro Power Company, marking the start of a period of recovery.

In 2009, the number one 2.5 megawatt turbine was replaced by a 10.5 megawatt unit; two and three were rehabilitated, and in 2013, number four was also replaced and upgraded to 7.8 megawatts, increasing the output, at least on paper, to 32 megawatts. By 2016, the total combined installed capacity at Mulungushi and Mita Hills was 56 megawatts, a small but significant amount given Zambia's pressing energy needs and shortages.

Zambia was once known for its cheap and plentiful power, which enabled the mines to develop. They consume around 50 per cent of national electricity output, perhaps unsurprising for a sector that contributes 70 per cent of foreign-exchange reserves. Hydroelectric power remains a significant development advantage for the country, which has around one-third of the water reserves of southern Africa.

The estimated demand for power in Zambia rose from 1 600 megawatts in 2008 to 2 200 megawatts eight years later. On paper, at least, this should be met by the current production from nine hydropower stations. However, poor water management and delayed new projects have led to incessant load-shedding across the country.

For example, the 750-megawatt Kafue Gorge Lower hydro project has been on the table since the mid-1990s, and the subject of countless donor-funded consultancies. One comprehensive study in 1997[4] identified the potential for an additional 6 000 megawatts from Zambia's network of rivers and lakes, offering 'significant export opportunity'. At a time when 65 per cent of the then 1 000 megawatts of power produced was provided to the copper industry, the report envisaged increased electricity usage by as much as 100 per cent within 15 years. It also noted South Africa's projected shortfall of 5 000 megawatts by 2010 and the opportunities for Zambia to export power to the republic.

After more than 15 years of delay, the project for Kafue Gorge Lower was finally awarded in late 2015. But the new power station will probably come on line only in five years, at best. Meanwhile, the predictions of growth in demand have proved remarkably accurate – so now this project is about catching up rather than getting ahead.

One cannot imagine another Mulungushi happening quickly in the modern era, if at all – to the great cost to the Zambian people desperate for power and jobs. Despite the knowledge that Zambia was behind the curve, and in spite of the presence of donors over many decades, the power sector was allowed to fail the Zambian people. The private sector has waited for years in some cases for projects to be approved. Such delays have seemingly been driven and encouraged by government inertia and room for petty manoeuvre.

Zambia has a national development plan, various industrialisation and job-creation strategies, and a 2030 Vision. There is no shortage of good analysis and ideas. Yet action – not more visions and strategy – is what is required to deliver development. Financing will also have to be put in place and, as with Mulungushi in the 1920s, it will most likely have to come from the private sector. That will require this investment being repaid over time, and with profit.

To get good ideas moving, a little of the Mulungushi 'can do' spirit and business zeal, which delivered an astonishing feat of engineering in an inaccessible valley 90 years ago, would not be out of place today.

The African resource challenge

Until recently, aid donors were seen as the principal means to develop Africa. This argument was put forward at the 2005 Gleneagles G8 summit when, led by Tony Blair and Gordon Brown, a call was made (and heeded) to double the flow of official development assistance to the continent. By 2014, net global aid flows reached $161 billion, from $60 billion in 2000 and $35 billion in 1980.[5] By 2016, Africa received $40 billion in annual aid, more than double the amount in 2000.[6]

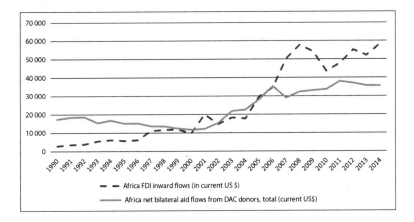

Figure 9.1: FDI and aid flows to Africa (in current $ millions), 1990–2014

Source: Development Assistance Committee of the OECD, 'Geographical distribution of financial flows to developing countries', Development Co-operation Report, and international development statistics database, www.oecd.org/dac/stats/idsonline; http://unctadstat.unctad.org/wds/TableViewer/tableView.aspx?ReportId=96740

Much has been learnt from the delivery of aid over the past quarter century. Since 2000, more than $500 billion has been spent by donors in Africa. A similar amount was lavished on Africa during the Cold War, but much of this was spent for reasons of strategic superpower interests and perceived loyalty, such as in the former Zaire, or on Soviet clients, rather than on development.[7]

Immediately after the Cold War, development aid was usually granted with tightened conditionality. These terms quickly became a source of tension with national governments. There followed a trend towards 'budget support', whereby the donors allowed some governments to control and apportion the spending of aid directly into their budgets. This approach has had varied success in improving governance, and in some cases there has been a reversion to direct project funding on account of various accounting and oversight failures. Although budget support significantly reduces donor transaction costs and improves harmonisation of spending, it has at best inconclusive effects on poverty alleviation.[8]

However, the overall record is unimpressive. As Daron Acemoglu and James A. Robinson have noted: 'The idea that large donations can remedy poverty has dominated the theory of economic development – and the thinking in many international aid agencies and governments – since the 1950s. And how have the results been? Not so good, actually. Millions have moved out of abject poverty around the world over the past six decades, but that has had little to do with foreign aid. Rather, it is due to economic growth in countries in Asia which received little aid.'[9]

Not surprisingly, since 2000, a number of changes and challenges have emerged to the Western aid model to Africa. The most significant is the advent of Chinese spending.[10] Using a broad definition of aid (including financial assistance for projects), China and the US provided $94.3 billion and $107.9 billion, respectively, over the period 2000–2013. (This is examined later.)

A further trend has been the ability of African countries themselves to generate development funding through the issuance of debt.[11] By 2014, 21 African countries had international credit ratings, more than double the number a decade earlier. African economies have been able to gain access to international funds seeking higher-yield investments in emerging economies, a trend that intensified following the fall in interest rates in developed economies after the 2008 financial crisis. In 2014, for example, there were new bond issues from Zambia, Kenya, Côte d'Ivoire, South Africa, Senegal and Ghana, which, between them, raised more than $7 billion, bringing the cumulative total raised since 2006 to $25.8 billion.

Bond issues are not the only source of 'new' money for Africa. There has been a steady rise in FDI flows, from $6.3 billion in 2000 to $42 billion in 2013.[12] Similarly, there are growing private-equity interests. The US-based Carlyle Group secured nearly $700 million, for example, for its first sub-Saharan African fund in 2014. There are other similar interests across the continent, from cement to flowers to banking.[13]

The increased flow of remittances from the African diaspora is a related financing trend. Officially, these payments amount to $40 billion, but may be as high as $160 billion, or one-twentieth of continental GDP, given that an estimated 75 per cent of all transfers are outside the formal banking system. For instance, a quarter of Eritrea's population of 6 million live abroad and send back an estimated 38 per cent of GDP. One in every three Eritrean households depends on remittance income, while three-quarters receive at least one form of remittance.[14] Generally, the smaller the country, the higher the dependency on remittances as measured as a percentage of GDP. Cape Verde, where the figure is 34 per cent, Liberia (26 per cent) and Burundi (23 per cent) are among the most dependent.

While leaders have been keen to develop new sources of inflows, there is also greater awareness of the systems of governance that enable illicit outflows.

The AU's high-level panel on illicit financial flows has calculated, for example, that the continent loses more than $50 billion in illicit financial outflows owing to fraudulent schemes by both businesses and governments aimed at avoiding tax payments. This figure, says the panel, has nearly tripled since 2001. In total, the continent is calculated to have illegally lost about $850 billion between 1970 and 2008, including $217.7 billion from Nigeria and more than $81.8 billion from South Africa. Such flows are the result of 'trade mispricing, payments between parent companies and their subsidiaries, and profit-shifting mechanisms designed to hide revenues', noted the study.[15]

The existence of tax havens facilitates these types of flows. However, the key enablers of such flows are weak systems of governance in Africa, and a lack of confidence in both policy and the rule of law. Acting on these fundamentals has proven highly problematic for governments.

It is how aid capital is used that separates development successes from failures. Vietnam is an example of the former.

Aid used well: Vietnam's lessons

If there was ever a country that had an excuse not to develop, it is Vietnam. Destroyed by successive wars over hundreds of years with China, Japan, France and the US, divided by colonialism and imposed foreign administrative systems, mountainous and with a difficult geography and challenging neighbours, ethnically divided and dogmatically committed to socialism, Vietnam should be one of the poorest countries in the world.

After reunification in April 1975, the government lost a decade with socialist policies, including collectivised agriculture, which resulted in famine and economic collapse. Vietnam started to reform in the mid-1980s, allowing farmers, at the start of the *doi moi* (renovation) process, to keep a slice of their production.

In the mid-1990s, when its *doi moi* reform programme had only just begun to take hold, most of its industries were state-owned and state-run, and the bulk of the fleet of its national airline were Soviet planes (to be avoided in the interests of self-preservation). Although motorbikes were starting to become popular, most people still moved around on foot and in carts, and by means of clunky Eastern Bloc cars, motorised tricycles, belching buses and a steam-powered railway. The country was obviously poor, conditions invariably tough and the standard of living low.

Twenty years later, the country was virtually unrecognisable. Hanoi is no longer dour and Ho Chi Minh City has recovered its status as one of the great cities of Asia. Despite myriad problems, including rickety infrastructure, inflation and financial overheating, Vietnam has been one of the fastest-growing economies in the world for the past two decades, averaging 8 per cent GDP growth from 1990 to 1997, 6.5 per cent from 1998 to 2003, and over 5 per cent since 2004, in spite of periodic global travails.

It is not as if the country's difficult history has been forgotten. Rather, the Vietnamese have successfully put the past behind them and chosen to look forward. Its recovery, as much from its own failures as from war itself, contains many lessons for others attempting the same.

Given half a chance, the super-industriousness and entrepreneurialism of the Vietnamese has shone through, just as it does in other environments given a similar break. From 1990 to 2005, Vietnam's agricultural production nearly doubled, transforming it from a net food importer to the world's second-largest exporter of rice. Although coffee had been introduced by French colonists in the mid-19th century, the industry withered due to war and central planning. Following *doi moi*, the introduction of private enterprise has caused a surge of growth in the industry. By 2000, as noted in Chapter 4, from virtually nothing, Vietnam had become the world's second largest coffee producer after Brazil, with annual production of 900 000 tonnes. By 2010, coffee production was over 1.1 million tonnes, second only in export value to rice.

Fish products, cashews, textiles and electronics industries also boomed. The garment sector, alone, has added a million jobs since 2010.

Although aid has played a role in this regeneration, it is a story of mobilising all possible sources of foreign and domestic capital.

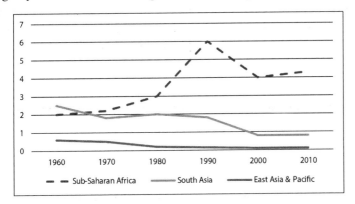

Figure 9.2: Net official development assistance received (% of gross national income), 1960–2010

Source: OECD Development Aid at a Glance, Statistics by Region, Africa 2015 edition, https://www.oecd.org/dac/stats/documentupload/2%20Africa%20-%20 Development%20Aid%20at%20a%20Glance%202015.pdf

Vietnam has been the recipient of significant external aid over the past 40 years. During the Soviet era, from 1975 to 1989, it received an estimated $1 billion annually. As in all such centrally planned economic experiments, it was good money after bad, and failed dismally, at least if the aim was to develop Vietnam (rather than keep it ideologically and strategically 'on side'). With the advent of *doi moi*, from 1993 to 2004, Vietnam received a total of $14 billion in official development assistance, mainly from Asia, the US, multilateral bodies (notably the World Bank and the Asian Development Bank) and EU members – about half of what was pledged. During the 2000s, the annual amount pledged more than doubled from $2.5 billion at the start of the decade to over $6 billion by 2008.

Donors point out that the impact of aid has been much greater in Vietnam as a result of local ownership and a sectoral focus. In the 15 years from 1993, for example, the single largest sector of expenditure was transport (28 per cent), followed by energy (22 per cent).[16]

Even so, the focus was never on aid as the principal means of development. Pick up an English-language newspaper in Vietnam and it is likely that you will find detailed listings of the scale and type of FDI by country and sector. There will also be lists of possible private-sector investment schemes in public infrastructure projects. FDI volumes increased from virtually zero in 1990 to an annual average, by 2015, of $10 billion.[17] Aid is useful in Vietnam because it complements the country's plans, rather than supplanting them.

A torrent of money cannot overcome weak governance

Traditional donors have a mixed record when it comes to improving governance and may, indeed, sometimes compound problems, as the case of Mozambique illustrates.

Mozambique has long been viewed by donors as a success story. Following its chaotic independence from Portugal in 1975, the East African country was a major recipient of Soviet and Eastern Bloc support, mainly in the form of materiel, and some Western humanitarian and development aid. Aid from the West increased massively during the 1990s, with the end of the civil war in 1992 and the advent of democracy, doubling from just over $1 billion at the time of the democratic elections in 1994 to $2.3 billion by 2013.[18]

In 1994, devastated by protracted political conflict and economic mismanagement, Mozambique was officially one of the poorest countries in the world, with a per capita annual income of just $160.[19] With the end of the civil war, during the 1990s and 2000s, Mozambique's GDP grew spectacularly, at over 7 per cent per annum. Its population also increased by 80 per cent during this time, from 15 million in 1995 to over 27 million 20 years later.

By the end of the first decade of the 2000s, Mozambique was riding high. In 2012, the national currency, the metical, was the best performing in the world against the dollar, while investment poured in. Even Portuguese nationals, who had fled *en masse* after independence in 1975, were trickling back to the former colony in search of better prospects and to escape Europe's economic troubles.[20]

The development of coal deposits in the province of Tete and huge offshore gas finds in the north hit the media with headlines such as 'Massive gas discovery transforms Mozambique backwater into boomtown'[21] and 'Boom time for Mozambique, once the basket case of Africa'.[22] According to Standard Bank, gas was forecast to add $39 billion to the economy over the next 20 years, boosting GDP per capita from approximately $650 in 2013 to $4 500 by 2035, and in the process creating 700 000 jobs.

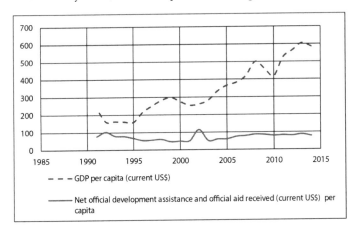

Figure 9.3: Mozambique – aid and GDP per capita (current $), 1985–2020

Source: World Bank national accounts data and OECD national accounts data files; Development Assistance Committee of the OECD, Geographical distribution of financial flows to developing countries, Development Co-operation Report, and international development statistics database, www.oecd.org/dac/stats/idsonline

In 2015, however, things started going badly again for Mozambique. The immediate cause of the crisis was the halting of aid from the IMF, the World Bank and other international mechanisms after donors found Mozambique had failed to declare debts of more than $1 billion taken out by state-linked companies. In 2013, Credit Suisse raised $500 million on behalf of Empresa Moçambicana de Atum, a hastily established state-owned tuna-fishing company. Russian bank Vneshtorgbank raised another $350 million, supposedly to pay for a fleet of fishing boats. But once raised, these funds were diverted to other purchases, including high-tech coast-guard speed-boats, while the fishing industry was left barely operational. The loans brought Mozambique's total debt close to $10 billion when its GDP was a shade under $16 billion.[23]

Once the debts were revealed, the metical plunged by nearly 40 per cent (the sharpest fall experienced by any African currency apart from Zambia's kwacha), despite the fact the central bank fruitlessly spent $1 billion in reserves in its defence.[24] By December 2015, the government had to resort to exchange controls to preserve its reserves. With most of its debt dollar denominated, the crash made Mozambique's external obligations unsustainable. So severe was the economic crisis that, in July 2016, the Mozambique Finance Ministry suspended the national budget because of 'adverse national and international macro-economic conditions'. Earlier, and underlining the severity of the crisis, ratings agency Moody's had downgraded Mozambique from 'a lowly B2 to a dismal B3'.[25]

Why, with all these resources and economic potential, did things unravel so badly for Mozambique? In the end, the failure was due to poor governance and weak institutions. The saga therefore raises questions about both the effectiveness of foreign aid in improving governance and the nature of politics in Mozambique.

At one level, by the World Bank's own admission, Mozambique's rapid growth had only a moderate impact on poverty reduction. Its social indicators remain poor: the adult literacy rate is 56 per cent and life expectancy at birth just 50.3 years. Malaria, a disease closely linked with poverty and weak institutions, remains the most common cause of death, responsible for 35 per cent of child mortality and 29 per cent of deaths in the overall population.[26] For all its growth and hubris, Mozambique remains very low in the UN's human development index – 180th out of 188 countries, with 55 per cent of its population living in poverty.

According to one view, the increase in aid levels in Mozambique has caused inequality to diminish through investment in human capital, and has acted as a catalyst for growth. But, even for its proponents, 'the argument that foreign aid dependency in Mozambique negatively affects governance is valid and grounded in good research. It can be observed that the aid does reduce transparency in the central government and [does] call governance into question.'[27]

Mozambique sits at an unimpressive 133 out of 140 on the World Economic Forum's *Global Competitiveness Report*, which assesses the quality of institutions, infrastructure, educational systems, and trading and other efficiencies.[28]

While the country is feted in some donor capitals for its progressive ideals, corruption remains pervasive in Mozambique, with officials from the governing party, Frelimo, at the centre. Mozambique also has a long history of political violence and, since 2014, the willingness of both Frelimo and the opposition, Renamo, to once again resort to arms has raised concerns that Mozambique's long-heralded peace process, at least partially grounded in government patronage, is less stable than previously thought.

Mozambique ranked 112th of 168 countries in Transparency International's 2015 Corruption Perception Index.[29] According to the Anti-Corruption Resource Centre, the prevalence of corruption is a 'concern for both the public as well as donors, who support almost half of the state's budget. Corruption manifests,' it notes, in 'various forms, including political, petty and grand corruption, embezzlement of public funds, and a deeply embedded patronage system. Checks and balances are weak, as the executive exercises strong influence over the legislative and the judiciary. Corruption also affects several sectors in the country, such as the police, public administration, judiciary, and public financial management.'[30] As a result, a small elite intimately linked with the ruling party dominates the economy, while the rest pick up the scraps.

The donor community appears to have failed to understand the nature of Mozambique's political economy and, more specifically, the extent to which members of the political class could and would manipulate the system for their own benefit. The rigour and robustness of checks and balances put in place with donor support have proven to be paper thin and unable to withstand the vested interests of Frelimo leaders, who seemingly operate with impunity. Obvious warning signs, including non-transparent tendering processes, have been routinely overlooked. For too long, donors were either willingly blind to the lack of accountability, or lacked the capacity to monitor Mozambique's public-financial-management mechanisms. Too much emphasis was placed on maintaining positive relationships and 'open dialogue', and not enough on robust investigation into what was actually happening. Again, Mozambique illustrates the challenge of trying to import governance through external assistance where the donors are reluctant to upset their relationships by using robust language.

The overall lesson from Mozambique is that resources and economic potential are, by themselves, not enough. To create a positive effect for the whole country, strong governance, robust institutions and transparency are essential. Economist Paul Collier has identified a number of ways to spend aid money better in weak markets, including by subsidising political-risk insurance and investments in high-risk but possibly catalytic areas.[31]

Or is the answer, perhaps, for investors into Africa – public and private alike – to do things more like China?

Chinese answers?

An interview in 2008 with an adviser to the then freshly inaugurated French president, Nicolas Sarkozy, illustrated the changes and challenges facing France in its Africa policy. When asked what drove French policy in this era, he replied: 'Three numbers: 4, 14 and 1.6 billion.' When asked what these meant, he said that 1.6 billion is the estimated population of sub-Saharan Africa by 2020, a fast-growing, youthful market; 14 is the distance in kilometres across the Strait of Gibraltar, separating Africa from Europe, 'showing we cannot ignore the security and economic reality'; and 4 was the age of President Sarkozy when his predecessor Jacques Chirac had served in the Algerian War alongside (among many others) Sergeant Gnassingbé Eyadéma, who would become president of Togo – which illustrates 'the change of generations [since the] ancien regime'.

The adviser added: 'And China has emphasised all of these factors, showing us that Africa is not just a problem to be solved, but a business opportunity to be embraced.'

There is a plethora of literature on China's changing role in Africa.[32] For example, in Continental Shift: A Journey into Africa's Changing Fortunes,[33] authors Kevin Bloom and Richard Poplak are sympathetic to China's newfound role as deal maker, purchaser of commodities and provider of infrastructure as a key driver of African change. Undoubtedly, since China's rise in the 1990s, when its annual trade with Africa was less than $5 billion, it has injected more funding into Africa, piqued interest, delivered much needed infrastructure and boosted trade by as much as twenty times.[34]

Certainly, Chinese contractors and business people are willing to go to places and work in conditions that few in the West would any longer contemplate. Travel to the furthest reaches of the Horn, and there is a Chinese contractor – whether it's surfacing the winding pass descending from Asmara to Keren in Eritrea, or building new roads, culverts and bridges in Lalibela in neighbouring Ethiopia.

But such apparently indisputable progress can, in the absence of governance, come at a cost. The DRC, ranked by the World Bank in 2014 as the world's fifth poorest country (with an annual GDP per capita of just $442),[35] is also judged as the richest in mineral wealth, estimated at having $24 trillion in reserves. The DRC possesses some of the world's richest copper resources, half of the world's cobalt (used for specialist steels and alloys, including in jet engines and gas turbines, magnetic and stainless steels, and cutting tools), 80 per cent of the world's reserves of all known coltan (used in mobile phones and other personal electronics). The country is also the fifth leading producer of tungsten and the sixth of tin.

In September 2007, the Congolese government announced a $9 billion deal, higher than the total national budget, with two Chinese state companies whereby $3 billion would be invested in mines and $6 billion would be used for infrastructure. In return, China's Sinohydro Corp and China Railway Engineering Corp would receive a 68 per cent stake in a joint venture with Congolese state copper miner Gécamines, and rights to two large copper and cobalt concessions.[36] After objections were voiced by the IMF and local NGOs about the lack of transparency and concerns that the deal burdened the DRC with unsustainable debt, it was revised in 2009 to $6 billion, with half going to mine development and half to infrastructure projects while removing the sovereign guarantee that had covered the mining loan. Anti-corruption NGO Global Witness calculated that China was concessioned 10 million tonnes of copper and 600 000 tonnes of cobalt in exchange for building 2 400 miles of roads and 2 000 of rail, 145 health clinics, 32 hospitals, two universities, electricity-transmission projects and two hydroelectric dams. The mines were, at the time of signing, expected to produce as much as $120 billion in revenues, or 11 times the DRC's GDP.

The IMF was able to exert substantial leverage, given a pending $12.3 billion debt-relief deal with the DRC that was eventually signed in June 2010. It did not want the Congolese to take on fresh debt at the very moment it was granting debt forgiveness. China's Exim Bank, the financier of the deal, pulled out in 2012, after its demands around taking over the

Congolese parties' 32 per cent stake and the shortening of the reimbursement period from the initial 25 years were not met, and because there were signs of discord between the various Chinese companies. The project resumed in 2014, after a prolonged series of negotiations.

In some regards, though, China is little different from other investors and donors. For one, it is concerned, just like other actors, with getting bang for its investment buck. In fact, the structure of Chinese resources-for-infrastructure and other semi-aid deals in Africa would suggest that, unlike Western donors, it is even more concerned about its return. Indeed, Chinese FDI is positively correlated with political stability. Not for nothing is the biggest recipient of Chinese investment in the continent South Africa. Of course, 'China's investment is more visible in the poor rule of law countries (including Angola, Burundi, the Central African Republic, the Democratic Republic of the Congo, Eritrea, Guinea, and Zimbabwe) because China *has* invested in those locations whereas Western investment generally stayed away from them'.[37]

Ultimately, the biggest difficulty in the relationship between China and Africa is not the nature of Chinese engagement, however, or whether its governance standards adhere to Western norms, but whether its African partners can forge deals that provide value for money, benefit to their economies and the capacity building needed for their local industries. China shares the concerns of other donors and investors because the answer to making an investment successful lies in supporting the development of local skills, the institutions of governance, and in finding the means to reduce those risks inherent in African investments.

De-risking Africa: Interview with Donald Kaberuka

Donald Kaberuka was elected as the President of the African Development Bank in 2005, where he served for two terms, which came to an end in September 2015.[38]

'I took over the presidency at a time of the Blair Africa Commission and the Gleneagles G8 summit. The philosophy at the time was "can we do more of the same" in doubling aid to Africa, cancelling debt and so on. There was no shift in the paradigm, no matter how much Blair and Bush meant well.

'At the same time, I did not think that doubling aid to Africa would happen. I was not even convinced that it was a good thing. Instead I was focused on trying to find ways whereby aid could be flipped to leverage private capital. To do this, however, I had to shift the focus of the bank from poverty reduction to private-sector growth. Three things had to occur. First, we had to reduce the cost of doing business. Second, we had to address the risk profile of the continent. And third, we had to expedite economic integration.

'This required pushing infrastructure programmes, putting governance at the centre of everything, and improving cross-border infrastructure through reducing non-tariff barriers and freeing up the movement of goods. We had a saying – "not by money alone". It required smarter government.

'It also required lending as much to business as to government. When I took over, the lending ratio was ten to one: $3 billion to government and $300 million to the private sector. Selling this change was, however, very difficult, since the focus was on poverty reduction, including addressing HIV/Aids. To do so, I needed allies. The people in the Bush administration were helpful, as was the Secretary for International Development in the Blair government [Hilary Benn]. It was also important to get South Africa a seat on the board of the bank, to leverage South Africa's weight and power, and the help of [the Minister of Finance] Trevor [Manuel].

'Now private-sector lending at the Bank is $4 billion annually. Some 40 private-equity funds are involved. There is a new Africa infrastructure fund, complementing our big push on infrastructure, which saw $28 billion invested, including $12 billion in transport alone. On integration, we were successful in our efforts to connect African countries with their neighbours through roads and electricity, aside from the Mano River area [in West Africa] and with bridges in Kazungula [across the Zambezi], between Kinshasa and Brazzaville, and between the Gambia and Senegal.

'In essence, we shifted from being a large NGO concerned about poverty reduction to being a funder focused on private-sector growth. If we had not made this transition, we would have been stuck with doing little projects, which should have been done by the likes of Oxfam.'

What about failures? – 'We failed in trying to develop cooperation around technological solutions, due to national rivalries. If I did it again, I would also give equal weight between promoting governance and the physical things that we build, since governance makes things happen automatically. This was most obvious in South Sudan, where on the very morning that fighting broke out, I had obtained board approval for a $25 million electrification project. Similarly, though I was the first bank president to set foot in the CAR [Central African Republic], the conflict expanded.'

What about the chasm between the list of projects and their bankability in Africa? – 'The problem is not technical, but rather political, for example as to whether you allow independent power producers per se. Projects require de-risking from an early phase, which requires in large measure political will, patient money and technical responses. Often it's a case not of new funding, but getting projects going for which money is already available, but which are stuck.'

What is the biggest lesson of your 10 years at the bank? – 'It is possible to build African institutions if one has an agenda and you can figure out how to go round various bottlenecks and not be another budget-consuming bureaucracy.'

*   *   *

The return on African investments is widely publicised as being above the market norm. One study of publicly traded companies operating in Africa for the period 2002–2007, mostly in the manufacturing and services sectors, found that their average return on capital was around two-thirds higher than that of comparable companies in China, India, Indonesia and Vietnam.[39]

The reason for this is that the levels of perceived risk do not support those offering lower returns or those spread over a longer-term time frame. 'At present, the concentration of investments is in relatively short-term maturities,' notes the World Bank. This reflects 'investors' reluctance to engage in sectors such as infrastructure, where the returns are spread over a longer time frame, yet the rate of return on foreign investment is higher in Africa than in any other developing region.'[40] Put differently, as one analyst has noted, 'returns are an expectation of the risk'.[41] Investors speak with a sense of disquiet over the levels of concern – perceived or real – about corruption, arbitrary taxes and tax-regime changes, policy instability, and the absence of a clear process and realistic timeline for legal redress when things go wrong. 'In Ghana and Nigeria,' says one London-based oil and gas specialist, 'we anticipate that we will lose 70 per cent and 80 per cent in our LGD [loss given default][42] modelling, respectively, compared to around 2 per cent in the UK. This,' he notes, 'reflects high levels of African risk.'[43]

The de-risking of African investments requires policy and regulatory stability, and clarity on the rule of law and the steps for redress. It hinges on an open, non-confrontational relationship between business and government. It also entails a thorough, independent and objective assessment of the potential risks.

Conclusion: Managing risk, mobilising resources

The perennial question for Africa has been, is there enough money for development? This is, in fact, the wrong question. The right question to ask is, given the colossal funds that are available, do African countries have the strength of governance, institutions and rule of law that are needed to be able to use the money available effectively?

There are a number of key constraints to mobilising capital in Africa. During the 2000s, investment interest in Africa was driven by a combination of commodity prices, comparative low rates of return elsewhere, the desire for a good-news story about the continent, and occasional hubris in overcoming bad data, or the absence of it, and relying instead on anecdotal evidence. In the wake of the commodity slowdown, however, international financiers have been increasingly risk-averse towards the continent. For example, African private-equity deals fell from $8.1 billion in 2014 to $2.5 billion in 2015.[44]

The fear of missing out on the African boom and the desire for a good story about the continent have more recently been supplanted by concerns about how much has really changed in the 2000s, and about whether the proceeds of the boom were used primarily for elite redistribution rather than investing in people and infrastructure. This is exacerbated by the (high) value expectations of African asset sellers, which have not caught up with the reality of the commodity downturn, in part reflecting the role and cost of African banks, in notable cases saddled with non-performing loans that they are reluctant to strike off their books. Finally, difficulties in making investments have been heightened by a scarcity of foreign exchange and the absence, overall, of a stable policy regime.

The severe governance challenges of most African countries make constructing a persuasive investment case difficult. As a result, although the potential capital available for investing is high, very little has been used in a manner that delivers obvious results. And while many African countries also have the capability to garner significant internal funds, they have been unable to do so because their banking systems are underdeveloped.

Moreover, the African business environment is generally poor in terms of data, which hinders the provision of credit. This reflects the small number of listed businesses and relative lack of liquidity. Of the 21 bourses in the African Securities Exchanges Association, the South African bourse in 2013 accounted for $1.1 billion of a total market capitalisation of $1.6 billion.[45] Compare this, for example, with the value of London's Alternative Investment Market (for smaller, growing companies), which has 1 000 listings with a market cap of $100 billion.

As a result, a de-risking strategy for investors in African business has to take the following into consideration:

- Due diligence: How much can be found out about the key actors? To what extent is their business model dependent on related party transactions – that is, on their political contacts?
- Quality of the local management team: What is the skill set they have, and what is required? Are they open about their relationship with government, and about the expectations of corruption? To what extent is there a need for an external team on the ground?
- Relationship with government: To what extent will the business be dependent on government income? Does government have sovereign guarantees in place? Is the relationship with government dependent on key individuals and is it at risk from a change of regime? How much interface is required to manage the relationship with government?
- Regulatory and policy risk: Is there policy clarity or a threat of policy change? Is there a threat of nationalisation? How efficient is the bureaucracy, and how large is the hassle factor with government? How many licences are required in the sector? (The greater the number, such as in power generation, the greater the increase in pressure points for cor-

ruption.) Is there a threat of politicking around pricing and ownership around elections?

Given these legitimate concerns of investors, government can greatly assist the process by simplifying and streamlining the investment application and approval process, upholding contractual law within set time limits and acting on promises to deal with corruption. It can also establish a system of public accounting that enables easier assessment of the overall economic environment and locating new companies in which to invest.

Overall, the aphorism 'improve it and they will come' is not an exaggeration when describing the relationship between capital (foreign or domestic) and the overall economic environment. If countries make the tough decisions that result in good governance, the money will flow in. If tough decisions are not made, or if they are not followed up with action, no amount of money from any donor or investor, no matter how well intentioned, will deliver the economic growth and jobs needed to satisfy the continent's young and growing population.

Such uncertainty – and poor performance – has been compounded by the absence of viable and realistic development plans on the part of African governments – the subject of the next chapter.

Chapter 10
Planning for success

Five steps for success:
- Use the planning process to instil a sense of urgency to promote growth and create jobs as the immediate imperative.
- Emphasise the government's partnership with business, and not, as many plans do, the primacy of government.
- A useful plan depends on ruthless prioritisation, appropriate resourcing and careful sequencing.
- Governments should recruit the best available people for the job in planning and elsewhere.
- The role of foreign governments and institutions should be circumscribed.

Challenge and opportunities: African countries face the twin constraints of lack of financial resources and insufficient appropriately skilled people to deliver complex national development plans. These deficiencies are compounded by the need to manage constituencies of losers resulting from hard choices. Consequently, although there are plenty of plans, the record of implementing their objectives is poor.

Key statistics: By the early 1970s, 32 African countries had drawn up national plans. Now many African countries have visions that project a trajectory between 2020 and 2035, including Malawi 2020, Cameroon 2035, Gabon 2025 and Ivory Coast 2020. According to the World Bank's Worldwide Governance Indicators,[1] between 1996 and 2014, overall government effectiveness in sub-Saharan Africa remained static. An Afrobarometer survey conducted in 2014/15 that examined the populations of 32 African countries found the most pressing problem cited was unemployment.[2]

The names of Windhoek's streets are evidence of Namibia's difficult past – but also its pragmatism.[3]

Where Fidel Castro Street intersects with Independence (formerly Kaiser) Avenue, there are signs to Christus Kirche, Reiterdenkmal and Alte Feste. Kenneth David Kaunda, Dr Kwame Nkrumah, and Nelson Mandela are among those honoured with street names that reflect Africa's liberation history, and today they form a criss-crossed pantheon of local heroes and German colonists.

The German colonial period was short, just 30 years, but brutal. It entailed the slaughter of between 25 000 and 65 000 Herero and 1 000 Namaqua tribesmen, accounting for 50 to 70 per cent and 50 per cent of their populations, respectively. This was followed by 75 years of South African occupation, reinforcing the colonial patterns of identity and racial privilege.

Today space is made, deliberately, for both German-Namibian and Afrikaner-Namibian cultures. Aside from day-trippers from Angola and Zambia, South Africans and Germans make up the majority of Namibia's 1.5 million international tourists a year. They go not only because of its natural beauty, but because it feels safe and welcoming. There are still German schools, and their cultural quirks are not only tolerated but encouraged.

Just a quarter century ago, however, Namibia – or South West Africa as some knew it – was only (and frequently) in the news for conflict and a failure to compromise.

Interviewed in State House,[4] on the corner of Robert Mugabe and Laurent-Désiré Kabila avenues, President Hage Geingob explained that the country's notable, if under-appreciated, record of stability and improving prosperity is based on a combination of respect for a liberal constitution, democracy and private enterprise (factors that were outlined in Chapter 2).

Peace, Geingob acknowledges, is just the start. 'I have declared a war on poverty,' he states, admitting, however, that 'it doesn't mean that we will automatically defeat it.'

We run through a thumbnail SWOT analysis of Namibia. Its strengths include political and economic stability among a small population of just 2.3 million, ranking 143rd largest in the world, rattling around a vast, resource-rich territory, the world's 34th largest. An exporter of gem-quality diamonds and the world's fifth largest uranium producer, the country is dependent on mining for more than half of its foreign-exchange earnings and some 11.5 per cent of GDP, though the sector employs just two per cent of the workforce.

The economy continues to grow. Although life expectancy went down from 1991, when it was 61.2 years, it climbed again during the 2000s to 64.7 in 2015, reflecting a rise in real per capita income from $2 000 to $5 210.[5] As the government has accurately stated, 'At independence, the economy was very small and the majority of people excluded from any meaningful economic activity and effective participation in society. Poverty in some regions was as high as 90 per cent. ... In many respects, Namibia at independence and Namibia today are miles apart.'[6]

But the fundamental weakness, as the president unerringly points out, is that the economy has not created enough jobs. The official unemployment figure is 28 per cent; unofficially, it may be twice as high if indigent farmers are included.

In part, the unemployment rate reflects a rise in the population numbers from just 1.4 million at independence. Windhoek's population alone, for example, has grown from around 150 000 in 1990 to 380 000 in 2016.

To keep up with this rate of population growth and to fuel employment, the government has had to borrow money. The current-account deficit reached 14.3 per cent of GDP in 2015. Successive fiscal deficits have seen debt climb from around 15 per cent (of GDP) in 2009 to around 36 per cent in 2015, much of it spent on the public sector and on infrastructure. As a result, the size of the civil service, employing over 100 000, is disproportionately large for a country of Namibia's size. Geingob says: 'A contributing factor to this scenario is the fact that at independence, the government, in the spirit of national reconciliation, retained those civil servants who had served under the apartheid system and added to them from groups that had previously been excluded.'[7]

Geingob is particularly concerned with rising youth unemployment, which is over 50 per cent. 'This relates to jobless economic growth, to the nature and standard of education, and mindset,' he says. 'We are a land of job-seekers rather than job creators.'

While unemployment is all of a weakness, a possible opportunity and, if not handled correctly, a distinct threat, the same could be said for

Namibia's relationship with South Africa, which is entwined 'culturally and economically', notes the president. Namibia imports more than 70 per cent of its requirements from 'down south' and receives around one-third of its government revenues from the South African-administered Southern African Customs Union. 'When "South Africa sniffs," as the saying has it, "we catch a cold". But we also invest in South Africa, through our pension fund, so this is a two-way partnership that requires transparency and accountability, which equals trust.'

To keep things moving, especially in the face of a regional economic slowdown, the government has responded with the Harambee (literally, 'pulling together') Prosperity Plan, released in April 2016.

'The problem in Africa with development planning is a lack of implementation,' says Geingob. 'We have meaningful ideas which come out in visions and glossy documents, but it ends there, and there is no implementation to back it up and see it through. We need to learn,' says the man who established a formidable reputation during his 12 years as prime minister from 1990 in instituting a management ethic, 'to distinguish in this regard between efficiency and effectiveness. You can efficiently send an email to make an appointment, but it may not be effective – the person may never arrive for the meeting. As long as goods and services fail to reach our people who need it most, then government is not effective.'

Designed to run in a first phase until 2020, Harambee sets out 15 goals and 41 targets across five key thematic pillars: effective governance, economic advancement, social progression, infrastructure development, and international relations and cooperation.

In building on Namibia's legacy of political stability, an independent judiciary, sound economic management and an active media, Harambee's objective is for Namibia to become 'the most competitive economy in Africa by 2020' – in the process, reducing the country's debt to GDP ratio to less than 30 per cent.

The focus, initially, is on the things that don't cost money, such as reducing the number of days it takes to register a business, or revitalising the energy market by promoting independent power producers. Specific targets include constructing 20 000 new houses and 50 000 rural toilets nationwide over the four years of the plan, and ensuring that there are 121 new businesses owned by rural youths by 2020.

With a small team of advisers in State House responsible for writing and implementing the plan, Geingob is personally engaged with overseeing its delivery. 'I have matched the ministers' experience and qualifications with their portfolios, within limits. I have identified fixed timelines and established performance contracts. But the main driver,' he acknowledges, 'is the presidency. If it was anyone else, it would be a problem. If I do it, then government will listen.'

At the centre of the plan is the private sector. Despite SWAPO's Marxist rhetoric, and the fact that there is a cadre of now 40- and 50-somethings who were educated in various Eastern Bloc countries that no longer exist, including Czechoslovakia, East Germany and Yugoslavia, 'even former revolutionaries realise that the private sector is not the enemy, that it, and not the government, has to create jobs' says the president. It's that pragmatism thing again.

He admits there are a lot of priorities, but narrows his top three down to 'instituting a governance architecture'; providing 'reasonably priced housing'; and 'fixing the education system, including vocational training'. He describes the school system as 'horrible', while there is a need to shatter social taboos. 'Because of our apartheid background, people think that it is demeaning to use their hands in work. But we need to learn from Germany, and others, the value of these tasks.'

Although legislation has been formulated for a New Equitable Economic Empowerment Framework, stipulating the transfer of 25 per cent of ownership of white-owned businesses to previously disadvantaged Namibians, Geingob dismisses this as a bad idea. 'Already we know that it is not going to happen. We are not here to work against one group. We need to learn to hold hands. We don't want to send the wrong signals to investors. Rather we need fair play.'

Harambee was discussed at town-hall meetings in all of Namibia's 14 regions. 'We are a resource-based country, and many of the investors who come here come for these [resources]. We need to find ways to add more value to them, but to do that, we need to provide a conducive investor environment ... and they, in turn, have to help us to address the divides in our society. This is a social responsibility, since if we fail to do so, it will defeat us all.'

Namibia is not alone in realising that its destiny is its own responsibility.

Among the lessons from other countries that have successfully planned for development, from Singapore to Chile, are the importance of local ownership of the problem and the solution in ensuring a continuous focus on economic growth, skills and education, and attracting appropriate expertise, including on the reform process itself, if necessary from outside.[8]

Corruption has to be controlled and there needs to be an administrative structure capable of delivering transformation. And leadership has a key role to play. As Yong Ying-I, permanent secretary to Singapore's Public Service Division, said of Singapore's former prime minister Lee Kuan Yew: 'He was superb judge of talent, with the magnetic leadership to draw outstanding people to work with him.' Lee knew the importance of being backed up by efficient administrative machinery to carry out his government's programmes. He personally drove the overhauling of a bureaucracy that had become ridden with lackadaisical and complacent mandarins.[9] And in successful examples, like Singapore, the state's plans and actions were guided by commercial principles rather than short-term political impulses, not least since sustainability demanded that its investments pay for themselves.

It is critical not to set unrealistic goals. Malawi is a perpetual example of this failing. For example, its Vision 2020 statement, prepared in 1998, states: 'By the year 2020, Malawi as a God-fearing nation will be secure, democratically mature, environmentally sustainable, self-reliant with equal opportunities for and active participation by all, having social services, vibrant cultural and religious values and being a technologically driven middle-income economy.'[10]

In May 2002, to deliver on this vision, the government launched the Malawi Poverty Reduction Strategy. Its review in 2005 concluded that there had been a failure by ministries and departments to translate the activities into their budgets, slow implementation of the devolution process, and that plan priorities were ignored in the allocation of funds.[11] Undeterred, the government prepared the Malawi Growth and Development Strategy 2006–2011 (MGDS I), a document running to 265 pages, containing 55 pages of goals and 97 key indicators. The 2012 review of that plan noted: 'Its focus of poverty reduction and employment creation was rather weak and little progress has been made in addressing these challenges.' It was also observed that the plan 'suffered from a weak monitoring and evaluation system which was rather fragmented and the measurability of performance outcomes was further complicated by poor baseline data'.[12] The follow-on plan, MGDS II, is similarly ambitious, covering 2011 to 2016, and running to 271 pages, with 128 pages of goals and 100 key indicators, for a government that is weak, lacks will and has remained pinned in the bottom five poorest countries for the last 50 years.

There have been four broad eras of African state planning since independence. In the 1960s and 1970s centralised planning tended to predominate. The focus then was the role of the state, with state-owned enterprises operating in most of the productive sectors. Plans typically had a three- to five-year lifespan. In general, they failed to deliver the promised results owing to weaknesses in the planning, overambitious targets and lack of political will to drive full implementation.

Next came the era of structural-adjustment programmes. These focused on reducing the role of the state, the privatisation of many state enterprises and the downsizing of many public-sector institutions. They also focused on limiting government spending to reduce budget deficits, and on creating macroeconomic stability.

But the negative consequences of these programmes for the poor were considerable. Hence, the 2000s saw the introduction of poverty-reduction strategies which sought to alleviate some of the worst social effects of structural adjustment. Debt relief was often made conditional on a country having such a strategy, and this was a major motivating factor for many countries. But the focus on social welfare often came with a cost to the productive sector of the economy, raising the issue of their long-term sustainability.

Over the last decade there has been a shift to more comprehensive national-development strategies and plans, often including broader global development goals. But, in broadening the approach, the plans have become large, complex and challenging to deliver, and often the accurate data needed for effective planning and performance measurement has generally been lacking.

The following sections examine the mechanics of creating and executing a national development plan, using the experience of Zambia as case study. This example explores why good plans have failed to achieve their intended results, and why those that have produced results were effective.

220

How planning might work

Former Zambian president Guy Scott recalled that when he took over as Minister for Agriculture in 1991, he asked for all the reports on how to improve Zambia's performance in the agricultural sector to be brought to his office. What appeared was a huge pile of paper, yet very little of what had been recommended in those reports had actually happened.

Much the same fate has befallen all six of Zambia's national development plans: planning but no delivery. Such plans often present a very sound analysis of the issues at play and describe potential solutions. However, the policy recommendations have usually been very general, requiring further elaboration to make them actionable. These problems have been routinely compounded by lack of capacity in the civil service to deliver them, and a lack of political leadership and will to set priorities and make choices.

Indeed, often the blame can be laid firmly at the door of the politicians for favouring short-term political interests to the detriment of the longer-term approach needed to solve the problems of the next generation. But good leaders by themselves are not enough: they need to be supported by a system that enables them to achieve results.

In 2016 two of the authors were invited by the Industrial Development Corporation of Zambia and the opposition United Party for National Development (UPND) to undertake a study into what was required to revitalise Zambia's economy. The country had failed to diversify its economy during the years of high commodity prices. It was suffering considerably from declining copper prices, underinvestment in infrastructure, the stresses of a rapidly growing population, and a toxic mix of bureaucracy and corruption, which was acting as a major constraint on business. Despite a population of 15 million, the economy supported the formal employment of only 625 000 people, of whom 256 000 were government employees. Also, as noted above, the country suffered from a lack of educated and experienced people capable of planning and delivering a national strategy.

Over several months, we toured the country, and read widely, interviewing more than 150 people in order to gain a better understanding of both the issues and the potential solutions. We were particularly struck by the lack of a common understanding of the problems facing the country and the lack of data upon which to base discussions and decisions. The ground truths were scarcely understood.

Very few people, for example, had an understanding of the extent of Zambia's central-government debt or of when repayments fell due. The same was true of the history behind Zambia's electricity shortages. For example, we unearthed a report from 1997, which very accurately predicted the power deficit being experienced in 2016 and suggested a course of action to avert the crisis. Nothing, however, was done. The most depressing moment was when we asked a senior member of the Zambian Electricity Supply Commission about their catch-up plan. His answer: 'Improved rainfall.'

Given that the six previous Zambian national development plans had failed to be implemented, we concluded that any new plan – if it were to work – had to take account of the capacity available for delivery and would, therefore, need to be very focused and include a range of early confidence-building measures aimed at establishing momentum. With Zambia's population set to grow to 25 million by 2030, we also concluded that the key issue for the country, like many other in sub-Saharan Africa, was to create the conditions for sustainable job creation. Finally, during our research, we had observed that Zambia's mining industry, although it provided a huge share of the tax revenue for the country, was in serious decline and lacking much needed investment.

Our plan was structured around three productive sectors: agriculture, tourism and mining. These were underpinned by five enabling sectors: finance and debt; transparency; governance; electricity; and logistics. Under each sector, we drafted five actions to be completed within six months, and five further actions to be completed after 18 months. The six-month actions were generally aimed at establishing confidence, seeding the conditions for further reform or delivering quick wins. The 18-month actions were about delivering more substantive reform. The actions had to be specific, realistically achievable and aimed at job creation.

Towards the end of our project in Zambia, we spent a considerable amount of time socialising the plan with key stakeholders to ensure that it had wide acceptance. We envisaged the plan being driven and monitored by a small team based in State House, with ministers allocated specific tasks to deliver, and with formal review meetings chaired by the president initially every three months. Such an approach echoes that followed successfully elsewhere in Africa, for example in Senegal under the Plan Senegal Emergent, which aimed to increase both public- and private-sector productivity.[13]

As foreigners, we were aware that we had, however, only a limited role to play in Zambia even if the government did wish to adopt our plan.

Insiders and outsiders

'Strengthening the coordination and management of the engendered and rights-based multi-sectoral and decentralized response to HIV and Aids' read the door decal on the Land Cruiser in the car park at the Lusaka Club. Such bureaucratic handbrakes only encourage government inertia and give room for petty manoeuvre.

That is not to say that outsiders cannot add value to development processes. They can bring enormous value to business. Through short, sharp interventions, they can identify measures for cost cutting, restructuring, product selection and promotion, process and costs of mergers, sales and acquisitions – all areas where they have obvious and genuine expertise. Those conducting detailed due-diligence reviews of processes and people can help to facilitate investment, and good results.

McKinsey, for one, played an important role in Morocco's economic reforms by identifying sectoral priorities. Facilitators can also play an important role in coalescing ideas. And it is sometimes useful to obtain an outsider's perspective, free from institutional constraints, using them as the military, for example, would use 'red teams': to test prevailing assumptions and logic. In particular, given the need to de-risk African economies, external advisers have a role to play as intermediaries between government and business where they can identify and help manage the constraints that hinder investment.

But there is a danger, conversely, that external consultants do not have sufficient vested interest, beyond their immediate financial rewards, in the implementation and the outcome. And there is a related risk that, in coming from outside, especially with baggage from other assignments, their ideas are not domestically grounded, or even sourced. Donors and governments also have to be aware of the consequences of employing

223

non-commercial people in roles that are supposed to be about private-sector development, and in which these individuals may lack experience or to which they are ideologically antithetical.

It is undoubtedly difficult to do well the type of analysis required for reform of processes. It goes beyond the 'issue tree' template favoured by consultancies, which dissects subjects graphically, first vertically, into components and, left to right, into further details. Instead, solutions require an appreciation of the complex overlay of politics, economics, business and security, which are normally far from the domain of the traditional consultancy. There is also a need fundamentally to distinguish between thought leadership, where an assessment is made as to how the environment is changing, and longer-term scenario generation, which entails the specific, time-bound policy prescriptions required.

All this means there is a need to accept that process – specifically, political process – is as much a part of the problem as the solution.

Indeed, the complexity of past national plans is not the fault of national leaders alone. Some blame must be laid at the door of the international community for insisting on adding in many objectives that, although important, are not critical. A consequence of such all-encompassing plans is that donor assistance becomes dissipated, effectively allowing donors to pick and choose from a wide menu what to support, rather than focusing their efforts on the core issues.

Given Africa's chronic requirement for jobs in the coming 40 years, development plans should be focused on economic growth and job creation.

Delivering the plan

Within any plan, actions need to be clearly articulated, tangible, visible, resourced and seen as both challenging and realistically achievable. These actions also need to obviously link to the government's declared programme, because, this way, successful completion can be used to communicate the government's wider programme. The plan also needs to be very clear about who is responsible for delivering an action; actions with multiple leads have a much lower chance of success.

A major challenge for such a planning approach is that it is difficult for a government to deliver meaningful change over a single term in office.

Facing a similar predicament and speaking at the launch of the first Singaporean national development plan, Lee Kuan Yew said: 'We, the grown-ups of today, must bear the hardships of today for the sake of the next generation. ... If any politician claims he can change a society within a few years, he is a humbug.'[14] Of course, in a democracy the reality is that re-election is the key objective of the party in government. Therefore, a dual approach that seeks to both deliver results synchronised with the term of the government and to get cross-party buy-in to the plan will probably offer the best chance of long-term success.

If the government's ability to deliver is weak, it is logical for it to actively find ways to extract itself from all but the most essential functions, freeing the private sector to take over where appropriate. This issue should be considered during the planning process. One Zambian interviewee explained that his business model was to find areas where the government's intervention was low, and then to build up a new business before the government woke up and intervened with new regulations and other bureaucracy.

At their core, ministries and governments can be thought of as operating four parallel work processes. They are continually trying to understand what is happening around them; they are planning and controlling their activities; they are communicating and influencing in an attempt to shape people and events; and, finally, they are assessing their progress. All of these processes rely very heavily on accurate management information which, as already noted, is often in short supply. Second, all of these processes interact and, therefore, the key goal for the team controlling the execution of the plan is to ensure that the processes stay synchronised in such a way that positive momentum is developed and progress is achieved. This requires a sustained commitment and a disciplined approach. As soon as important officials start to send their deputies to key synchronisation meetings, momentum is rapidly lost.

Experience from President Ellen Johnson Sirleaf's 150-day plan[15] for Liberia at the start of her second administration, in 2012, shows that engaging civil society generated real pressure, motivating the government to deliver on its promises. Such an approach relied on a willingness of government to engage in robust dialogue and the ability of civil-society organisations to provide an independent monitoring role.

For many African countries under pressure to produce rapid growth, a dual approach is probably required. To get things moving, a core planning team linked to specific delivery units will need to be established. And a sustained effort will need to be made to restructure, change culture, and train and educate the civil service. This demands more than just vision statements and team-building exercises. Examples will need to be made and vested interested tackled.

The importance of people

Kishore Mahbubani, dean of the Lee Kuan Yew School of Public Policy, attributes success to the implementation of three exceptional policies: meritocracy, pragmatism and honesty. 'Indeed, I share this "secret" MPH formula with every foreign student at the Lee Kuan Yew School, and I assure them that if they implement it, their country will succeed as well as Singapore. Meritocracy means a country picks its best citizens, not the relatives of the ruling class, to run a country. Pragmatism means that a country does not try to reinvent the wheel. As Dr Goh Keng Swee, independent Singapore's first finance minister, would say, "no matter what problem Singapore encounters, somebody, somewhere, has solved it. Let us copy the solution and adapt it to Singapore". Implementing "honesty" is the hardest thing to do. Corruption is the single biggest reason why most Third World countries have failed. The greatest strength of Singapore's founding fathers was that they were ruthlessly honest. It also helped that they were exceptionally shrewd and cunning.'[16]

The dilemma facing many African countries is that they need rapid economic growth and job creation, and do not have a lot of time in which to make their civil services more effective. Yet they have consistently failed to significantly improve their human talent pool.

In reviewing a decade of sub-Saharan African government reform, the IMF highlighted in 1997 that many countries began civil-service changes in the 1980s after 10 years of rapid civil-service job growth, coupled with erosion of wages, in real terms, especially for upper-grade staff. It noted that 'it was difficult for governments to retain competent staff and incentives to accept bribes were high'.[17] Donors have continually focused on ballooning costs, the phenomenon of ghost workers and the shortage of skills in critical areas.

The World Bank's Worldwide Governance Indicators attempt to measure six aggregate governance indicators for over 215 economies, over the period 1996 to 2014.[18] One of these measures, government effectiveness, is compiled by using data that captures perceptions of the quality of public services, the quality of the civil service and the degree of its independence from political pressures, the quality of policy formulation and implementation, and the credibility of the government's commitment to such policies.

Of course, these figures conceal a mixed picture. Mauritius improved over time and scored highly in 2014 at 83. Rwanda achieved a score of 11 in 1996, but increased to 56 in 2014. The DRC has scored consistently poorly, at four in 2014. Malawi has experienced a declining trend since 2011 with a score of 25 in 2014. Despite many attempts at civil service reform in sub-Saharan Africa, its regional ranking is little changed. For the entire region, the analysis reported a marginal decline in the percentile ranking from 28 to 26 over 19 years. The trajectories of Rwanda and Mauritius both show that improvement is possible, but it takes time and consistent effort.

A familiar theme of conversation in Africa is the difficulty of obtaining work permits for expatriate workers, particularly for technical specialists. Companies and other organisations are continually being told to employ local workers and that they must reduce their expatriate workforce. Organisations point out that local workers are cheaper to employ than expats and that they would happily engage them, but appropriately qualified and experienced people are not available. It has seemed like a never-ending debate, and one that is adding much friction to companies trying to do business. In the end, this issue needs to be resolved by hard focus on what will, over the long term, create the most jobs for the whole country.

Part of the issue of lack of talent in the region has been the difficulty in retaining talented, qualified professionals. The World Bank estimates the number of migrants from Zambia to be 1.5 per cent of the population (approximately 235 000).[19] A 2011 survey of the Zambian diaspora[20] estimates that of those who had left, three-quarters had obtained a first degree or higher. The study also notes that 71 per cent of respondents were prepared to be physically present in Zambia to transfer knowledge and expertise. It also highlights that corruption, nepotism and inefficiency in the public service frustrate and discourage those who would consider returning.

Although the figures in the report need to be treated with some caution, it is clear that there are many professional people within the Zambian diaspora who, with the right incentives, could be encouraged to return, and that these incentives have more to do with fair treatment, opportunity and easy of doing business than straight financial inducement.

Liberia provides an interesting case study on how to improve the stock of human talent. In 2000 it was estimated that 45 per cent of Liberia's skilled workers lived outside the country, with a large proportion residing in the US. The government introduced two successful programmes, Transfer of Knowledge Through Expatriate Nationals (TOKTEN) and the Senior Executive Service (SES) to encourage skilled people to return. TOKTEN aimed to recruit expatriates on short contracts to fill specific gaps or to train others, whereas SES sought to recruit 100 skilled Liberians on three-year renewable contracts.[21]

There have been many stirring words written about the importance of people, but this extract from Singapore's strategic economic plan, written in 1991, titled 'Towards a Developed Nation', is highly illuminating of the thinking a quarter century into that country's development transformation: 'The single most important factor towards achieving developed country status is enhancing Singapore's most important resource, its people. They should be equipped with a high standard of competence; a high level of basic education; a high degree of industry relevance in training programmes; effective programmes for mid-career training; and nurturing important human resource qualities, such as the work ethic and creativity.'[22]

To tackle the issue of the deficit in human capital, both short- and long-term actions are likely to be needed. In the short to medium term, the critical gaps need to be identified, home-grown talent needs to be located and incentivised to return, and external talent needs to be attracted to fill the gaps. Concurrently focused scholarship schemes, such as those run in Singapore and Chile, need to be set up to fast-track the development of suitable graduates and they need to be tied to returning to the country to work in key positions. Over the longer term, there needs to be a real focus on developing the education system and tuning it to the needs of the nation.

Conclusion: Plan to fix the problem

The chances of our plan for Zambia being implemented sank with the re-election of the government of Edgar Lungu. Even though his government was going to be forced down a reform path by the IMF because of its cash-strapped fiscal position and burgeoning international debt, Lungu's was the same party that had got them into the trouble in the first instance. They would reform not because they believed in it, but because they had no other options. So, when the pressure came off, they were unlikely, history suggests, to stick to the tough and politically unpopular reforms.

This experience illustrates the need for any plan to take into account vested interests in the political economy if it is to have any hope of success. These interests have to be identified, acknowledged and dealt with. While writing a plan is a good start, it does not by itself fix the problem. For success, a much more balanced approach, which matches the plan with the capacity to deliver, is required.

Further guidelines are also needed. First, the numbers of actions need to be kept to a realistically achievable number. Drawing up a long list of government interventions ignores the capacity reality of most developing countries in Africa, and will end in disappointment.

Second, any plan, and indeed every action, needs to be careful socialised and iterated in its formulation, and continually updated as the plan is implemented, with new actions replacing those delivered. Local ownership of the plan and its actions is essential.

Third, there is a need for strict timelines. These should be given a specific date for delivery or implementation.

Fourth, how the plan is driven, both within and across government, needs careful thought. Although some form of central team, probably working from the president's office, will be needed to maintain coherence, care must be taken to ensure that ministers, permanent secretaries and the civil service are bought into the system, so they can play an active and constructive part in its delivery. Building in early, achievable successes will be key to establishing confidence and in developing momentum.

And, finally, although general recommendations are possible, each country is unique and requires a plan of its own, taking into account its specific strengths, weaknesses, opportunities and threats.

There are clear limits for outsiders. The ability of donors or advisers to create political incentives for internal actors to do 'what's necessary' is constrained by the imperative to stay in power whatever the external aid incentive on offer. This is why local ownership is *sine qua non* of any successful reform: it cannot be desired more by outsiders than locals. It is also why successful reform initiatives have to win the argument for change domestically. And it explains why the disincentives for leadership – fear of external isolation, even opprobrium – also have to be signalled and sometimes employed.

It is seldom the case that where there is a poorly managed or dysfunctional government – marred by corruption or clientelism – the people in charge do not know what a well-functioning government looks like. They are bombarded with advice and models of international best practice, the most efficient management and information systems, and so on. The reason reforms often don't work is because it is not in certain key officials' interests to see them implemented; they actually benefit from the existing dysfunctions. To varying degrees, this scenario has impaired development efforts in many African states.

And in all this, there is a need to avoid the temptation of grandiose or silver-bullet solutions. It's not only that these will never happen, or won't solve fundamental problems. When one reads of nuclear programmes in South Africa or space programmes in Nigeria, for example, the conclusion is inevitable for any investor worth half his salt: they smell corruption and avoidance of the key issues. National plans can be absolutely critical to a country's growth or they can be little more than paperweights. The question is not so much about planning, but about whether a national design can be envisioned that is both relevant to the most important challenges facing a country and can be implemented by a determined leadership. Creating a plan is not the end of the process but merely, if successful, the beginning of a reallocation of resources to address the most important problems and the creation of a government structure motivated to implement the plan.

Chapter 11
Leadership and delivery

Five steps for success:
- Leadership should use democracy to instil a disciplined nationalism, explaining the country's development path.
- The emphasis of leaders should be on execution and attention to the details of governance.
- Leadership requires utilising the full range of personal diplomatic skills and patience.
- Accountability of government officials should be ensured through transparency.
- Strong leaders are willing to delegate authority.

Challenges and opportunities: Changing a country's economic trajectory and dealing with an issue as big as Africa's projected population growth require strong political leadership. Such leadership not only needs to set out a vision and make the tough choices when resources are scarce, but it also needs the energy, commitment to the common good and attention to detail to drive delivery. Improving governance, strengthening institutions and acting transparently are vital reforms for countries in need of foreign investment, and here strong leadership is also vital.

Key statistics: Ten[1] of the 16 countries[2] in the 'very high alert' or 'high alert' categories in the 2016 Fragile States Index are in sub-Saharan Africa.[3] Six[4] of the bottom 10 countries[5] in Transparency International's 2015 Corruption Perceptions Index are African.[6] According to the World Economic Forum, the 10 most competitive economies in sub-Saharan Africa are (with their global rank in parenthesis): Mauritius (46), South Africa (49), Rwanda (58), Botswana (71), Namibia (85), Côte d'Ivoire (91), Zambia (96), Seychelles (97), Kenya (99) and Gabon (103), out of 140 economies measured. African countries also occupy 15 of the bottom 20 places in the same survey.[7]

On assumption of office as president of Nigeria in 1999, I [Olusegun Obasanjo] discovered that the accumulated debt of Nigeria to the Paris Club[8] was some $30 billion. Some of the projects that constituted the debt were dubious, if not outright fraudulent. One typical example was a turn-key project for $8 million where the money was drawn out with no site clearance let alone the foundations being laid. And yet, there was a video of the purported commissioning of the project. This happened in Enugu State, one of the 36 states of Nigeria. Obviously, it involved collusion and corruption between the state government and the lender and promoter of the project. All the same, the loan was a commitment and it had to be repaid.

Such had become the practice of Nigerian debt to the international community.

I did not waste time on the merit or demerit and impropriety of any of these projects, which previous governments had accepted and on which interests or penalties were already being paid in the event of failure to meet interest payments. I concentrated on seeking debt relief from the governments of creditor countries, which have bound themselves together as a cartel in what they called the Paris Club. Nigeria was spending almost $3 billion annually to service all its debt. This was a heavy burden on the economy of the country. Yet a failure to service the debt would incur penalties. There were only two ways out for Nigeria: to renege on the commitment previous governments had reached with Paris Club or to negotiate debt relief. To renege would lead to Nigeria being isolated and facing heavy punishment in the international economic community and market.

The most sustainable and prudent course was negotiation. But what sort of negotiation? Previous administrations had negotiated postponement of repayment and servicing terms, which kept increasing the quantum of debt, making it more and more burdensome and unbearable, especially with the price of a barrel of oil below $10 when I assumed office in 1999.

I embarked on shuttle diplomacy to clean up the image and perception of Nigeria in the eyes of the world and to seek debt relief. I visited most Western capitals to present anew Nigeria's case. One such visit was to Washington DC where I met President Clinton and the president of the World Bank, Jim Wolfensohn. I raised the issue of debt relief with both of them and asked Jim for both support and advice. He advised that Nigeria should urgently embark on comprehensive reform to impress its creditors.

If Nigeria was doing well in its economic reform and management, it would get the World Bank's support.

That constituted my marching orders. In my first term, from 1999 to 2003, I visited many countries and world leaders, some more than once, to campaign for debt relief. There I got apparently sympathetic hearings, but not much action from political leaders. After my first term, I realised that my talks at the highest political levels needed follow-up at the levels below. So I head-hunted Ngozi Okonjo-Iweala from the World Bank, appointing her as Nigeria's Minister of Finance. My plan was that she would manage the follow-up at a lower level. Even then, the fact that Nigeria was the sixth largest oil-exporting country in the world was regularly used as the reason to deny debt relief. I would then explain that Nigeria's population of almost 150 million at the time and its stage of development should justify such relief.

Gradually, the message started to sink in. But Nigeria needed a creditor nation that believed in the reforms, programmes and progress that it was making. That country was the UK under Prime Minister Tony Blair with Gordon Brown as his Chancellor of the Exchequer. With the firm support of both, the UK spearheaded the movement at the meeting of G7 to plead for debt relief for Nigeria. At that time, the UK was Nigeria's largest creditor. Brown was on firm moral ground to plead for and lead the crusade for debt relief for Nigeria.

In the end, Nigeria obtained debt relief of about $18 billion and paid up about $12 billion to rid itself of this burden. It was a great breakthrough and the consequent savings were channelled to the Millennium Development Goals, one of the promises made to the creditors. With debt relief having been agreed by the Paris Club, Nigeria was in a strong position to negotiate debt relief from other creditors too.

The second big challenge under my presidential watch was the issue of sharia law. As a country shared almost 50:50 between Muslims and Christians, sharia has always been part of the legal and judicial systems in the north, but only at the customary, or so-called magistrarial levels. Even then, the Nigerian constitution has provision for establishing a Sharia Court of Appeal if the need ever arises. Sharia was, therefore, never an issue because it dealt with personal issues, such as marriage, inheritance, and minor and civil issues, such as debt, boundary disputes and land matters. Only very occasionally did it deal with criminal issues which, where necessary, were forwarded to the High Court for confirmation.

The initiator of the sharia controversy, the then Zamfara State governor, Sani Yerima, raised the issue, however, for self-serving and self-preservation reasons, not for genuine or authentic religious conviction. When he stood for the governorship of his state under the banner of the All People's Party, the man who later became the National Security Adviser (NSA), General Aliyu Mohammed, sponsored a candidate under the banner of the then ruling party, the People's Democratic Party (PDP). The PDP candidate lost the election but it would appear that the NSA, intending to find fault against the governor, started surreptitiously to collect evidence of misconduct and corruption against the governor. Meanwhile, I made several attempts to reconcile them, but to no avail. I even took both of them on an official visit to China, an opportunity to bring them together. When it appeared that the NSA persisted, Governor Yerima decided to make himself untouchable.

He invited the imams, Muslim leaders and priests in his state, and informed them that he was turning Zamfara into a full sharia state. He promulgated a law declaring Zamfara as a sharia state. And, true enough, he became untouchable. Wanting not to be seen as acting in isolation, he instigated imams in other Islamic states in the north to agitate for a full sharia law declaration. In all, 12 states out of 19 in the north promulgated full sharia law.

Muslims in the country were all watching closely to see what I would do. A wrong statement or action on my part would be seen as incendiary, because an 'infidel', anti-Muslim president would be seen as trampling on the holy religion of Islam. But, at the same time, Christian clergymen and leaders both within and outside Nigeria were calling on me to stamp out the new phenomenon of wholesale sharia in states where there was a Muslim majority but with a substantial contingent of Christians too. They pointed out that Nigeria is a secular or multi-religious society, and not a Muslim state. Throughout this controversy, the only statement I made was to the effect that if the sharia that the governor of Zamfara was touting was genuine, it would survive and thrive. If not, it would fizzle out.

To justify his action and to prove his 'shariness' to those whom he had recruited to his 'political' sharia, Governor Yerima cut off the hand of a thief – a traditional Muslim punishment. After that, sure enough, the sharia fervour started to fizzle out. Muslims, who had expected me to kick back against sharia, thereby giving them ammunition to cause mayhem, and Christians, who felt angry and disappointed that I did not roll out military tanks to crush the proponents of sharia, both felt winners and losers at the same time. But Nigeria was surely the unquestionable winner. Eventually, Yerima weaned himself off the Muslim clergy and sharia crumbled in his state.

A few months later, Yerima visited me in my official residence and, greeting my young female cousin, hugged her familiarly in my presence. I jokingly remarked to Yerima that this action was not sharia-compliant. Yerima retorted, 'Didn't you say sharia would fizzle out and has it not fizzled out?'

At that point, the matter had turned into a joke. If mishandled, it would have become a serious disaster for Nigeria. I received more letters from within and outside Nigeria on the sharia affair than on all other issues put together in my eight-year presidency.

*　　*　　*

A cool head and adroit diplomacy are expected of statesmen and women. As the examples from Nigeria above illustrate, while there are common challenges, African states are increasingly differentiated, not just in terms of their geography, but also in population size, economic and social make-up, and their political record. Some are stable and have solid human-rights regimes; others are emerging or descending into conflict. Below are four examples that illustrate aspects of delivery: Ethiopia and Botswana – one large country and one small; one largely without commodities and one commodity-dependent; and, respectively, one is classified (by Freedom House) as 'not free' and the other as 'free'.[9] Mauritania is also cited as an example of the challenges and opportunities for reform in the Sahel, a region with particular and extreme challenges. Finally, the chapter examines a key economy in West Africa, looking at Côte d'Ivoire's record in catching up from conflict.

Is Ethiopia's economic single-mindedness enough?

In Ethiopia, it is hard not to be impressed by the clarity of strategic vision, single-mindedness and focus on execution.[10]

'We see China becoming expensive, but Africa being unready to take advantage, partly because the continent's labour costs are expensive,' says Ethiopia's prime minister, Hailemariam Desalegn. 'However, in Ethiopia, to achieve our advantage in light manufacturing, we have kept such costs low. This starts with government wages. If you make government wages large, it impacts on and inflates the market.'

Ethiopia, confirms its leader, whose official salary is less than $400 a month, has 'the lowest salaries for government officials in Africa. We also have productivity-based salary increases, not just simple increments.'

Hailemariam, who is from the minority Wolayta community in the south of the country, became prime minister in August 2012 at the age of 47, on the death of Meles Zenawi. As a young man, he wanted to become a doctor, but was put off by a visit to hospital in Addis Ababa with his sick father. Instead, he trained as a civil engineer, along the way acquiring a master's in hydrology from Finland's Tampere University. On his return, at just 27, he became a dean of the Water Technology Institute, a position he found 'very challenging' given his age and experience. Making the step into politics, he was appointed Deputy Governor of the Southern Nations, Nationalities, and Peoples' Region[11] at the age of 35 and, a year later, became governor, serving for nearly five years until 2006. After a time as a special adviser to Meles, he was promoted to Deputy Prime Minister and Minister of Foreign Affairs in October 2010.

Without much in the way of natural resources, a population rising fast towards 100 million[12] and landlocked since the independence of Eritrea in 1991, Ethiopia's development options appear limited. Fifty-five per cent of the population are under 24 and, as a consequence, the government is obsessed with creating jobs.

The absence of natural-resource-driven growth has been something of an advantage to Ethiopia, especially during the commodity-price downturn. Ethiopia has emerged as one of the fastest growing – perhaps *the* fastest growing – of Africa's economies. Even though double-digit growth has become something of an official mantra, independent appraisals still put it at over 10 per cent from 2003 to 2013 – this against a sub-Saharan regional average of 5.3 per cent.[13] This economic performance has significantly reduced national poverty levels, down from 45.5 per cent in 1995 to under 30 per cent 15 years later.[14]

'First and foremost, we have to focus on our comparative and competitive advantages in a global setting,' says the prime minister. 'Our first priority is agriculture – the need to mechanise and to get more out of it.' Farming still accounts for 80 per cent of Ethiopia's employment. 'We have a strategy to support smallholder farming, and to increase the demand for agriculture. But this alone,' he says, 'is not sustainable. We have to think about the next steps.'

In part, these next steps are about increasing the value obtained from agriculture by moving from subsistence to export crops. The next phase of Ethiopia's economic transformation involves, underlines the prime minister, improving skills in the search for what his predecessor, Meles, referred to as 'relative comparative interest'.[15]

'We have to be focused on technical and vocational training. Otherwise, we will have a young population which is not skilled, has the wrong attitude, and one which does not understand the market. This involves more than just technical skills. It is about preparing people, supporting entrepreneurs and small and medium size businesses,' he says.

Hailemariam recognises that local sources of capital and labour can only supply so much. 'We are intent on attracting more FDI, based on our competitive advantage, which is focused on labour-intensive light manufacturing.'

The figures bear this out. In 2005 Ethiopia's annual FDI inflow was $200 million, equivalent to 3.6 per cent of GDP, similar to Chinese inflow ratios during the 1990s. Now it has increased tenfold. FDI from the US alone, between 2013 and 2015, totalled $4 billion, including a $200-million investment in a flower exporting company, and a $250-million expansion by Coca-Cola.

The most important task for the government, from the prime minister's vantage, is to get investors into 20 industrial parks dotted around the country. 'These parks,' he stresses, 'are not just sheds, but comprehensive programmes, including everything from one-stop services to proper utilities, environmental management, and training and skills development provisions – all of the facilities and services appropriate to a modern city. To make these parks work,' he says, 'we need also to understand why they fail in Africa and elsewhere.'

Forty kilometres out of Addis is the Eastern Industrial Zone, which, by 2016, had more than 20 Chinese investors, attracted by low or zero tariffs on imported manufactured goods, and tax holidays of up to seven years. The centrepiece of the park is the Chinese Huajian Group's 'Shoe City', a shoe factory employing 3 200 workers making 180 000 pairs of shoes a month for export.[16]

'We are aiming at 50 000 jobs per park,' says the prime minister. This sector is where the issue of labour costs makes a difference. Ethiopian workers earn, on average, a tenth of their Chinese counterparts' wages. For example, Addis's shoe factories pay between 700 and 800 birr ($30–35) a month.

As one travels north-east of the capital, past newly constructed public-housing units, one comes to another park, in Legetafo. Although the roads here are still under construction, little more than mud tracks in places, factories are springing up everywhere, from food processing to packaging, soap and, again, shoes. These products are not only for the export market.

Top Shoes has just installed five new Taiwanese-supplied machines alongside the company's four existing processing units to manufacture rubber sandals and flip-flops, which wholesale to domestic consumers at under $1.00 a pair. However, whereas each machine can stamp out 5 000 shoes a week, they are vulnerable to fluctuations in domestic demand. At the time of our visit, just two of the nine machines were steaming and clunking away.

There are considerable challenges in operating manufacturing businesses where virtually all the component parts and materials are imported, and where electricity is unreliable, necessitating investment in backup generators. Nevertheless, it appears, the government is working hard to make Ethiopia attractive enough for such challenges to be worth overcoming.

Yet the prime minister notes the need to source domestic capital as a fillip to foreign investment, 'especially in textiles, garments, footwear, and agro-processing'. The Ethiopian government is also focused on delivering a badly needed expansion in the regional rail network and in electricity generation. Such improvements are desperately needed to soak up the number of young people coming onto Ethiopia's job market, estimated at 2 million every year,[17] a situation that is made more urgent by growing migration to the cities. The country's current urbanisation is still very low, at just 19 per cent of the population. However, this is set to change.

Ethiopia's competitive advantage – its low cost of labour – is not the only issue about which the prime minister is disarmingly forthright.

The success of Ethiopia's transition and its ability to create jobs en masse will hinge on encouraging an indigenous business class as a strong domestic base for growth. A shortage of capital stands in the way, partly because the government uses so much of it for its infrastructure projects and partly because of the government's desire to maintain control and a corresponding failure to open up certain sectors to outsiders.

'We need to make the political economy more receptive to capital,' explains the prime minister. 'If it is favourable for rent-seeking and if government officials are involved in patronage and in short-term looting, it discourages the local private sector to invest in productive areas. This demands that we stamp out corruption. But it also means,' he adds, 'that we remove the deficits in infrastructure, rules and procedures, and finance to encourage private-sector investment in productive, value-addition activities.'

As Ethiopia looks to attract investors in textiles from Turkey and construction materials from India, among other industries, the country needs, says Hailemariam, 'not only to have one foot on the ground, but also another looking for the next step, which means looking for areas to leapfrog, including in bio-tech and nano-tech.' This means, he admits, 'engaging in and spending on research and development to enable competitiveness'.

The creation of quality jobs will take 20 to 30 years at least, he says. 'But we know where we have started from, and where and how we want to go to create jobs. First, we have to start with low-cost, labour-intensive and low-technology solutions.'

The prime minister is equally forthright about the individual responsibility of Ethiopians. 'Our biggest constraint is the attitude, outlook and exposure of our people. We have a huge rural population. You need to create an understanding among them of the need for value creation in a way that requires everyone working very hard and working differently – for example, in the change from subsistence to rural agriculture. You also have to convince people that white-collar jobs are not everything, that agriculture can be a modern occupation.

'All this,' he explains, 'requires a good communications strategy, including [communicating] the threats if we don't change our ways. In South Korea the threat that used to motivate people was of the dangers of communism. Our danger is a danger of poverty and of the country's disintegration if we don't tackle these problems, and become active and hard-working.'

For all of these challenges, there have been some remarkable Ethiopian successes. Ethiopian Airlines, as covered in Chapter 7, and the country's flower industry, discussed in Chapter 4, are examples of successful business development in very different industries

Shoe City came about as a result of a personal invitation by Meles to the company's founder to open a plant during a 2011 trip to China. Little surprise, then, that Prime Minister Hailemariam was 'shocked' by Meles's death. 'It was a traumatic moment. I did not think I could run the country in his absence, or how I would do so. But we were able to navigate it with the support of colleagues. When I realised that the ultimate decisions in this country are taken by myself, you can only imagine how stressful that is. This is why I opted for a more consultative and collective leadership process in politics and with the private sector.' He meets the latter three times annually in strategy sessions, quarterly on competitiveness issues, and monthly to assess progress on exports.

Hailemariam acknowledges that 'the most important thing in leadership is to be trusted by the people. We have to show by example our zero tolerance towards corruption, to not use public money for personal enrichment, and to show sacrifice. If you cannot do this, you can't expect others to do so.'

When asked about how he defines success, the prime minister replies: 'It is about bringing meaningful change in the lives of our people. It's not just about figures or growth, but about changing lives. Growth,' he adds, 'has to be shared to be sustainable.'

Despite the clarity of planning and the willingness to make sacrifices, concerns about the long-term sustainability of the Ethiopian model were highlighted by police crackdowns in 2016 against protests in the Oromo and Amhara regions. The protests were triggered by attempts by the government to re-allocate land in these regions, which are home to nearly two-thirds of the country's population. These groups see Ethiopia's governing coalition as dominated by Tigrayans, who form around 6 per cent of the population; they are the group who led the guerrilla war against the military regime of Mengistu Haile Mariam. The message is clear: economic growth and prosperity depend on getting the politics right. In fact, many of the protests have targeted foreign investment, highlighting the indivisibility of domestic peace and the ability to attract and retain foreign investment.

A combination of its stabilising regional security role and its traumatic domestic political record suggests that the international community will, for a while, give Ethiopia something of a free pass on its human-rights record. This might not, however, be in the donors' longer-term interests. Paradoxically, the government's bigger challenge might come with economic success. As it gets wealthier, the demands of its middle class for greater freedoms may well combine with the demands of those who feel excluded. If this happens in an economic crisis, as was the case in Indonesia in the late 1990s, the pressure for change could become overwhelming, and possibly unmanageable. History suggests that a continual strengthening of democracy would provide the answer to Ethiopia's long-term development challenges.

Botswana: The challenge beyond commodities

Just a few kilometres from the new Sir Seretse Khama International Airport in Gaborone is De Beers Global Sightholder Sales.[18] Previously known as the Diamond Trading Company (DTC), this is a sorting, valuation and sales centre. In 2014 it handled over 32 million carats of diamonds (worth more than $7 billion) for global distribution. In the vicinity of the angular glass-and-stone building are the national vault, the Bureau of Standards, various diamond-cutting and polishing workshops, and the national archives.

The DTC was moved from London in 2012 as part of a deal struck around the renewal of the lease on the giant Jwaneng and Orapa mines, which have the world's richest diamond deposits. Botswana's goal is to gain a greater share of downstream benefit from its principal export. Every five weeks, 86 authorised sightholders, or clients, meet in Botswana to buy parcels of rough diamonds. As part of the same beneficiation drive, the government also established the Okavango Diamond Trading Company, which independently handles 3 million carats of diamonds a year.

Sorting the diamonds is a complex, technological, labour-intensive process. It takes 1 500 employees, including 550 sorters, to sort the unpolished gemstones into 11 344 categories, which make up the 500 or so parcels on sale at each sight.[19]

With its cranes, traffic jams, new hotels and shiny skyscrapers, Gaborone is today a far cry from when Sir Seretse led the country to independence on 30 September 1966. Then, Botswana was one of the least developed and poorest nations in the world, its per capita income just $83, and most of its people dependent on subsistence agriculture. At independence there were fewer than 30 000 people in salaried employment, only about 50 university graduates, a low literacy rate, and scant access to healthcare, sanitation, water, telephones, electricity, public transport and other services. The country depended on British foreign aid to survive.

By the turn of the 21st century, Botswana's per capita GDP, at $7 300, was 15 per cent greater than that of its powerful neighbour South Africa. The reason for the success has centred on the state's partnership with De Beers to develop its diamond resources. Producing more than a quarter of the world's diamonds, the industry accounts for 35 per cent of Botswana's GDP and around 85 per cent of exports.

Botswana's dependence on diamonds, its best friend since independence, is almost total, a fact not lost on successive governments.

Finding the means to add greater domestic value has been a particular focus of the government of Ian Khama, eldest son of the independence leader, who became president in 2008 at 55. The Botswanan 'system' permits a new president to take over before the end of his predecessor's term, allowing him time in office before contesting a national election in his own right.

A former defence force commander, and still a keen aviator, Khama is forthright and clear about the foundation of the country's success. 'It is based on a cultural and traditional commitment to democracy,' he says, 'and what democracy entails. Unlike some, who twist the concept of democracy to suit themselves, we have stuck to these principles, in that everything we do should be in the interest of our citizens. This explains our tough stance on corruption – which is all about self-interest and self-promotion. From democracy and good governance,' he observes from his modest offices in Gaborone, 'stems everything else, including the prudent financial management of the economy.'

The commitment to democracy, Khama says, 'has little to do with colonial legacy, not least since the British capital of the territory was outside [the country], in Mafikeng. Rather, it is both cultural and dependent on leadership. More than being just a good intention, or rhetoric, the commitments to democracy and good governance are now deeply ingrained.'

Botswana has made several attempts at stimulating diversification. The Financial Assistance Policy, terminated in 1999, provided labour and capital subsidies to new ventures, but very few of the 3 000 operations that were launched under this programme survived. The Citizen Entrepreneurial Development Agency policy, which replaced it, offered low interest loans along with mentoring and support programmes.

In 2005 the Brenthurst Foundation helped to assemble a group of international specialists at the invitation of the government of Botswana to help devise a strategy for economic diversification. Out of these preliminary discussions emerged the Botswana Economic Advisory Committee (BEAC), later the Council, which was to oversee this strategy.

Khama points to tourism as a success story in the drive for diversification. Botswana has increased slightly its numbers of international visitors from 1.4 million arrivals in 2006 to 1.5 million in 2014.[20] In 2013 travel and tourism directly supported 31 000 jobs, or 4.6 per cent of total employment. The direct contribution of travel and tourism to GDP is estimated at $510 million, or 3.2 per cent of the country's total GDP in 2014.[21]

One of the early BEAC recommendations was to work to reduce the costs of doing business to below that of its nearest and greatest competitor, South Africa, with the aim of becoming the 'Mauritius of southern Africa' in the services sector. This strategy would not require subsidies, but would need a general improvement in the competitiveness environment by addressing the high value of its currency, one of the effects of natural-resource dependency and inflows, and the costs of banking and telecommunications.

The president referred to certain tensions between growth and stability that have to be constantly managed – the exchange rate, for one, in terms of balancing the need to keep inflation within a 3 to 6 per cent bracket yet low enough to ensure export competitiveness with Botswana's major trading partners. In the same context, he highlighted 'a difficult choice' that had to be made about what to do with the national airline, another BEAC hot topic, namely whether and how to prune costs versus using it as a strategic asset to bring in tourists and business people. Another early but still-born recommendation focused on positioning the airport as a regional cargo hub, along the lines of Memphis or Hong Kong.

The government replaced the BEAC with a joint government–private sector forum to get things done. Was the council a failure, then? 'It did good work, especially on strategic issues, but to make such bodies effective,' countered the president, 'you need to have all ministers and their permanent secretaries present.'

Still, in the BEAC's favour, the move into the diamond beneficiation business has created more than 2 000 jobs. But there are limits to this initiative, not least the comparative global costs of cutting and polishing the stones. This processing costs at least $45 per carat in Botswana but just $10 in India. And in South Africa the cost is at least three times higher than the Botswanan figure, which has encouraged the relocation of some SA-based businesses to the neighbouring country. Although the move of diamond trading from the UK has resulted in the relocation of 80 families to Gaborone, boosting local housing and other services, the relocation of the DTC has not yet led to the sort of boom in business travellers that had been envisaged, not least as sightholders often prefer to 'pop into' Botswana for a day from Johannesburg.

There are other challenges, notes President Khama, with diversification into manufacturing. 'When you sit next to a neighbour with an economy the size of South Africa's, who are extremely active in trying to attract FDI and who are calling themselves a regional gateway, it is more difficult. I find that labelling personally unfortunate, as it says that we in the region, around South Africa, should not be manufacturers, but only the market. This is not the only way that South Africa has stifled attempts at industrialisation in neighbouring states. They have also put in place trade measures to do so too. Yet they have a bigger market, more developed infrastructure, seaports and airports, and other big advantages. Still, we have tried to sell ourselves as being at the *centre*,' he stresses, 'of the southern African region, which is why we have invested in logistics.'

On specific failures, Khama singles out electricity: 'We used to rely on imports from Eskom in South Africa. When it became clear that Eskom could not adequately supply to its own market, and this made us vulnerable, we had to bring forward our plans to be energy self-sufficient by 2012. But we were let down by the contractor, as a result of which we are still now running helter-skelter to be not only self-sufficient, but an energy exporter in two to three years' time.'

When viewed through the prism of East Asia's success, it seems that, more than anything, success at diversification requires a laser focus on growth and development. What has Khama learnt about the role of leadership in this task?

'In my case,' smiles the president from behind a desk and next to shelves cluttered with martial bric-a-brac, 'I have no doubt that the military background had a big influence, especially on the nature of decision making and management. It was a very big plus in my life to have gone through the military. It prepares you for anything in life, and it's something that I will retain and won't let go of.

'In part, it also about what sort of character you are. I have pushed the issue of dignity and of showing compassion and care for fellow citizens during my time, especially those disadvantaged. Of course, your parents also have an influence. I was fortunate in having a father in this job too, and a mother concerned with charitable causes. These things together have helped me to deal with challenges.'

Here, in tackling poverty, Botswana had an advantage in Khama's leadership ethos. 'Always starting from a bad situation, you can make good.' But he concedes that there is a problem of apathy among his citizens. The guarantee of income from diamonds demotivates business to 'get out there'.

'Occasionally, we get offered opportunities, but we are laid back in leaping at them because of having diamonds. Also, there is a syndrome of dependency on government, since we were once so poor and have done a lot through social interventions. Many people probably get assistance who should be looking after themselves – this is a trend. The question they always have is, "What is government going to do for me?"

'Maybe what we have achieved through diamond revenues has made us complacent. But, we have to remember,' he points out, 'that diamonds are not forever.'

Reform in the Sahel

Nouakchott's fish market at the Plage des Pêcheurs (the fishermen's beach) is a place of great energy. Teams of men, some in oilskins, most barefoot, heave colourfully decorated pirogues up the beach. Others store away outboard engines and pack handmade nets. Boys and girls sell drinks and food, and donkey carts lug bags and boxes of fish. The concrete tables in the marketplace are piled with fish, the floor littered with discarded heads and entrails, while traders seal cooler boxes for the refrigerated trucks parked outside.[22]

Hundreds of traditional, open fishing boats line the shore. The seas off Mauritania's 754-kilometre coastline contain some of the world's richest fishing grounds, generating a quarter of the country's exports. But the industry is under pressure. As much as 1.2 million tonnes of fish are caught in Mauritanian waters annually, though fishermen complain that they have to go as far as 30 kilometres offshore to make their catch. In July 2015 the EU renewed a 20-year agreement with Mauritania allowing EU vessels to trawl up to 281 500 tonnes annually in return for commercial payment and an aid package to support local fishing and environmental controls. Commercial trawlers can net up to 250 tonnes of fish daily; a pirogue might do 5 tonnes a year. Chinese, Russian and South Korean trawlers are, like the Europeans, drawn to the area by increasing consumer demand and declining stocks back home. It is estimated that more than a third of the fish caught off West Africa is illegal, unreported or unregulated, losing $1.3 billion in annual income.

Plans are afoot to extract more value from fishing and better integrate the industry into the Mauritanian economy. Doing so will require a break from the past, including making considerable investment in infrastructure, implanting a new set of policies and ensuring a new way of doing things.

This industry will be a key test for a country which, if it walks its own talk, could become a regional exemplar.

Together with water scarcity, populist temptations including Islam, and fictions of local statehood across an area of more than 6 million square kilometres, the Sahel scene is set for chronic failure. Throw in climate change and soil degradation (already estimated by the UN Food and Agriculture Organization as affecting over 80 per cent of the Sahel) and a predominantly young population, and one should expect migration, both south and north, on a grand scale. The region's population is projected to increase from 135 million to 330 million by 2050 and an estimated 670 million by 2100.

Until now, the role of the international community has been to manage the tactical extremes, and to try to bolster state, and especially military, capacity in places where there are fundamental issues of control of society and territory at stake. This approach is likely only to stave off rather than solve these problems, especially where it's not always clear who the government and the good guys are.

Nouakchott – the 'place of winds' – was created afresh as the capital upon independence from France in 1960, when just 10 000 lived in what was little more than a fishing village. Now home to perhaps 1.5 million people, or a third of Mauritania's population, the city is pockmarked with grey concrete residences under construction. There are no physical city limits to the urban spread across the apparently endless expanse. 'If you have a thing about sand,' observes one diplomat, 'you should not be here.' Sprawl and poverty place different but extreme strains on infrastructure.

The country's troubled political history has not helped either. There have been a dozen coups or attempted coups since independence, the first in 1978, which ended the rule of independence leader, Moktar Daddah. A military junta controlled the country until 1992, when the first multi-party elections were held. Another bloodless coup in August 2005 oversaw a transition to democracy. Although Sidi Ould Cheikh Abdellahi was inaugurated in April 2007 as the country's first free and fairly elected president, his term ended abruptly in August 2008 with a putsch led by General Mohamed Ould Abdel Aziz. The general was subsequently elected president in July 2009 and re-elected to a second, and apparently final term, in 2014 with 82 per cent of the vote. Both events, however, were boycotted by various opposition movements.

Although there have been significant reforms – in the freedom of the media, for example – Mauritania's political system remains classified 'not free' by Freedom House. The country's divisions appear to run deeper than its democracy. There remain ethnic and racial tensions among three major groups: the Arabic-speaking descendants of slaves (Haratines), who make up around 40 per cent of the population; Arabic-speaking so-called 'white

Moors' (Bidhan), forming 30 per cent; and the remainder, Afro-Mauritanians originating from the Senegal River Valley to the south. As Bidhan Mauritanians occupy most elite positions in government and business, there is a tense public debate about slavery and its effects.

Despite such differences and adverse conditions, there is a strong sense of national attachment and resourcefulness. 'We still think like nomads,' explains a veteran local politician, 'to our cost. We dump rubbish where we choose, and have no permanence. It reflects in the way in which we drive.' Mauritania is one of the few countries where you will be routinely overtaken while waiting at a red traffic light, a place where old Peugeots and battered Mercedes taxis come to die. 'But being nomads,' he smiles, 'also means we can survive the toughest conditions.'

Mauritania's image outside of the country remains tainted. This is compounded by challenges in doing business. It is ranked 168th out of 189 countries in the World Bank's 2016 Ease of Doing Business indicators. Investors say they are hampered by erratic tax practices, and an inefficient and corrupt legal system.

None of this, however, is lost on government. The prime minister's chief of staff, Mohamed Djibril, admits that dealing with corruption and ensuring inclusive government are items two and three on the government's list of top three priorities – the first being to 'develop the private sector, without which it is impossible to create jobs'.

There are deeper challenges, though. Ahmed Mahmoud Dahan, a former Minister of Foreign Affairs and, later, Islamic Affairs, and now the head of the Institute for Strategic Studies in Nouakchott, says the state was 'established by the colonial authorities principally for extraction. After independence, it was replaced by a state to serve the executive. As a result,' he says, 'power is all-important, as the state is virtually the sole source of jobs.' Predictably, therefore, in the government, until now 'there has been little incentive for change'.

This view is echoed by Prime Minister Yahya Ould Hademine. With a background in the state iron-ore mining company, Hademine also has clear ideas of what needs to be done. Appointed in August 2014, the Canadian-educated technocrat identifies the first constraint as the fact that 'Mauritania was not a state before independence. We have had to construct institutions and educate our people to enter modernity. Now, after 50 years, we have reached the level of countries like Senegal, at least, which has been doing this for hundreds of years.' This situation was made more difficult by 'a big 20-year drought in the 1970s, which seriously affected our livestock-based society, and increased the rate of urbanisation. But then we had to provide new infrastructure in the cities – potable water, roads, services, policing – as well as attempt to deliver,' he says, 'over a large territory.'

On top of these constraints, he says, there is also a need for increased investment, an improved legal system and justice. These efforts have been complicated by the rise of 'violent extremism'. The government has identified three fields for growth and jobs: fishing, agriculture and livestock. 'We aim to add more value to fishing,' says Hademine. 'Whereas Morocco has just half of our production, it has 500 000 workers. Senegal produces one-quarter of what we do, but has 400 000. We have just 36 000. The Free Zone initiative in the [northern port of] Nouadhibou aims to change this, as will the development of smaller ports along the coast.' The government plans to spend as much as $1 billion on the fishing industry alone.

It's slightly more complicated, however, given that the local fishing industry is dominated by Senegalese. Many menial jobs go to foreigners, mostly from West Africa.

'In agriculture,' says the prime minister, 'the plan is to prepare the land to the south along the Senegal River, where we have hundreds of thousands of hectares available. We already produce 80 per cent of our rice requirement in this area.' A focus on these areas would build on the success of the mining sector, he says.

What about the to-and-fro steps regarding democracy?

'You have to understand that Mauritania is not exactly like all African countries,' replies Prime Minister Hademine. 'Our population has a long cultural history. In the Middle Ages they conquered Spain and Morocco, so convincing them of the need for new rules of governance requires a different approach from other African populations who learnt how to read with the coming of the colonial power. Our path is thus one of small steps.'

These 'steps' include the debate around inclusive government, which some see as a proxy, however, for extending the president's rule to a third term. With a proactive leadership role in the AU and the Arab League, the government is surprisingly defensive about its international engagement. Even though it has made a long-term regional commitment to fighting violent extremism, France is routinely fingered as the culprit when things go awry, as is Israel, since Nouakchott cut ties with Jerusalem in 2009. And there is a suspicion that foreign workers and investors take jobs from Mauritanians, hence there are strict terms companies need to follow when transferring jobs from expats to locals, which can be a balancing act between local empowerment and appeasement, on the one hand, and continued competitiveness on the other.

Yet, ironically, Mauritania's greatest strength lies in its relationship with the international community. In the Sahel, it is a standout country given its relative security, enabling it to link, rather than divide, North Africa and sub-Saharan Africa.

Côte d'Ivoire: Catching up from conflict

In 1983 President Félix Houphouët-Boigny declared his birth place of Yamoussoukro, 250 kilometres from Abidjan, to be Côte d'Ivoire's administrative capital. Strung out across wide boulevards lined with tall street lamps, more Parisian than provincial, there was a new parliament, convention centre and an international airport capable of taking Concorde. The centrepiece was the Basilica of Our Lady of Peace, named in gratitude for the country's stability since independence, and built on a coconut plantation donated by the president himself. With its 158-metre-high, 100-metre-diameter dome and expansive piazza inspired by Saint Peter's Basilica in Rome, it was completed in 1990, involving 1 500 workers from 36 companies working a 24/7 schedule over three years. With 7 400 square metres of stained-glass windows – including one depicting Palm Sunday and featuring Houphouët, the architects and contractors – and seven hectares of marble, the basilica is listed as the largest church in the world, capable of hosting 200 000 worshippers inside and out.

The trickle of pilgrims and visitors to the 'Bush Basilica' in Yamoussoukro suggests that Houphouët's dramatic gesture was misplaced in a country where just a third of the population is Christian. Such grand gestures were much less valuable to the young country than the investment in a generation of skills during Houphouët's 33 years in office.

To the contrary, construction of the new capital signalled the start of quarter century of financial and political crisis in Côte d'Ivoire.[23]

The country gained its independence from France in August 1960, when Houphouët, a nurse who became one of the country's wealthiest farmers, assumed the presidency. He inherited an economy geared towards the export of cocoa, coffee and palm oil, which made up 40 per cent of the entire region's exports. Côte d'Ivoire's economy was dominated by a sizeable population of French 'settlers', numbering about 50 000 in the 1970s out of a local population of just 7 million.

The president promoted agriculture, a sector in which mainly immigrant Burkinabé smallholders worked on farmland owned by urbanised Ivorians, cultivating coffee, cocoa and rubber.

As many as a quarter of the population today are foreigners.[24] On the Boulevard Valéry Giscard d'Estaing, leading to Abidjan's airport, there is a crossroads, 'Le Carrefour du Kumasi', named after the Ghanaian city. The Abidjan suburb of Treichville, around the port, is dominated by Senegalese. And there has been a more recent influx of migrants from the Sahel.

For two decades after independence, Côte d'Ivoire maintained an annual rate of economic growth of more than 10 per cent. Agricultural output increased threefold over this period.[25] By the 1970s, the country had become the world's third largest coffee producer (behind Brazil and Colombia) and the leading producer of cocoa. Even today, the country produces 40 per cent of the world's cocoa crop. It was Africa's largest producer of pineapples and palm oil, and, overall, its economy was second only to Nigeria's in West Africa. GDP doubled in the 1960s, as did literacy, and virtually every town had roads and electricity. Not for nothing was Abidjan labelled the 'Paris of West Africa', its Plateau district a cosmopolitan hub of commerce, people and nightlife.

But these manifestations of development flattered to deceive, and the collapse was sudden.

A decline in the price of cocoa coupled with the burden of excessive state spending caused growth to crash in 1979, a fall from which it did not recover until the mid-1990s, and then only temporarily. In the process, per capita income fell from $1 230 in 1979 to under $600 by 1995,[26] exacerbated by a threefold increase in population from 4 million at independence to 12 million by 1990. A decline in external trade was made worse by the overvaluation of the regional CFA Franc, a situation that favoured the spending habits of the elite.

When Houphouët stayed beyond his anticipated exit on the 25th anniversary of independence, business adopted a wait-and-see attitude rather than investing in the economy. And a culture of corruption had begun to bite. As Houphouët's rule faltered, administrative weakness was exposed. The private stabilisation fund for cocoa established in the 1990s was empty, raided with impunity by the administrative elite. Political crisis and change paralleled economic stress. GDP tumbled as the country's external debt trebled. Between 1985 and 2008, the share of the population estimated to be living below the poverty line increased fivefold to 49 per cent.[27]

In the process, Côte d'Ivoire exhibited five trends that typically serve as a harbinger of policy radicalism, socio-economic upset and even state failure:[28] economic crisis, usually signalled by an absence of growth; widespread corruption, including a focus on redistribution rather than wealth creation; exclusion of a large chunk of the population from opportunity on the basis of social division (education or gender) or racial division (including ethnic and religious aspects); large-scale migration, including immigration; and the presence of the wrong leader at a crucial time.

The situation worsened with the chaos that followed Houphouët's death at the age of 88 in 1993. Lacking the old man's national appeal, those who followed found it all too easy to play the identity card – xenophobia – spurred on by a combination of economic difficulties and the widespread immigration encouraged in earlier times.

The political career of Alassane Dramane Ouattara, commonly known as 'ADO', the president since 2010, illustrates the complexity – and temptation – of ethnic politics in the region. With a PhD in economics from the University of Pennsylvania, the president had worked for the IMF before and after his stint as prime minister, and as governor of the Central Bank of West African States in Dakar.

'During the crisis of the 1980s,' he recalls, 'I was called from the Central Bank to help stabilise the situation. Although I wanted to go back to the bank, in November 1990 I was appointed as prime minister. The results of the measures we carried out were quite good. The deficit was curbed and governance improved. The president had been in power for 30 years and governance problems were massive.

'Then the president died, and the economic problems,' he notes, 'moved into a second political phase of problems. The new president

[Henri Konan-Bédié] tried to reverse all of the reforms, including the traditional openness of our society and our economy. He even,' he says with a smile, 'tried to declare me ineligible for the presidency.'

Konan-Bédié was forced out in late 1999 by a military coup led by General Robert Guéï. Then Laurent Gbagbo came to power in October 2000 following elections marred by violence. Ouattara was disqualified from running due to his allegedly being of Burkinabé nationality. Protests culminated in a September 2002 armed uprising, when troops mutinied, launching attacks in several cities, and France deployed soldiers to stop the rebel advance.

When Guéï was killed, Ouattara took refuge in the French embassy, and Gbagbo returned home to negotiate an accord resulting in a government of national unity. Amid ongoing violence, Gbagbo's original mandate as president, which expired on 30 October 2005, was extended until elections were finally held in October/November 2010.

Despite a high voter turnout of over 80 per cent and a clear victory for Ouattara, Gbagbo simply would not accept the results. His pursuit of a course of destructive and violent action was, in the words of one diplomat based in the country at the time, 'the crystallisation of Côte d'Ivoire's economic and political collapse; while the international intervention to ensure the installation of a democratically elected leader was a clear effort to put the country back on to a path of economic and political liberal growth. It worked.'[29]

Gbagbo was eventually evicted from his hideout in Abidjan in April 2011 by UN forces. In November 2011, he became the first former head of state to be extradited to The Hague by the International Criminal Court.

'When I was prime minister, life expectancy was nearly 60 years,' reflects Ouattara. 'By 2010, it had fallen to just 50. The situation was terrible. There was complete disorder in the army. The judicial system was non-operational. More than 3 000 people had been killed.

'So, our first objective was to bring security to the country. Once this was achieved, we had to get back to the fundamentals of good economic policy. This included reinstating a democratic system, which had suffered under the ethnic politics of Gbagbo,' he says, '[and] where just 5 per cent of the population controlled the army and police. But we learnt from the American experience in Iraq. We did not fire the entire army but engaged in an extensive process of DDR [disarmament, demobilisation and reintegration].

'The reintegration of the militia was made easier,' he acknowledges in an easy-going manner, 'by the economic growth we enjoyed. This was in part due to our reforms but was helped by better terms of trade. The price of cocoa saw farmers earn twice the revenues between 2012 and 2016, and their production is also up by 50 per cent.'

The average real growth rate reached 8.5 per cent annually between 2012 and 2015, one of the highest in sub-Saharan Africa. It reflects rising investment across sectors, including government. Whereas just 5 per cent of the budget was earmarked for investment in 2012, says Ouattara, this had risen four years later to more than 30 per cent.[30] Côte d'Ivoire has become Africa's catch-up country.

'At the same time,' says the president, 'we have put emphasis on infrastructure, especially energy.' Electricity output nearly doubled to 2 000 megawatts from 2012 to 2016.

Ouattara admits that things on the 'social front' have not gone as well as on the economy and security fronts. One tactic he adopted was to set up presidential councils – on education, higher education, electricity, water and infrastructure. 'Once we get the full picture from them, then I take a decision on the way forward.'

Another 'weak point', he admits, is in the judicial system. And reconciliation, he says, 'has not been done as well as I would have liked'.

The government has drafted a $50 billion, five-year national development plan. With its 1 400 projects, say critics, the plan is too unfocused. This reflects the challenge of building a competitive economy, and in so doing 'upgrading the software', says Eric Kacou, a locally based, Harvard-trained economist, 'to create a vibrant private sector, and not just support a class of traders and middlemen'.[31]

As the saga of the economic collapse in Houphouët's declining years illustrates, there are clear limits (and costs) to government, macro-led growth. Prosperity tends to flow from microeconomic policy specifics and not the margin from trade or big projects, or living off government quotas and contracts. The success of the transition from public- to private-sector growth will determine the country's economic and political future. This transformation will require, in Côte d'Ivoire as elsewhere, incentivised performance and employment in economic activity, and not simply rewarding proximity to power.

Ouattara agrees. 'Ivorians have not been business-minded in the past. The country was living off cocoa, through farming and through intermediation in logistics. Most industries belonged to the French, and many of these were sold to Lebanese after the French were chased away by Gbagbo in 2004.' Although there are incentives for local firms in tendering, Ouattara does not believe in 'institutionalising advantages to favour the locals. This type of scheme is against me as a liberal. Such liberal policies have worked well for Côte d'Ivoire for decades, and will continue to do so.'

What lessons does he have for other African leaders?

'The first is that you really have to work hard. I am sorry to say that in many countries the leaders are only there to try to please people. Instead, they need to get to the details, and manage the country like an enterprise.

'Secondly, success depends on having an open process, which requires determining what people want, and adjusting policies to suit.

'Thirdly, it is very important for African economies to strengthen their systems of freedom, including the institutions that go with this, and freedom of expression, which goes with innovation and development. This requires a strong but disciplined opposition, which is part of this process.

'Success,' he says, 'requires addressing the future. Our big challenge is how to ensure the youth do not get discouraged. We have created 2 million jobs in the past few years, and we have one of the lowest unemployment rates in Africa, which is one reason why we attract so many workers from elsewhere in the region. But I am not satisfied with this. If we are to prevent major disturbances in the future we have to address the concerns of the youth. This means,' he observes, 'addressing education and focusing on technical education and not just classical education.

'I think I was very lucky', Ouattara says. 'I always tell my ministers that the fact I worked for an organisation like the IMF has helped me, where quality and competence are important, and performance can be measured. In my second stint there – between 1994 and 1999 – I focused on Latin American and Asian countries, particularly in managing problems of debt and inflation management, but also in understanding the growth record, especially in Asia.

'Being in the US as a student and later too in my career, also helped to shape my views on liberal policy and democracy. These two attributes are essential for Africans. The era of the old socialist ideals, where you are spending money you don't have and you cannot find work, is gone. And if you are to get yourself out of a difficult situation,' he says, 'I have learnt you have to do this for yourself.'

Conclusion: Constituencies of winners

There has been no shortage of African leaders who have asked for sacrifices from their citizens. However, their calls have usually not been coupled with a national vision and with the execution of detailed policies to convince people of a new future. Those with means are instead tempted to join the portion of the economy dominated by patronage not because they are ill-meaning, but because that is the easiest way to ensure their escape from poverty to prosperity.

The coming demographic surge and the concomitant challenge posed by huge numbers of unemployed young people should allow willing African leaders to create a narrative that justifies difficult decisions. The great growth in populations and the threat of restive young people are easily understood issues, especially as they are a continuation of trends that have been occurring for quite some time. Large numbers of urban unemployed youth will not be a distant crisis in a strategically unimportant rural area, but will become an obvious threat to the heart of the state.

Basing the narrative on this demographic threat can also be a national unifier because no particular group can be blamed for it.

Many African national plans to date have been wasted opportunities. Broad statements that cover many issues over long time frames with limited hopes for execution will not mobilise the constituencies that African leaders need to drive reform. These plans have to be fundamentally changed if they are to convey the urgency and resolve needed to address key issues and to focus limited resources.

Devising a national narrative – an engaging script – is essential to explain the chosen course of action, the need for hard and sometimes painful choices, and to win public support. No knockout blows are likely to result from conducting reforms, and pursuing development, as in war. As Lawrence Freedman observes, in politics, as in business and warfare, initial successes are hardly ever decisive: power has to be consolidated through governance, ongoing innovation and delivery.

Of course, African leaders will have to develop their own tactics to put across the sense of urgency and prove that they are materially attentive to the needs of their citizens. President Álvaro Uribe's performance in Colombia bears study, as he was instrumental in turning that country around within a decade from a failing to a functioning state. Presented with a huge security challenge, he nonetheless refused to stay in Bogotá, opting instead to go out every weekend to visit municipalities and talk to local people. He often gave them his personal phone number and encouraged them to call him if they had a security-related problem. Uribe used these visits to understand the challenges and drive change.[32] African leaders will have to give similar thought to what kinds of profiles they should adopt in order to change the prevailing political culture.

A particular challenge for African leaders is to identify and cultivate constituencies for reform. At the start of the reform process, it is much easier to see who will lose out than who will ultimately benefit. The benefits of long-term reforms are difficult to sell to a needy population. New investment and entrepreneurial activity take time and it may not be possible for those who will ultimately become better off to envision their own successful futures in 10 or 15 years. Or, as one South African local-government councillor put it to us, 'You can't eat policy.'[33]

On the other hand, those who depend on the old order can immediately see the writing on the wall and will fight viciously to defend the status quo. Among the finer political arts is for leaders to move to where constituencies invest in the future rather than simply doing the political maths of the moment; this will be critical to developing long-term support for reform.

In cultivating constituencies for reform, leaders should show ostentatiously that they are competent, focused and able to deliver.[34] Their personal example could incentivise more of society to cast their lot with reform. Leaders who delay and move slowly will be less able to attract supporters who will inevitably have to wait longer to see the fruits of their allegiances.

Conclusion

Kashim Shettima is the governor of Borno State, the epicentre of the Boko Haram insurgency. Elected in 2011, he does not hide his obvious frustration or mince his words about the challenges faced by society there: 'Underneath Boko Haram is the cause – extreme poverty. All of this born out of economic deprivation.'

The poverty has been aggravated by Nigeria's high rate of population growth. From an official population of 185 million today, by 2020, Shettima notes, 'Nigeria will be at 206 million people; by 2030, 262 million; and, by 2050, 398 million, making it the third most populous country in the world.' By then, he says, '70 per cent of Nigerians will live in northern Nigeria', with its 'cocktail of desertification, youth unemployment and low output. There is no part,' he says, 'of the north immune from this madness.'

The road north to Jaji from the capital, Abuja, offers plenty of evidence of the scale of the challenge. Stores line the highway, selling bottles of palm oil, guinea-fowl eggs, corn, and soil-encrusted yams. In one of the so-called 'tanker towns', more than a hundred fuel tankers have pulled over for the drivers to take refreshments 'of various sorts', explains our guide. Small businesses operate ceaselessly in the heat and amid the dust, cooking and selling food, making furniture, changing and patching tyres, and repairing cars, trucks and motorbikes.

The chaotic roadside scenes are a reminder of the strength of the human spirit, the seemingly irrepressible ingenuity of Nigerians and the costs of weak governance.

An agricultural economist by training, Shettima rattles off statistics illustrating Nigeria's plight: 'While we import potatoes from South Africa, tomato paste from China and cabbages from the United States, which are repackaged in Dubai, 70 per cent of our farmers are in the drudgery of subsistence agriculture. Whereas our cows produce a litre of milk per day, Europe can do 40 times this amount. While entrepreneurial capitalism is embedded in the very psyche of Nigerians,' he laments, 'we lack the technical skills and organisation.'

As a result, despite its rich soils and plentiful rainfall, Nigeria is a net food importer. Even though agriculture employs two-thirds of the labour force, the UN's FAO calculates that over the past 20 years, value-added per capita in agriculture has risen by less than 1 per cent annually. The FAO estimates that Nigeria has forfeited $10 billion in annual export opportunities from groundnut and palm oil, cocoa and cotton alone. Nigeria consumes 5 million tonnes of rice a year, at least 3 million of which are imported. Though it is the largest producer of cassava in the world, the average yield is estimated at under 14 tonnes per hectare; the potential yield is up to 40 tonnes. Equally, productivity of other cereals remains low, at around 1.2 tonnes per hectare compared with, for example, South African farms, which average three times this yield.[1]

The reasons for the poor agricultural performance are high interest rates and the resultant lack of investment, the lack of large-scale commercial plantations, scant use of fertiliser, and an absence of extension services. Underlying this poor performance have been the dominance of crude oil as a source of national revenue and the lack of will to diversify as long as the price was high.

Nigeria and the many challenges it is facing should serve as a warning to other African states and their leaders. Oil, a geological endowment that few countries can match, did not insulate Nigeria from the extraordinary challenges its government now faces. Indeed, oil may have made everything worse. Unless reform is undertaken now to produce sustainable economies that create jobs, Africa's fast-growing population, desperate for employment, will soon overwhelm state institutions in many countries. In fact, Africa has seen a 2.5 times increase in the number of public protests since 2000. And, not surprisingly, the protestors' top three demands are salary increases, better working conditions and calls for the dissolution of government and for the head of state to step down. Without progress, these sorts of protests are likely to increase in number, threatening the stability of the continent and the tenure of its governments and leaders.

Admittedly, Nigeria has many social fault lines and economic challenges, but other countries have faced similar conditions and difficulties, and done well. Indonesia, for one, shows how things might be different, despite the fact that country experienced a rapid post-independence increase in population, a reliance on natural resources (particularly oil) for export income, a challenging and discontiguous geography and topography, religious and ethnic schisms, and weak infrastructure. The difference between the two population giants of sub-Saharan Africa and South East Asia is, in blunt terms, leadership. Indonesia experienced much improved economic growth following Suharto's forced takeover in the mid-1960s from the independence icon Sukarno. Despite the misty-eyed retro mythology surrounding Sukarno, his rule was neither democratic, nor did it deliver development. Instead, as corruption and inefficiency throttled growth, he relied on a combination of personal charisma, anti-Western gesturing and grand-scale heroic architecture to get by. By the time he left government under house arrest, inflation was at 1 000 per cent. For all his corruption, nepotism and the repressive nature of his dictatorship, Suharto brought economic order and growth in three decades of rule. Not for nothing is he known as *Bapak Pembangunan* ('Father of Development') to the serial polygamist Sukarno's *Bung* ('buddy').

Suharto's plan focused on improving agro-yields, and gradually liberalising and internationalising the economy to secure investment in export-oriented manufacturing industries. Indonesia produced its first rice surplus in 1983 as a result of improved yields and per capita output. By the late 1980s, Indonesia had become not only an agricultural exporter, but also an exporter of textiles, footwear, clothing and consumer goods.[2] In the 1960s and early 1970s, Indonesia's per capita income was less than Nigeria's. As Figure 1 shows, by the mid-1980s, however, with Nigeria beset by political instability and mismanagement, Indonesia had started to surge ahead. While things have evened out since the oil price rise of the 2010s and as governance has improved in Nigeria, Indonesians are today still on average richer than Nigerians. However, inequality in Indonesia is much lower comparatively.[3]

An imperative of long-term growth and good governance is what separates Indonesia's development trajectory from Africa's. It also explains why South East Asia has enjoyed growth in jobs, as opposed to just economic growth. This necessitated a plan for improved prosperity that entrepreneurs can take advantage of – a plan that was also implemented by successive governments, including Suharto's and those since, each of them steadily improving on and extending the country's governance framework. While Indonesia's success illustrates the importance of setting the context, Suharto's

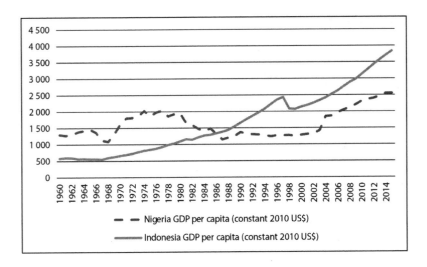

Figure 1: Different paths, different policies: Nigeria and Indonesia, 1960–2014

Source: World Bank national accounts data and OECD national accounts data files, http://databank.worldbank.org/data/reports.aspx?source=world-development-indicators&preview=on#

downfall after three decades of rule paradoxically illustrates the most important reason of all for Indonesia's success – a commitment to popular welfare. Contrary to the notion that an authoritarian state is required for development, Indonesians were willing to accept Suharto's autocratic regime only when it delivered growth. When Suharto's excesses outweighed his successes and the corruption proved too great a burden to bear, the old system of 'guided democracy' gave way to parliamentary democracy.[4]

Other sectoral studies in this book provide similarly important observations for how African leaders might transform the oncoming demographic wave into a positive economic dynamic. In particular, we have demonstrated that other countries, particularly in Asia and South and Central America, have resolved similar crises, turned their economies around, lifted their people out of poverty and created the jobs and housing that were needed. Although it is late in the day, action can still be taken that will make a huge difference to the lives of millions of young Africans in search of jobs and to the lives of those yet to be born.

Changing the narrative

As we have noted from the outset in this book, development is no longer a mystery but a well-understood process that a fair number of countries have successfully undertaken. The foundations for success lie in getting the politics and leadership right. After that, important lessons learnt by other countries can be implemented.

Central to the turnaround of many countries, enabling them to implement pro-growth policies, was creating a sense of urgency, a realisation that business as usual would lead to disaster. Several Asian countries, including our case studies of Singapore and Indonesia, and also South Korea and Taiwan, were able to use their crises to create a narrative that allowed leaders to implement difficult policies and to explain why changes were needed. Leaders were able to show first that the state itself, protector of the current population, would be threatened if difficult decisions were not made immediately.

Secondly, by implementing good policies, leaders were able to convince their citizens that the sacrifices demanded would not be in vain but would, in fact, result in a better economy and society for their children because the government was a competent steward of the economy.

Themes for driving reform

Each African country must devise a reform agenda that is appropriate for its circumstances. African countries naturally have different histories and trajectories; they are organised in different ways. Their economies are different: some are oil rich; some are single commodity dependent; some are more urbanised than others; some are failed or failing; most, but not all, are dependent on food and fuel imports. Some are big geographically, but with small populations. Just three – the DRC, Nigeria and Ethiopia – account for nearly 40 per cent of sub-Saharan Africa's total population. Others are tiny: 15 countries[5] make up just over 2 per cent of the continent's population. Not all small African countries are rich but, with the exception of South Africa, all relatively rich countries have small populations.

But there are also commonalities. Most countries are poor, have weak governmental structures, are not orientated to promoting private-sector growth, and have not convinced their citizens of the urgency of reform. Most are facing the prospect of a huge population boom in their cities.

As a result, there are several common themes across the case studies that should inform African government leaders. Firstly, short-term benefits from reform are very difficult to perceive, but big changes are possible over a five- to ten-year time frame. The scope of the changes we suggest in agriculture, mining, manufacturing and other sectors are significant, but the benefits will take time to become apparent. However, the power of compound growth rates can soon assert itself. Whether it is the rise in fortunes of Singapore, agriculture in Vietnam, or manufacturing in Mexico, countries can change fundamentally over a decade or two. The lack of very short-term deliverables (indeed, there may be short-term pain) makes the creation of a narrative all the more important.

Secondly, there has to be a premium on getting things done. To tackle national priorities, there needs to be a hard-headed, ruthless prioritisation that focuses available government capacity on delivering the essential elements of a reform programme. For instance, the aversion to employing foreigners, who could supply badly needed skills, should be abandoned. Foreign human resources should be regarded as assets that are needed to drive progress. Outsiders, of course, cannot guarantee execution and it would spell trouble if the outsiders want the problem fixed more than the local citizens. African leaders must be seen by their own bureaucracies as just as unwilling to accept failure as Asian leaders were during their critical growth periods. Certainly, part of Rwanda and Ethiopia's success is that the leaders are vitally interested in government performance.

In particular, leaders need to be supported by an effective civil service. If the civil service, as an institution, does not work efficiently, people will fall back on other networks to make 'stuff happen'. Therefore, ensuring the civil service is both trusted and effective needs to be high up the agenda.

Governor Shettima observes in the context of Nigeria's challenges that '[President] Buhari has brought something remarkably un-Nigerian: integrity along with austerity'. This focus is required because, as the governor puts it, 'corruption has become intolerable. While there are tolerable and intolerable levels of corruption, today it has become the aim on its own, which is unsustainable.'

A focus on implementation does not have to be the exclusive preserve of well-meaning authoritarian regimes. 'It is in our enlightened self-interest to work for the interests of the people,' says Shettima. 'People hate Nigeria's leadership with a passion. They are contemptuous about it. We need a much more realistic approach to solving problems.' Doing so will demand strong leadership to challenge the system of spoils based largely on ethnicity, religion and geography, and supplant it with a meritocracy. Transparency and rule of law are key. These are traits supported by a democratic system of government.

Thirdly, there has to be a focus on what the state must do and what it should not do. Our case studies reveal that there is a vital role for the state in setting up a business environment that promotes confidence and growth, and in developing robust institutions. Given the limited human and material capacity of African governments, it is also important to understand what states should not do, so that they can focus on the initiatives that they are required to lead. In many African countries, excessive bureaucracy is serving to constrict economic growth by adding a huge administrative burden to businesses. The onus should be on government to reduce bureaucracy by, for example, cutting the number of permits required by businesses to operate and by making it straightforward to obtain them; or, to take another example, by simplifying – or removing – visa regulations to make it easy for tourists and business people to visit.

Fourth, tremendous energy and attention must be devoted to developing a healthy private sector. Businesses in many African countries are currently incentivised to live off the patronage that the state provides because there are few other ways to make money. If jobs are to be created, businesses must assume their proper role of generating investment and creating employment. It is critical that the banking and insurance markets are made to work more effectively with proper, but not onerous, supervision.

Government must also provide and sponsor infrastructure, so that the transactional costs that businesses face are limited. Our case studies of successful projects reveal that competent states undertake complex things, like building ports or canals. The exact mix will vary from country to country. Even the most efficient firms cannot compete on a global level if they pay too much for erratic electricity supplies, if the roads prevent prompt shipments, and if their goods are held up in dysfunctional harbours.

Finally, the proper role of financial resources should be understood. There remains significant international goodwill towards the continent – for reasons both of altruism and self-interest. If African leaders create a policy context where resources, including aid, can be used productively, international assistance will be bountiful. This can be most useful in supporting democratic institutions, infrastructure and skills. But outsiders cannot solve Africa's problems: at best they can help, though they can also make them worse when they act in isolation. African leaders are mistaken if they believe that any estimate of likely international assistance will be enough to deal with their challenges in the near future or that blaming the international community for insufficient aid will gain them any credibility among their citizens. Instead, they should concern themselves with the detail of domestic reform.

Our experience in planning in many countries highlights that it is both possible and necessary to distinguish between cross-cutting and specific sectoral actions when planning reforms. Moreover, despite being founded on solid analysis of the constraints, African reform initiatives are often characterised by sweeping, big-picture reforms with unrealistic goals. There is a need to break these down into deliverable actions. Table 1 brings together these 'deliverables', the various actions for success recommended in this volume.

Table 1: Summary of steps for success

People and cities	
	• Cities must be seen as drivers of Africa's diversified growth and jobs. Urban-centred growth represents a dramatic change from the export of natural resources, which has been central to most African economies.
	• Urgent action is the only way to address the pending urban-population explosion.
	• Focus on city-level funding and authority as a means to redefine the resources to enable local governments to meet the challenge of quickly expanding populations.
	• Promote density of housing and cost-efficient transport solutions to realise the urban dividend.
	• Focus on the provision of local security as the door through which much else follows.

Democracy and development	• Democracy and development are indivisible. Democratic government represents the interests of the general population, and not just an elite.
	• The bouts of stability that authoritarians can bring must be viewed sceptically, given the superior global economic performance and stability of democratic governments over the long term.
	• Democracies must be crafted to address the particular political, economic and demographic challenges that countries face.
	• Democracy is vital to the empowerment of cities because only democratic leaders are able to devolve power.
	• A democracy playbook' is necessary to meet the threats to democratic elections and institutions.
Infrastructure	• Infrastructure development requires a long-term approach to support projects that may take many years to complete, and to maintain the confidence of investors.
	• Clear revenue models for capital infrastructure projects must be developed at the outset.
	• The critical role of the private sector in infrastructure development will be influenced by the extent of public-sector monopolies.
	• Infrastructure must be carefully linked to policy on trade, connectivity, skills and openness.
	• The construction of housing can be supported by giving local authorities greater autonomy, pursuing a policy of increasing density in cities, simplifying the procedures for land title and supporting initiatives for affordable housing.
Agriculture	• Eliminate government distortions of agriculture pricing.
	• Deal with fears of food shortages through better market forecasting.
	• Ensure government policies embrace modern farming practices, including mechanisation, economies of scale and greater yields.
	• Ensure security of long-term title for farmers, whether by leasehold or freehold.
	• Improving logistics is critical to success in both food production and non-food agriculture exports.

Mining	• Improve policy and investor certainty. Stable, efficient and transparent regulatory and administrative processes are vital investment determinants for mining companies. • Develop a compelling, forward-looking, realistic narrative with the mining sector about the role it will play in national development, and stick to it. • Further beneficiation is dependent on cheap electricity and domestic manufacturing opportunities. • Appreciate the logistics systems needed for investment in bulk minerals (especially iron and coal) and the immense costs involved. • Government policy has to reflect the realities of fluctuations in commodity prices and the long-term needs of investors.
Manufacturing	• Attract manufacturing businesses migrating from China, understanding exactly what these businesses require to 'move to Africa'. • Attracting manufacturing business will depend on being more competitive than one's worldwide rivals. • Government should tackle bureaucratic delays and reduce opportunities for corruption, as these are essential elements of setting the business environment for success. • Use trade policy, preferences and agreements to drive industrial development rather than 'industrial strategy'. • Higher-value 'mindfacturing' depends on developing basic manufacturing skills and complementing them with relevant education, research and training institutions.
Services	• The service sector needs to be actively nurtured by governments, with a focus on providing the required infrastructure and regulatory environment. • Keep government costs (and overheads) low, and match ambition with pragmatism, and growth will follow, as has been shown in the case of airlines like Ethiopian and Emirates. • Assist the development of a domestic tourism industry by making access easier than that of competitors. This includes making it easy to acquire visas and reducing the costs and hassle of running hotels, through single-permit processes.

	• Establish conditions to encourage foreign banks to assist the rapid acceleration in the development and sophistication of local banking systems.
	• Actively support the development of the insurance industry and recognise its regional nature by removing protectionism and providing effective regulation.
Technology	• Openness to the international economy is a requirement if African business is to benefit from new technologies and for the development of such technologies locally.
	• Efficient government depends on its integration with technology to improve service delivery from healthcare to education.
	• Regulatory and political barriers must be eliminated to extend broadband access to more citizens.
	• Investment in research and development should be encouraged through tax breaks.
	• Government should accept the reality of job losses from technology in some sectors, while seeking to maximise gains in others.
Mobilising resources, de-risking investment	• Foreign aid can help, but investment will come from the private sector; it is therefore critical to adopt a business-friendly mindset.
	• Creating stability and certainty in the policy, legal and regulatory spheres is key to a successful investor strategy.
	• Aid will not overcome weak governance. Improved state performance and delivery have to be locally generated and owned.
	• Chinese engagement should be embraced but care should be taken to ensure value for African people rather the enrichment of elites.
	• Aid must be aligned to national plans and tailored to reducing the costs of doing business.
Planning	• Use the planning process to instil a sense of urgency to promote growth and create jobs as the immediate imperative.
	• Emphasise the government's partnership with business, and not, as many plans do, the primacy of government.
	• A useful plan depends on ruthless prioritisation, appropriate resourcing and careful sequencing.

	• Governments should recruit the best available people for the job in planning and elsewhere.
	• The role of foreign governments and institutions should be circumscribed.
Leadership and delivery	• Leadership should use democracy to instil a disciplined nationalism, explaining the country's development path.
	• The emphasis of leaders should be on execution and attention to the details of governance.
	• Leadership requires utilising the full range of personal diplomatic skills and patience.
	• Accountability of government officials should be ensured through transparency.
	• Strong leaders are willing to delegate authority.

If African countries are to meet the challenges coming their way and provide jobs for their young, fast-growing populations, their leaders need to make their countries both attractive and competitive in both a regional and international sense.

Reform or perish

Throughout this book, we have argued that rapid reform is needed if the continent is to secure the prosperous future it, and its people, so deserve. However, Africa is not confronting the coming crisis by accident. It is facing it as a consequence of decisions taken, or not taken, by its leaders. Zambia, for example, had forecast very accurately its predicted electricity demand in the period 2010 to 2015 two decades earlier. Leaders knew what needed to be done to avert a power shortage and there were plenty of investors ready to provide capital. Nevertheless, little happened because vested interests and inertia got in the way.

This is not to pretend that reform is easy. Reform is about challenging the status quo and there will be powerful individuals and groups who will fight hard to prevent change. Given Africa's rising population and growing cities, inaction will ultimately end badly for all, even the elites. Africa's leaders do not enjoy the goodwill that their predecessors from the fight for independence did: they will be judged solely on what they have delivered to their constituencies.

The challenge for African leaders is to harness the considerable growth potential of the continent, along with international interest and goodwill, for the benefit of their people, before they are overwhelmed by the challenges of rapid population growth and urbanisation. It is urgent that the critical reform initiatives begin now because it will be too late once the large populations of young people with smartphones and high expectations arrive in the cities.

Notes and references

Introduction

1 There have been 630 African conflicts since 1990. See the presentation by Paul Williams, 'Conflict in Africa: Why it persists', African Centre for Strategic Studies, Washington DC, 24 October 2016.

2 World Bank, 'While poverty in Africa has declined, number of poor has increased', http://www.worldbank.org/en/region/afr/publication/poverty-rising-africa-poverty-report, accessed December 2016.

3 We are grateful to Ambassador Phillip Carter for this notion.

4 World Bank, The Current Economic Position and Prospects for Zambia, May 1966, ii.

5 See Population Pyramids of the World, Zambia, https://populationpyramid.net/zambia/2030/, accessed December 2016; Zambian Association of Manufacturers audit, cited in 'Bringing back the "glory days" of Zambian manufacturing', The Bulletin and Record, March 2012, 14–15; D. Limpitlaw, 'Nationalisation and mining: Lessons from Zambia', The Southern African Institute of Mining and Metallurgy, 111, October 2011; and World Bank, 'Zambia', Overview, http://www.worldbank.org/en/country/zambia/overview, accessed December 2016.

6 Steven Radelet, 'Africa's rise – interrupted?' Finance & Development 53(2), June 2016.

7 World Bank, 'Sub-Saharan Africa', http://data.worldbank.org/region/SSA, as measured in real (2005) gross national income per capita, accessed December 2016.

8 See World Bank, http://www.worldbank.org/content/dam/Worldbank/document/Africa/Report/Africas-Pulse-brochure_Vol7.pdf, accessed June 2016.

9 See World Bank, http://data.worldbank.org/indicator/SL.UEM.TOTL.ZS, accessed December 2016.

10 See World Bank, http://documents.worldbank.org/curated/en/2014/01/18829981/youth-employment-sub-saharan-africa-vol-1-2-overview, accessed December 2016; see also http://www.brookings.edu/blogs/africa-in-focus/posts/2014/08/12-youth-unemployment-africa-mcarthur, accessed December 2016.

11 Abdi Latif Dahir, 'It's bleak: Africa is in a slump for the first time in twenty years', Quartz Africa, 11 October 2016, http://qz.com/806292/imf-sub-saharan-africas-gdp-economic-growth-will-fall-to-its-worst-level-in-two-decades/, accessed December 2016.

12 This is the theme of a number of contemporary titles on Africa, including: Vijay Mahajan, Africa Rising: How 900 Million African Consumers Offer More Than You Think. US: Prentice Hall, 2008; Kingsley Moghalu, Emerging Africa: How the Global Economy's 'Last Frontier' Can Prosper and Matter. London: Penguin, 2014; Charles Robertson, The Fastest Billion: The Story Behind Africa's Economic Revolution. London: Renaissance Capital, 2012; and Kevin Bloom and Richard Poplak, Continental Shift: A Journey into Africa's Changing Fortunes. Johannesburg: Jonathan Ball, 2016.

13 '1.2 billion opportunities', The Economist, 16 April 2016, http://www.economist. com/news/special-report/21696792-commodity-boom-may-be-over-and-barriers-doing-business-are-everywhere-africas, accessed December 2016.

14 'One million people out of poverty in Rwanda,' CNBC Africa, 30 June 2016, http://www.cnbcafrica.com/video/?bcpid=1572473874001&bckey=AQ~~,AAABbep-pM1E~,YSfB5eRxPEbUu52DyyunfxqhQ1KV6HP4&bctid=5012356830001, accessed December 2016.

15 World Bank, 'Can Africa claim the 21st century?', http://go.worldbank.org/Z7KUASD0N0, accessed December 2016.

16 'Africa's middle class: Few and far between', The Economist, 24 October 2015, http://www.economist.com/news/middle-east-and-africa/21676774-africans-are-mainly-rich-or-poor-not-middle-class-should-worry, accessed December 2016.

17 GDP growth in sub-Saharan Africa improved to 4.6 per cent in 2014, up from 4.2 per cent in 2013, but weaker than the average of 6.4 per cent during 2002–2008. See, for example, http://www.worldbank.org/content/dam/Worldbank/GEP/GEP2015b/Global-Economic-Prospects-June-2015-Sub-Saharan-Africa-analysis-pdf, accessed December 2016.

18 For details on these increases, see http://www.un.org/en/development/desa/news/population/2015-report.html; https://africacheck.org/factsheets/fact-sheet-africas-population-projections/; https://esa.un.org/unpd/wpp/publications/files/key_findings_wpp_2015.pdf, accessed December 2016.

19 Max Fisher, 'The amazing, surprising, Africa-driven demographic future of the earth, in 9 charts', The Washington Post, 16 July 2013, https://www.washingtonpost.com/news/worldviews/wp/2013/07/16/the-amazing-surprising-africa-driven-demo-graphic-future-of-the-earth-in-9-charts/?utm_term=.31a6a7c11bc5. Last accessed December2016.

20 See http://www.bbc.com/news/world-africa-34188248, accessed December 2016.

21 UN, 'World population prospects, the 2012 revision', vol. 1, 2013, 57–58, http://esa.un.org/wpp/Documentation/pdf/WPP2012_Volume-I_Comprehensive-Tables.pdf, accessed December 2016.

22 'The young continent', The Economist, 12 December 2015, http://www.economist. com/news/briefing/21679781-fertilit y-rates-falling-more-slowly-anywhere-else-af-rica-faces-population, accessed December 2016.

23 'The world's 10 youngest populations are all in Africa', World Economic Forum, https://www.weforum.org/agenda/2016/05/the-world-s-10-youngest-countries-are-all-in-africa/, accessed December 2016.

24 IMF, Regional Economic Outlook, 'Sub-Saharan Africa: Navigating headwinds', https://www.imf.org/external/pubs/ft/reo/2015/afr/eng/pdf/sreo0415.pdf, 25, accessed December 2016.

25 African Development Bank, OECD, UN Development Programme, African Economic Outlook 2015, 2015, xiii.

26 Ibid., xiv.

27 British Council, 'Can higher education solve Africa's job crisis?', 2014, https://www.britishcouncil.org/sites/default/files/graduate_employability_in_ssa_final-web.pdf, accessed December 2016.

28 Mark Anderson and Achilleas Galatsidas, 'Urban population boom poses massive challenges for Africa and Asia', The Guardian, 10 July 2014, http://www.theguardian.com/global-development/2014/jul/10/urban-population-growth-africa-asia-united-nations, accessed December 2016.

29 UN, 'World's population increasingly urban with more than half living in urban areas,' 10 July 2014, http://www.un.org/en/development/desa/news/population/world-urbanization-prospects-2014.html; see also http://www.prb.org/publications/datasheets/2013/2013-world-population-data-sheet/data-sheet.aspx, accessed December 2016.

30 Remi Jedwab, Luc Christaensen and Marina Gindelsky, 'The speed of urbanization and economic development: A comparison of industrial Europe and contemporary Africa,' presented to the World Bank-GWU Conference on Urbanization and Poverty Reduction, http://siteresources.worldbank.org/INTIE/Resources/475495-1368648404460/Jedwab_The_Speed_of_Urbanization_Tales_from_Europe_and_Africa.pdf, accessed December 2016.

31 World Bank, 'An analysis of issues shaping Africa's future', April 2016, http://documents.worldbank.org/curated/en/970911468563846454/text/104729-RE-VISED-PUBLIC-WB-AfricasPulse-Spring2016-vol13-v17-final.txt, accessed December 2016.

32 McKinsey & Company, 'What's driving African growth', April 2010, http://www.mckinsey.com/insights/economic_studies/whats_driving_africas_growth, accessed December 2016.

33 McKinsey & Company, 'Lions on the move', June 2010, http://www.mckinsey.com/global-themes/middle-east-and-africa/lions-on-the-move, accessed December 2016.

34 McKinsey & Company, 'Lions on the move II', August 2016, http://www.mckinsey.com/global-themes/middle-east-and-africa/lions-on-the-move-realizing-the-potential-of-africas-economies, accessed December 2016.

35 Frik Els, 'IMF warns of another 14% drop in metal prices this year', Mining.com, 12 April 2016, http://www.mining.com/imf-predicts-another-14-drop-in-metal-prices-this-year/, accessed December 2016.

36 'Africa discovers the downside of foreign borrowing', The Economist, 2 April 2016, http://www.economist.com/news/finance-and-economics/21695939-africa-discovers-downside-foreign-borrowing-ante-upped?zid=304&ah=e5690753dc-78ce91909083042ad12e30, accessed December 2016.

37 World Bank, 'Zambia', http://data.worldbank.org/country/zambia, accessed December 2016.

38 See 2015 Index of Economic Freedom. Washington DC: Heritage Foundation, 2015, http://www.heritage.org, accessed December 2016.

39 Mo Ibrahim Foundation, 'A decade of African governance, 2006–2015', 2016, http://s.mo.ibrahim.foundation/u/2016/10/01184917/2016-Index-Report.pdf?_ga=1.149205750.1138767584.1476258984, accessed December 2016.

40 Mo Ibrahim Foundation, 'The 2016 Ibrahim Index of African Governance: Key findings', http://mo.ibrahim.foundation/news/2016/progress-african-governance-last-decade-held-back-deterioration-safety-rule-law/, accessed December 2016.

41 'World Bank: Extreme poverty to "fall below 10%"', BBC News, 5 October 2015, http://www.bbc.com/news/world-34440567, accessed December 2016.

42 'Towards the end of poverty', The Economist, 30 May 2013, http://www.economist.com/news/leaders/21578665-nearly-1-billion-people-have-been-taken-out-extreme-poverty-20-years-world-should-aim, accessed December 2016.

43 UN, Sustainable Development Knowledge Platform, Sustainable Development Goals, https://sustainabledevelopment.un.org/sdgs, accessed December 2016.

44 The Malay name for the violent conflict of 1963 to 1966, which stemmed from Indonesia's opposition to the creation of Malaysia.

45 Commonly held to be Prime Minister Lee Kuan Yew, lawyer David Marshall, unionist Devan Nair, lawyer Eddie Barker, economist Goh Keng Swee, Lim Kim San, Ong Pang Boon, Othman Wok, S. Rajaratnam and Toh Chin Chye. See Founding Fathers. Singapore: The New Paper, 2015.

46 Greg Mills's discussion with Raila Odinga, 1 February 2016, Nairobi.

47 Milton Osborne, Southeast Asia: An Introductory History. Sydney: Allen & Unwin, 2013, 45.

48 We are grateful to Christopher Clapham for this point.

49 See 'Remarks by the President to the Ghanaian Parliament', https://www.whitehouse.gov/the-press-office/remarks-president-ghanaian-parliament, accessed December 2016.

50 Dambisa Moyo, Dead Aid: Why Aid is Not Working and How There is a Better Way for Africa. New York: Farrar, Straus and Giroux, 2009.

51 This debate is advanced in Greg Mills, Why Africa is Poor: And What Africans Can Do About It. Johannesburg: Penguin, 2010.

52 For a discussion on the nature of African political economy since independence, see Jeffrey Herbst and Greg Mills, Africa's Third Liberation: The New Search for Prosperity and Jobs. Johannesburg: Penguin, 2012.

53 See, for example, http://www.washingtonpost.com/sf/world/2015/07/20/a-remote-city-of-smugglers/. Also https://www.iom.int/news/iom-records-over-60000-migrants-passing-through-agadez-niger-between-february-and-april-2016, accessed December 2016.

Chapter 1

1 Mo Ibrahim Foundation, http://mo.ibrahim.foundation/news/2016/progress-african-governance-last-decade-held-back-deterioration-safety-rule-law/ , accessed November 2016.

2 He preferred to be identified by only his first name.

3 Telephonic discussion with Greg Mills, June 2016.

4 Measured at twenty foot equivalent units, or TEUs.

5 Wolfgang Fengler, 'Why Kenya needs a world-class port in Mombasa', *Africa Can World Bank Blog*, 4 April 2012, http://blogs.worldbank.org/africacan/why-kenya-needs-a-world-class-port-in-mombasa, accessed December 2014.

6 World Bank Ease of Doing Business Index 2012, Doing business, Mombasa, Kenya, http://www.doingbusiness.org/data/exploreeconomies/kenya/sub/mombasa/, accessed December 2014.

7 See Adam Smith international, http://www.adamsmithinternational.com/explore-our-work/east-africa/kenya/mombasa-county-youth-employment-programme, accessed December 2014.

8 Margaret Ngayu, 'Sustainable urban communities: Challenges and opportunities in Kenya's urban sector', *International Journal of Humanities and Social Sciences* 1, 4, April 2011, http://www.ijhssnet.com/journals/Vol._1_No._4;_April_2011/9.pdf.

9 See Adam Smith international, http://www.adamsmithinternational.com/explore-our-work/east-africa/kenya/mombasa-county-youth-employment-programme, accessed December 2014.

10 'Gunned down in Mombasa – The clerics that have died', *IRIN*, 28 July 2014, http://www.irinnews.org/report/100412/gunned-down-in-mombasa-the-clerics-that-have-died, accessed December 2014.

11 'Migrant crisis: Migration to Europe explained in seven charts', BBC News, 4 March 2016, http://www.bbc.com/news/world-europe-34131911, accessed November 2016.

12 'Everything you want to know about migration across the Mediterranean', *The Economist*, 4 May 2015, http://www.economist.com/blogs/economist-explains/2015/05/economist-explains-6, accessed November 2016.

13 We are grateful for Paul Collier's insights here.

14 'African cities: Left behind', *The Economist*, 15 September 2016, http://www.
economist.com/news/middle-east-and-africa/21707214-all-over-world-people-es-
cape-poverty-moving-cities-why-does-not?frsc=dg%7Ca, accessed November 2016.

15 Jeremy Barofsky, Eyerusalem Siba, and Jonathan Grabinsky, 'Can rapid urbanization in
Africa reduce poverty? Causes, opportunities, and policy recommendations',
Brookings Institute, 7 September 2016, https://www.brookings.edu/blog/
africa-in-focus/2016/09/07/can-rapid-urbanization-in-africa-reduce-poverty-caus-
es-opportunities-and-policy-recommendations/, accessed November 2016.

16 'If mayors ruled the world: A new Freakonomics radio podcast', Freakonomics, 10
April 2014, http://freakonomics.com/2014/04/10/if-mayors-ruled-the-world-a-
new-freakonomics-radio-podcast/, accessed November 2016.

17 Ibid.; see also Annual Bank Conference on Africa, opening session, 13 June 2016,
https://www.youtube.com/watch?v=37O58T4Jyx4&feature=youtu.
be&t=10m07s, accessed November 2016.

18 Email interview with Tim Harris, 4 December 2014.

19 Interview with Tim Harris, Cape Town, 13 January 2015.

20 This section draws on an article by Greg Mills and Lyal White first published in
November 2015 in the *Daily Maverick*. See http://www.dailymaverick.co.za/
article/2015-11-25-brazils-lerner-driver/#.WC3YG3ecaA8.

21 Interview, Bogotá, 8 November 2016.

22 See Paul Williams, *War and Conflict in Africa*. Cambridge: Polity, 2016.

23 2016 Ibrahim Index of African Governance: Key findings, Mo Ibrahim Foundation, 4
October 2016, http://mo.ibrahim.foundation/news/2016/progress-african-gover-
nance-last-decade-held-back-deterioration-safety-rule-law/, accessed November
2016.

24 For the international 'league table' on violent cities, see http://www.worldatlas.
com/articles/most-dangerous-cities-in-the-world.html.

25 See Western Cape Provincial Crime Analysis. Analysis of crime based on the 2015/16
crime statistics issued by the South African Police Service, 2 September 2016, dated 7
October 2016.

26 Buchule Raba, 'Cape Town's police-to-population ratio way below national norm',
Times Live, 27 July 2016, http://www.timeslive.co.za/local/2016/07/27/
Cape-Town%E2%80%99s-police-to-population-ratio-way-below-national-norm,
accessed December 2016.

27 Interview, Civic Centre, Cape Town, 24 November 2016.

28 Western Cape Provincial Crime Analysis. Analysis of crime based on the 2015/16
crime statistics issued by the South African Police Service, 2 September 2016, dated 7
October 2016.

29 This data is drawn from Jorge Giraldo-Ramírez and Andrés Preciado-Restrepo,
'Medellín, from theater of war to security laboratory', *Stability: International Journal of*

276

Security and Development, June 2015, http://www.stabilityjournal.org/articles/10.5334/sta.fy/, accessed November 2016.

30 Francis Fukuyama and Seth Colby, 'Half a miracle', *Foreign Policy*, 25 April 2011, http://foreignpolicy.com/2011/04/25/half-a-miracle/, accessed November 2016.

31 For details on the role of planning and architecture in this transformation, see http://www.architectural-review.com/archive/colombias-infrastructure-reclaimed-as-public-space/8684196.fullarticle; http://www.pps.org/reference/ten-strategies-for-transforming-cities-through-placemaking-public-spaces/; http://architectureindevelopment.org/news.php?id=49; and http://www.forbes.com/sites/ashoka/2014/01/27/the-transformation-of-medellin-and-the-surprising-company-behind-it/#35b9b3954752, accessed November 2016.

32 This is covered in Greg Mills, David Kilcullen, David Spencer and Dickie Davis, *A Great Perhaps? Colombia: Convergence and Conflict*. London: Hurst, 2016.

33 The population of the Department of Antioquia is 6 million. Of this number, approximately 2.5 million inhabitants are from Medellín. The inhabitants of Medellín and the wider metropolitan area together add up to 3.5 million.

34 By comparison, in 2000 there were 5 863 police officers in the metropolitan area. Information supplied by Anamaría Botero Mora, Agencia de Cooperación e Inversión de Medellín y el Área Metropolitan, 17 August 2015.

35 The number of graduate officers has increased from around 10 per cent in 1994 to 70 per cent of officers in 2015, a result, primarily, of the 2004 human resource strategy. Discussion with Medellín police, March 2015.

36 See Edwin Heathcote, 'Venice Biennale: Architects' social conscience', *Financial Times*, 20 May 2016, http://www.ft.com/cms/s/0/4a3b84a8-18fc-11e6-b197-a4af20d5575e.html?siteedition=uk#axzz4LY-VM2Tur, accessed November 2016.

Chapter 2

1 David E. Kiwuwa, 'Africa is young: Why are its leaders so old?', CNN, 29 October 2015, http://edition.cnn.com/2015/10/15/africa/africas-old-mens-club-op-ed-david-e-kiwuwa/, accessed November 2016.

2 Fareed Zakaria, 'A conversation with Lee Kuan Yew', *Foreign Affairs*, March-April 1994, https://www.foreignaffairs.com/articles/asia/1994-03-01/conversation-lee-kuan-yew, accessed November 2016.

3 Lee Kuan Yew, *From Third World to First: The Singapore Story, 1965 to 2000*. New York: HarperCollins, 2000.

4 'In his words', *AsiaWeek Magazine*, 22 September 2000, http://edition.cnn.com/ASIANOW/asiaweek/magazine/2000/0922/cs.singapore.words.html, accessed November 2016.

5 Freedom House, *Freedom in the World, 2015*. New York: Freedom House, 2015.

6 'The march of democracy slows', *The Economist*, 20 August 2016, http://www.
   economist.com/news/middle-east-and-africa/21705355-threats-democratic-rule-af-
   rica-are-growing-time-and-demography-are?zid=304&ah=e5690753dc-
   78ce91909083042ad12e30, accessed November 2016.

7 According to Freedom House's rankings, a 'free' country 'is one where there is open
   political competition, a climate of respect for civil liberties, significant independent
   civic life, and independent media'; a 'partly free' one in which 'there is limited respect
   for political rights and civil liberties', and which 'frequently suffer from an environment of corruption, weak rule of law, ethnic and religious strife, and a political
   landscape in which a single party enjoys dominance despite a certain degree of
   pluralism'; and a 'not free' country is one 'where basic political rights are absent, and
   basic civil liberties are widely and systematically denied'. See http://www.freedom-
   house.org/report/freedom-world/freedom-world-2013, accessed November 2016.

8 'The march of democracy slows', *The Economist*, 20 August 2016, http://www.
   economist.com/news/middle-east-and-africa/21705355-threats-democratic-rule-af-
   rica-are-growing-time-and-demography-are?zid=304&ah=e5690753dc-
   78ce91909083042ad12e30, accessed November 2016.

9 Ibid.

10 Office of the UN High Commissioner for Human Rights, http://www2.ohchr.org/
   english/law/compilation_democracy/ahg.htm, accessed November 2016.

11 Interview with Hakainde Hichilema, February 2016.

12 Interview with Raila Odinga, Nairobi, 9 September 2016.

13 'Are elections giving democracy a bad name?', http://www.kofiannanfoundation.
   org/articles/4696/, accessed November 2016.

14 This argument was framed around a narrow interpretation of the Namibian constitution, on the grounds that since the president had first been elected by a Constituent
   Assembly, his first term did not count toward the limit.

15 Joseph Siegle, 'Why term limits matter for Africa', Center for Security Studies blog, 3
   July 2015.

16 'Kagame says he is seeking a third term for the sake of democracy', Quartz Africa,
   http://qz.com/682038/kagame-pushes-back-at-third-term-critics-but-for-the-west-
   its-not-just-about-rwanda/, accessed November 2016.

17 Jeffrey Sonnenfeld, CEO exit schedules: A season to stay, a season to go, *Fortune*, 6
   May 2015, http://fortune.com/2015/05/06/ceo-tenure-cisco/, accessed
   November 2016.

18 Ibid.

19 Jeremy Barofsky, Eyerusalem Siba and Jonathan Grabinsky, 'Can rapid urbanization in
   Africa reduce poverty? Causes, opportunities, and policy recommendations',
   Brookings, 7 September 2016, https://www.brookings.edu/blog/africa-in-fo-
   cus/2016/09/07/can-rapid-urbanization-in-africa-reduce-poverty-causes-opportu-
   nities-and-policy-recommendations/, accessed November 2016.

20 Alberto F. Ades and Edward L. Glaeser, 'Trade and circuses: Explaining urban giants', NBER Working Paper No. 4715, April 1994, http://www.nber.org/papers/w4715, accessed November 2016.

21 Joseph Siegle, Michael Weinstein and Morton Halperin, 'Why democracies excel', Foreign Affairs 83, 5, 2005, 57–71. See also Morton Halperin, Joseph Siegle and Michael Weinstein, *The Democracy Advantage: How Democracies Promote Prosperity and Peace*. London: Routledge, 2010.

22 Deemed as part of China for this purpose.

23 Takaaki Masaki and Nicolas van de Walle, 'The impact of democracy on economic growth in sub-Saharan Africa, 1982–2012', WIDER Working Paper 2014/057, March 2014.

24 We are grateful to Terry McNamee for this input.

25 Sebastian Elischer, 'Taking stock of "good coups" in Africa', *The Washington Post*, 18 May 2015, https://www.washingtonpost.com/blogs/monkey-cage/wp/2015/05/18/taking-stock-of-good-coups-in-africa/, accessed November 2016.

26 Correspondence with Dr Joe Siegle, August 2016.

27 Ibid.

28 'Preventing conflict in the next century', *The World In 2000*. London: Economist Publications, 1999, 91.

29 See Background on the Conference on Security, Stability, Development and Cooperation in Africa, AU, http://www.au2002.gov.za/docs/background/cssdca.htm, accessed November 2016.

30 Afrobarometer, http://afrobarometer.org/sites/default/files/publications/Dispatches/ab_r6_dispatchno30.pdf, accessed November 2016.

31 The Becker–Posner Blog, 'Autocracy, democracy and economic welfare', http://www.becker-posner-blog.com/2010/10/autocracy-democracy-and-economic-welfareposner.html, accessed November 2016.

32 Daron Acemoglu, Suresh Naidu, Pascual Restrepo and James A. Robinson, 'Democracy does cause growth', June 2014, https://www.aeaweb.org/conference/2015/retrieve.php?pdfid=333, accessed November 2016.

33 Email correspondence with Guy Scott, 21 October 2016.

34 This is based on correspondence with the UPND team. See also 'UPND demands resignation of ECZ director Pricila Isaac', *Lusaka Times*, 13 August 2016, https://www.lusakatimes.com/2016/08/13/upnd-demands-resignation-ecz-director-pricila-isaac/, accessed November 2016.

35 See http://www.freemedia.at/IPIMain/wp-content/uploads/2016/08/2016-IPI-AMI-Zambia-Press-Freedom-Mission-Report-Final.pdf, accessed November 2016. See also http://ccmgzambia.org/wp-content/uploads/2016/08/CCMG-Preliminary-EDay-Statement-12-Aug-2016.pdf, accessed November 2016.

36 See http://zambiareports.com/2016/07/12/znbc-right-to-reject-unethical-up-nd-adverts/ and on the documentary itself, http://www.zambiawatchdog.com/high-court-orders-znbc-to-air-upnd-documentaries/, accessed November 2016.

37 The EU mission report, in noting the state broadcaster's bias, observed that news coverage on state radio and television 'largely excluded other parties, or only reported other parties negatively'. It also noted that 'provisions and application of the Public Order Act unreasonably restricted freedom of assembly to the benefit of the ruling party', see http://africanarguments.org/2016/08/17/zambias-disputed-elections-on-binned-ballots-and-systematic-bias/, accessed November 2016.

38 The official margin was initially 13 000, but the figures originally announced by the Electoral Commission of Zambia for Lundazi were 8 000 higher than the numbers that were then provided on the official certificates. The electoral commission put this down to an administrative error.

39 'Zambia general elections 2016: Observer group interim statement', http://thecommonwealth.org/media/news/zambia-general-elections-2016-observer-group-interim-statement#sthash.sswQUDgc.dpuf; and http://eeas.europa.eu/statements-eeas/2016/160816_01_en.htm, accessed November 2016.

40 Alexander Mutale, 'Zambian elections: clear, but narrow, win', *Financial Mail*, 19 August 2016, http://www.financialmail.co.za/features/2016/08/19/zambian-elections-clear-but-narrow-win, accessed November 2016.

41 'Zambian court throws out election petition case – Lungu to hold inauguration', *Africa News*, 5 September 2016, http://www.africanews.com/2016/09/05/zambian-court-throws-out-election-petition-case-lungu-to-hold-inauguration/, accessed November 2016.

42 Telephone conversation between Hakainde Hichilema and Greg Mills, August 2016.

43 See AU, African Peer Review Mechanism, http://www.au.int/en/organs/aprm, accessed November 2016.

44 Email correspondence, 28 October 2016.

45 Nic Cheeseman, 'Deconstructing the Magufuli miracle in Tanzania,' 17 October 2016, https://africajournalismtheworld.com/2016/10/17/deconstructing-the-magufuli-miracle-in-tanzania/?fb_action_ids=10154594723621419&fb_action_types=news.publishes, accessed November 2016.

46 Ibid.

47 See the results of a 2016 *Guardian* study at https://www.theguardian.com/world/2016/mar/07/revealed-30-year-economic-betrayal-dragging-down-generation-y-income, accessed November 2016. See also Chris Belfield, Jonathan Crib, Andrew Hood and Robert Joyce, 'Living standards, poverty and inequality 2016', Institute for Fiscal Studies, 19 July 2016; and Jonathan Cribb, Andrew Hood and Robert Joyce, 'The economic circumstances of different generations: The latest picture', Institute for Fiscal Studies Briefing Note BN187, 2016.

Chapter 3

1 This section is based on a route diagnostic carried out on Tazara, including interviews with several officials and businesses in Lusaka, Dar es Salaam, Kabwe and the Zambian Copperbelt in May and June 2015.

2 'Tazara's new CEO pledges to revive Chinese-built railway line', *Xinhua*, 24 April 2016, https://web.archive.org/web/20160703220928/http://news.xinhuanet.com/english/2016-04/24/c_135307983.htm, accessed November 2016.

3 See, for example, http://siteresources.worldbank.org/INTAFRREGTOPTRADE/Resources/PN35_Dar_port_reform_Feb_2013.pdf, accessed November 2016.

4 Interview, May 2015.

5 World Bank, 'Transforming Africa's infrastructure', http://web.worldbank.org/WBSITE/EXTERNAL/COUNTRIES/AFRICAEXT/0,,contentMDK:22386904~pagePK:146736~piPK:226340~theSitePK:258644,00.html, accessed November 2016.

6 Ibid.

7 See 'Investment trends and outcomes in the power sector in sub-Saharan Africa: Why are some countries more successful than others in attracting capital?', presentation by Anton Eberhard, 2015.

8 'Fact sheet: Infrastructure in sub-Saharan Africa', World Bank, http://web.worldbank.org/WBSITE/EXTERNAL/COUNTRIES/AFRICAEXT/0,,contentMDK:-21951811~pagePK:146736~piPK:146830~theSitePK:258644,00.html, accessed November 2016.

9 http://www.brasembottawa.org/en/brazil_in_brief/transportation.html, accessed November 2016.

10 See Logistics Barometer 2016 South Africa, http://www.sun.ac.za/english/faculty/economy/logistics/Documents/Logistics%20Barometer/Logistics%20Barometer%202016%20Report.pdf, accessed November 2016.

11 'Transport costs and specialisation', World Bank, http://siteresources.worldbank.org/INTWDR2009/Resources/4231006-1225840759068/WDR09_12_Ch06web.pdf. The India and China per tonne/kilometre rail freight costs were $0.19 and $0.15, respectively. See http://www.supplychain.cn/en/art/3455/, and http://fieo.org/view_section.php?lang=0&id=0,63,74,501, accessed November 2016.

12 Interview, London, 27 September 2016.

13 This section is based on a research trip by Greg Mills to Panama (and the canal) in November 2015 in the company of Dr Lyal White. It is adapted from an article published in the *Daily Maverick*, http://www.dailymaverick.co.za/article/2015-11-17-panama-locks-stocks-and-a-smokin-economy, accessed November 2016.

14 'What are the Panama papers? A guide to history's biggest data leak', *The Guardian*, 3 April 2016, https://www.theguardian.com/news/2016/apr/03/what-you-need-to-know-about-the-panama-papers, accessed November 2016.

15 See Paul Collier and Anthony Venables, 'Housing and urbanization in Africa: Unleashing a formal market process,' CSAE Working Paper WPS/2013 01,

Department of Economics, Oxford University, 9 January 2013, http://www.csae. ox.ac.uk/workingpapers/pdfs/csae-wps-2013-01.pdf, accessed November 2016.

16 'A 360° View. Africa construction trends report 2015', Deloitte, https://www2. deloitte.com/content/dam/Deloitte/za/Documents/manufacturing/ZA-ConstructionTrendsReport-2015.pdf, accessed November 2016.

17 'Urbanisation in Africa', African Development Bank, 13 December 2012, http://www.afdb.org/en/blogs/afdb-championing-inclusive-growth-across-africa/post/urbanization-in-africa-10143/, accessed November 2016.

18 Paul Collier and Anthony Venables, 'Housing and urbanization in Africa: Unleashing a formal market process,' CSAE Working Paper WPS/2013 01, Department of Economics, Oxford University, 9 January 2013, http://www.csae.ox.ac.uk/workingpapers/pdfs/csae-wps-2013-01.pdf, accessed November 2016.

19 This section is based on a research trip to Khayelitsha, Harare, Langa and Hanover Park in June 2016 arranged by the Office of the Mayor of the City of Cape Town. See also https://www.capetown.gov.za/en/stats/2011CensusSuburbs/2011_Census_CT_Suburb_Khayelitsha_Profile.pdf, accessed November 2016.

20 Interview, Cape Town, 13 June 2016.

21 'Stocktaking of the housing sector in sub-Saharan Africa', World Bank, http://www.worldbank.org/content/dam/Worldbank/document/Africa/Report/stocktaking-of-the-housing-sector-in-sub-saharan-africa-summary-report.pdf, accessed November 2016.

22 Ibid.

23 'Lions on the move II: Realizing the potential of Africa's economies', McKinsey, August 2016, http://www.mckinsey.com/global-themes/middle-east-and-africa/lions-on-the-move-realizing-the-potential-of-africas-economies, accessed November 2016.

24 'Stocktaking of the housing sector in sub-Saharan Africa', World Bank, http://www.worldbank.org/content/dam/Worldbank/document/Africa/Report/stocktaking-of-the-housing-sector-in-sub-saharan-africa-summary-report.pdf, accessed November 2016.

25 'The construction industry in the 21st century', International Labour Organization, 2001, http://www.ilo.org/public/english/standards/relm/gb/docs/gb283/pdf/tmcitr.pdf, accessed November 2016.

26 'Labour and work conditions in the South African construction industry', *Construction Industry Development Board, 2015*, http://www.cidb.org.za/publications/Documents/Labour%20and%20Work%20Conditions%20in%20the%20South%20African%20Construction%20Industry;%20Status%20and%20Recommendations.pdf, accessed November 2016.

27 'Stocktaking of the housing sector in sub-Saharan Africa', World Bank, http://www.worldbank.org/content/dam/Worldbank/document/Africa/Report/stocktak-

ing-of-the-housing-sector-in-sub-saharan-africa-summary-report.pdf, accessed November 2016.

28 See, for example, 'Lions on the move II: Realizing the potential of Africa's economies', McKinsey, August 2016, http://www.mckinsey.com/global-themes/middle-east-and-africa/lions-on-the-move-realizing-the-potential-of-africas-economies, accessed November 2016.

29 The scandal of Sweet Home Farm, 6 July 2010, see http://mnrowland.blogspot.co.za/2010/07/scandal-of-sweet-home-farm.html, accessed November 2016.

30 Ibid.

31 Cited in 'Stocktaking of the housing sector in sub-Saharan Africa', World Bank, http://www.worldbank.org/content/dam/Worldbank/document/Africa/Report/stocktaking-of-the-housing-sector-in-sub-saharan-africa-summary-report.pdf, accessed November 2016.

32 Paul Collier and Anthony Venables, 'Housing and urbanization in Africa: Unleashing a formal market process,' CSAE Working Paper WPS/2013 01, Department of Economics, Oxford University, 9 January 2013, http://www.csae.ox.ac.uk/workingpapers/pdfs/csae-wps-2013-01.pdf, accessed November 2016.

33 Discussion undertaken by Greg Mills with Andrew Charman of the Sustainable Livelihoods Foundation, Muizenberg, June 2016.

34 'Stocktaking of the housing sector in sub-Saharan Africa', World Bank, http://www.worldbank.org/content/dam/Worldbank/document/Africa/Report/stocktaking-of-the-housing-sector-in-sub-saharan-africa-summary-report.pdf, accessed November 2016.

35 Steve Johnson, 'China by far the largest investor in African infrastructure', *Financial Times*, http://www.ft.com/cms/s/3/716545c0-9529-11e5-ac15-0f7f7945adba.html#axzz4F2Zfy3qC, accessed November 2016.

36 As discussed on Bloomberg Television, 14 October 2016.

Chapter 4

1 'Africa: The commodity warrant', *Credit Suisse New Perspectives Series*, 14 April 2008.

2 FAO, Comprehensive Africa Agriculture Development Programme, 'Extending the area under sustainable land management and reliable water control systems, http://www.fao.org/docrep/005/y6831e/y6831e-03.htm, accessed June 2016.

3 Tendai Dube, 'Investing in Africa's agriculture is the next best thing', CNBC Africa, 13 August 2015, http://www.cnbcafrica.com/news/southern-africa/2015/08/13/africa-agriculture-investment/, accessed June 2016.

4 For details on African agriculture programmes, see http://www.fao.org/docrep/005/y6831e/y6831e-03.htm. This chapter is partly based on research conducted in Argentina, Zambia, Malawi and Ethiopia in 2016, and on interviews at the FAO in June 2016.

5   'Brazil's soybean production increases', *World Grain News*, 2 February 2016, http://
    www.world-grain.com/articles/news_home/World_Grain_News/2016/02/
    Brazils_soybean_production_inc.aspx?ID=%7BAF13567A-6BA0-4ACE-B858-
    10568A45C3AE%7D, accessed June 2016.

6   Jacob Taylor, 'India's Green Revolution', https://explodie.org/portfolio/in-
    dia-green-revolution.html, accessed June 2016.

7   Saby Ganguly, 'From the Bengal Famine to the Green Revolution', http://www.
    indiaonestop.com/Greenrevolution.htm, accessed November 2016.

8   See International Coffee Organization statistics on Vietnamese coffee market, https://
    infogr.am/_/IY6Z0hQyzw4MNXvhwNAu, accessed November 2016.

9   Chris Summers, 'How Vietnam became a coffee giant', BBC News, 25 January 2014,
    http://www.bbc.co.uk/news/magazine-25811724, accessed November 2016.

10 Interview with Tsegaye Abebe, Addis Ababa, June 2016.

11 Jan Greyling, 'A look at the contribution of the agricultural sector to the South African
    economy,' Grain SA, March 2015, http://www.grainsa.
    co.za/a-look-at-the-contribution-of-the-agricultural-sector-to-the-south-african-
    economy, accessed November 2016.

12 Department of Agriculture, Forestry and Fisheries, http://www.daff.gov.za/docs/
    statsinfo/Trends13.pdf, accessed November 2016.

13 'Western Cape fruit and wine exports blossoming', *Business Day*, 19 March 2015,
    http://www.bdlive.co.za/business/agriculture/2015/03/19/western-cape-fruit-
    and-wine-exports-blossoming, accessed November 2016.

14 South African Wine Industry Information and Systems, *Final report – Macroeconomic
    impact of the wine industry on the South African economy (also with reference to the impacts on
    the Western Cape)*, 30 January 2015, http://www.sawis.co.za/info/download/
    Macro-economic_impact_study_-_Final_Report_Version_4_30Jan2015.pdf,
    accessed November 2016.

15 A growing industry (agriculture), Western Cape Top 300, http://western-cape.
    top300.co.za/a-growing-industry-agriculture/, accessed November 2016.

16 See 'Crop prospects and food situation', FAO, 2 June 2016.

17 For details on the nutrition-development aspect, see, for example, http://web.
    worldbank.org/WBSITE/EXTERNAL/TOPICS/EXTCY/EXTECD
    /0,,contentMDK:20207804~menuPK:528430~pagePK:148956~piPK:216618~th
    eSitePK:344939,00.html, accessed November 2016.

18 See US Department of Agriculture, http://www.ers.usda.gov/datafiles/Food_
    Expenditures/Expenditures_on_food_and_alcoholic_beverages_that_were_con-
    sumed_at_home_by_selected_countries/table97_2012.xlsx, accessed November
    2016.

19 Washington State University, *Washington State Magazine*, 'Annual income spent on
    food', http://wsm.wsu.edu/researcher/wsmaug11_billions.pdf, accessed November
    2016.

20 See US Department of Agriculture, http://www.ers.usda.gov/data-products/ chart-gallery/detail.aspx?chartId=40044&ref=collection. Subsidies have also contributed to lower food prices in stimulating production, see http://www.usda. gov/wps/portal/usda/usdahome?navid=farmbill, accessed November 2016.

21 Interview, Rome, June 2016.

22 Information supplied to authors by the FAO, June 2016.

23 Martin Ford, *The Rise of the Robots*. London: One World, 2015, 24.

24 This section is based, in part, on a visit to Equalizer on 26 August 2016.

25 'World map with top 10 countries by wheat production', *Maps of the World*, http:// www.mapsofworld.com/world-top-ten/world-map-countries-wheat-production. html, accessed June 2016.

26 'The top 5 soybean-producing countries', Top 5 of Anything, https://top5ofanything. com/list/69ee35b6/Soybean-Producing-Countries, accessed June 2016.

27 At http://www.grainsa.co.za/pages/industry-reports/production-reports/, accessed November 2016.

28 The visits to Caledon were conducted by Greg Mills in August 2016.

29 See Foskor Pty Ltd, http://www.foskor.co.za/SitePages/Home.aspx, accessed November 2016.

30 J.P. Landman, 'Agriculture – A tale of two sectors', Nedbank Investment Research and Fund Management, 7 June 2016.

31 See the OECD's 2015/2016 'Agricultural outlook', http://www.agri-outlook.org/ specialfeature/, accessed June 2016.

32 This section is adapted from an article that appeared in the *Daily Maverick* in April 2016. See http://www.dailymaverick.co.za/article/2016-04-19-tobacco-road-ma-lawis-ten-oxcarts-worth-of-development/, accessed November 2016.

33 World Bank, GDP per capita, http://data.worldbank.org/indicator/NY.GDP.PCAP. CD, accessed August 2016.

34 Round-table discussion, Lilongwe, April 2016.

35 Spain exported $1.3 billion in oranges in 2015, South Africa $589.6 million, or 13.2% of the global market, see http://www.worldstopexports.com/oranges-ex-ports-by-country/. Brazil is the largest orange producer (with 35.73 million tonnes), followed by the US (15.86 million tonnes) and China (14.51 million tonnes). Egypt is in seventh place (with 3.17 million tonnes) and South Africa in 10th place (1.72 million tonnes); see http://worldknowing.com/top-10-largest-orange-producing-country-in-the-world/, accessed November 2016

36 Interview, Cape Town, August 2016.

Chapter 5

1 'The role of mining in national economies', International Council on Mining and Metals, October 2012, http://www.icmm.com/document/4440, accessed November 2016.

2   UN Development Programme, 'Managing primary commodity booms and busts: Emerging lessons from sub-Saharan Africa', http://www.sl.undp.org/content/dam/sierraleone/docs/annualreports/undp-rba-primary%20commodities%20boom%20bust%20april%202016.pdf?download, accessed November 2016.

3   He did not want his surname revealed. This section is based on a research visit by Greg Mills in June 2016 to find out about artisanal mining activities, which was initially recorded in the *Daily Maverick* at http://www.dailymaverick.co.za/article/2016-07-05-take-a-chance-welcome-to-the-golden-underground-world-of-zama-zamas/#. WDqXJ3ecbLF, accessed November 2016.

4   'What is artisanal and small-scale mining?' MiningFacts.org, http://www.mining-facts.org/communities/what-is-artisanal-and-small-scale-mining/, accessed November 2016.

5   Stats SA, 'The decreasing importance of mining in South Africa', http://www.statssa.gov.za/?p=4252, accessed November 2016.

6   Ed Cropley and Agnieszka Flak, 'Special report: Why South African mining's in decline', Reuters, 4 February 2011, http://uk.reuters.com/article/uk-south-africa-mining-idUKLNE71303020110204, accessed November 2016.

7   Information acquired from the South African Chamber of Mines.

8   With thanks to Neal Froneman for this point.

9   Interview, Durban Deep Mine, June 2016.

10   See African Natural Resources Center, African Development Bank, http://www.afdb.org/en/topics-and-sectors/initiatives-partnerships/african-natural-resources-center-anrc/, accessed November 2016.

11   These figures are based on a survey of seven Ghanaian mining companies. With thanks to ICMM's Tom Butler for this point; see also https://www.icmm.com/document/8264, accessed November 2016.

12   See 'The role of mining in national economies', ICMM, October, 2012, http://www.icmm.com/document/4440, accessed November 2016.

13   'Commodity shock knocks Africa's growth prospects – World Bank', *Mining Weekly*, 11 April 2016, http://m.miningweekly.com/article/commodity-shock-knocks-africas-growth-prospects-world-bank-2016-04-11, accessed November 2016.

14   As is the case with Zambian Consolidated Copper Mines.

15   Interview, London, 21 September 2016.

16   Paul Kiernan, 'Anglo American's troubled Brazil mine finally ships iron ore', 3 November 2014, *The Wall Street Journal*, http://www.wsj.com/articles/anglo-americans-troubled-brazil-mine-finally-ships-iron-ore-1415050405, accessed November 2016.

17   Telephonic interview, 24 September 2016.

18   'Mining company Vale authorised to sell portion of coal business in Mozambique', Macau Hub, 10 June 2016, http://www.macauhub.com.mo/en/2016/06/10/

mining-company-vale-authorised-to-sell-portion-of-coal-business-in-mozambique/, accessed November 2016.

19 Telephonic interview, 24 September 2016.

20 This section is based on research in Guinea undertaken in 2013 and first written about in Greg Mills, *Why States Recover*. London: Hurst, 2014, 52–65.

21 The others being (in 2013): Burundi, Liberia, Guinea-Bissau, Central African Republic and Liberia. See http://www.un.org/en/peacebuilding/, accessed November 2016.

22 Patrick Radden Keefe, 'Buried secrets', *The New Yorker*, 8 July 2013, http://www.newyorker.com/reporting/2013/07/08/130708fa_fact_keefe?printable=true&currentPage=all#ixzz2fiX7hKqN, accessed November 2016.

23 Ibid.

24 Discussion with Fodé Idrissa Touré, popularly known as Briqui Momo, then the presidential counsellor in April 2013. Touré had made his fortune in the Ivory Coast. He came back to Conakry and built a multi-storey building in the city. Each time he had completed a floor, he would stand on the top and throw money to the people in the street. That is how he received his nickname, Briqui Momo: '*momo*' is a term for old people and '*briqui*' means 'packs of money'. Briqui Momo died in September 2013. See also http://www.bloomberg.com/news/articles/2015-10-13/rio-runs-out-of-goodwill-in-guinea-as-giant-iron-ore-mine-lags, accessed November 2016.

25 This is based in part on interviews conducted by Greg Mills in Conakry in April 2013.

26 Frik Els, 'Iron ore price: Vale makes boldest oversupply move yet', Mining.com, 14 September 2016, http://www.mining.com/iron-ore-price-vales-made-the-boldest-oversupply-move-yet/?utm_source=digest-en-fe-160915&utm_medium=e-mail&utm_campaign=digest, accessed November 2016.

27 Megan van Wyngaardt, 'Rio to sell Simandou stake to Chinalco', 28 October 2016, *Mining Weekly*, http://m.miningweekly.com/article/rio-to-sell-simandou-project-stake-to-chinalco-2016-10-28, accessed November 2016.

28 A. Fraser and J. Lungu, 'For whom the windfalls? Winners and losers in the privatisation of Zambia's copper mines, http://www.revenuewatch.org/documents/windfalls_20070307.pdf, accessed November 2016. See also Ndangwa Noyoo, 'Nationalisation: A case study of Zambia, Rhodes University Summer School, 13 September 2011.

29 'Mine nationalisation lost Zambia $45bn, Eunomix study finds', *Mining Weekly*, http://www.miningweekly.com/article/mine-nationalisation-lost-zambia-45bn-eunomix-study-finds-2013-03-22, accessed November 2016.

30 This graph was drawn in part from Ndangwa Noyoo, 'Nationalisation: A case study of Zambia, Rhodes University Summer School, 13 September 2011', from the calculations of David Littleford, and from the author's own calculations, based in part on private Zambian Consolidated Copper Mines records.

31 At London Metal Prices, meaning an effective 25 per cent for those Zambian operations that did not sell at London Metal Exchange prices.

32 'Zambia: Selected issues', IMF, June 2015, https://www.imf.org/external/pubs/ft/scr/2015/cr15153.pdf, accessed November 2016.

33 Again, the royalty is calculated at average monthly London Metal Exchange prices, as opposed to a profit-based margin.

34 'A guide to understanding mineral royalty tax', Chamber of Mines of Zambia, February 2016.

35 Cited in *The Post*, 29 April 2016.

36 See https://vimeo.com/channels/1190374.

37 See Invest Chile, http://www.foreigninvestment.cl/index.php?option=com_content&view=article&id=123, accessed November 2016.

38 Ricardo French-Davis, *Reforming the Reforms in Latin America*. London: Macmillan, 2000.

39 This section is based on research conducted in Mauritania in October 2016 by Greg Mills.

40 See http://data.worldbank.org/indicator/EN.POP.DNST, accessed December 2016.

41 See http://data.worldbank.org/en/country/mauritania/overview, accessed December 2016.

42 Ibid.

Chapter 6

1 'An awakening giant', *The Economist*, 8 February 2014, http://www.economist.com/news/middle-east-and-africa/21595949-if-africas-economies-are-take-africans-will-have-start-making-lot, accessed November 2016.

2 KPMG, 'Sector report: Manufacturing in Africa', 2, http://www.kpmg.com/Africa/en/IssuesAndInsights/Articles-Publications/General-Industries-Publications/Documents/Manufacturing%20in%20Africa.pdf, accessed November 2016.

3 'Made in Africa: Is manufacturing taking off across the continent?', BBC Africa, 29 May 2014, http://www.bbc.com/news/world-africa-27329594, accessed November 2016.

4 World Bank, World development indicators, http://databank.worldbank.org/data/reports.aspx?source=world-development-indicators&preview=on, accessed November 2016.

5 Ibid.

6 This section is based on a research trip to Vietnam in February and March 2016. With thanks to Thomas Vester and Dafydd Lewis for their assistance in this regard. See Greg Mills, 'Lessons From Nam: Learning from Vietnam's manufacturing experience', *Daily Maverick*, 29 March 2016, http://www.dailymaverick.co.za/article/2016-03-29-lessons-from-nam-learning-from-vietnams-manufacturing-experience/, accessed December 2016.

7   World Bank, GDP per capita, http://data.worldbank.org/indicator/NY.GDP.PCAP.
    CD, accessed November 2016.

8   Data from *Saigon Times Weekly*, 27 February 2016.

9   Katrina Manson, 'Chinese manufacturers look to Rwanda', *Financial Times*, 6 May
    2015, http://www.ft.com/cms/s/0/8c3b27ec-e8e1-11e4-87fe-00144feab7de.
    html#axzz4K2HfVNKB, accessed November 2016.

10 World Bank, Doing Business, Economy rankings, http://www.doingbusiness.org/
    rankings, accessed November 2016.

11 This information is based on research trips to Lesotho in August 2015 and February
    2016.

12 Greg Mills, '"A fractious lot": Anatomy of (another) coup in Lesotho', *Daily Maverick*,
    3 July 2015, https://www.dailymaverick.co.za/article/2015-07-03-a-fractious-lot-
    anatomy-of-another-coup-in-lesotho/#.WE_OhtJ97IU, accessed November 2016.

13 Ibid.

14 *Business Day*, 30 October 2014, http://www.bdlive.co.za/economy/2014/10/30/
    little-change-in-jobless-rate, accessed November 2016. The data is drawn, between
    2000 and 2007, from Statistics SA's Labour Force Survey, and between 2008 and 2016
    from the Quarterly Labour Force Survey.

15 Greg Mills's visits to Newcastle and Ladysmith were conducted in November 2014.

16 This section is based on a set of interviews and visits conducted by Greg Mills and
    Dickie Davis in Port Elizabeth, Pretoria and Uitenhage, November 2016.

17 This section is based on a research trip to Mexico during October and November
    2015 in the company of Lyal White. See Greg Mills, 'In Mexico manufacturing is a
    race to the top', *Daily Maverick*, 12 November 2015, http://www.dailymaverick.co.
    za/article/2015-11-12-in-mexico-manufacturing-is-a-race-to-the-top/, accessed
    November 2016. Where not individually referenced, the information or interviews
    were obtained during this visit.

18 Literally, a factory in Mexico run by a foreign company and exporting its products to
    the country of that company.

19 With thanks to Enrique Dussel Peters for this quote.

Chapter 7

1   World Bank, 'Growth of the service sector', http://www.worldbank.org/depweb/
    beyond/beyondco/beg_09.pdf, accessed March 2016.

2   David Fine et al, 'Africa at work: Job creation and inclusive growth', McKinsey Global
    Institute, August 2012, http://www.mckinsey.com/global-themes/mid-
    dle-east-and-africa/africa-at-work, accessed December 2016.

3   Wim van der Beek, 'Five factors that differentiate Africa's fintech,' CNBC Africa, 13
    June 2016, http://www.cnbcafrica.com/news/financial/2016/06/13/fac-
    tors-that-differentiate-fintech-in-africa/?utm_source=CNBC+Daily+Newslet-
    ter&utm_campaign=74209677bf-RSS_EMAIL_CAMPAIGN_Daily&utm_medi-

um=email&utm_term=0_37ea1a8e5e-74209677bf-216248097, accessed December 2016.

4 'Dubai gets 2% GDP from oil after diversifying revenue sources', http://www. bloomberg.com/news/articles/2010-09-28/dubai-gets-2-gdp-from-oil-after-diversifying-revenue-prospectus-shows, accessed December 2016.

5 Ejaz Ghani and Stephen D. O'Connell, 'Can services be a growth escalator in low income countries?', World Bank, Policy Research Working Paper 6871, July 2014, http://www-wds.worldbank.org/external/default/WDSContentServer/WDSP/IB /2014/07/22/000158349_20140722093642/Rendered/PDF/WPS6971.pdf. p. 10, accessed December 2016.

6 World Bank, 'Growth of the service sector', http://www.worldbank.org/depweb/ beyond/beyondco/beg_09.pdf, accessed March 2016.

7 See FlySAA, http://www.flysaa.com/za/en/footerlinks/aboutUs/saaAwards.html. Last accessed December 2016.

8 Ilse de Lange, 'Comair challenges government bailout of SAA', The Citizen, 5 May 2015, http://citizen.co.za/376178/comair-challenges-government-bailout-of-saa/, accessed December 2016.

9 Greg Mills, 'Ethiopian Airlines: An example to SAA?', Daily Maverick, 17 June 2016, http://www.dailymaverick.co.za/article/2016-06-17-ethiopian-airlines-an-example-to-saa/#.WEASbHecbNA, accessed December 2016.

10 Uganda is ranked second in East Africa, with 44 per cent of its citizens having access to banking services, followed by Rwanda at 42 per cent, Tanzania at 40 per cent and Burundi at 7 per cent. http://www.theeastafrican.co.ke/business/Kenya-tops-list-of-banked-population/2560-2697138-jh9o4iz/index.html.

11 'Banking Africa's unbanked – time for a reality check', Business Day, 12 May 2015, http://www.bdlive.co.za/africa/africanbusiness/2015/05/12/banking-africas-unbanked-time-for-a-reality-check, accessed December 2016.

12 Email correspondence with Laurie Dippenaar, 29 October 2016.

13 This section is based primarily on a discussion in Johannesburg at the Bank's Rosebank HQ and email exchange with a Standard Bank strategist, 10 March 2016.

14 Email correspondence with Simon Dagut, 14 March 2016.

15 'For most urban Africans, owning anything other than a slum home is out of reach', The Economist, 14 December 2015, http://www.economist.com/news/middle-east-and-africa/21684033-unaffordable-houses-make-sub-saharan-africa-worlds-smallest-mortgage, accessed December 2016.

16 The average length of time to register land in sub-Saharan Africa is 58 days, compared to 22 days for OECD countries. The African average, however, is lower than that of South Asia (98), East Asia (73) and Latin America (63). See http://blogs.worldbank. org/opendata/youthink/chart-how-long-does-it-take-register-property, accessed December 2016.

17 This is based on interviews conducted at Hollard in Johannesburg and in Zambia, March 2016. See also https://www.lloyds.com/news-and-insight/press-centre/speeches/2015/07/the-challenges-and-opportunities-facing-the-south-africa-insurance-market-today; and http://www.businessinsurance.com/article/20150610/NEWS09/150619997/insurance-challenges-in-africa-exec, accessed December 2016.

18 This section is based on a series of conversations and correspondence with Aon and other insurance experts during March 2016.

19 In 1993 SAB spent $50 million for an 80 per cent stake in Hungary's largest brewer, Dreher. In 1996 the company gained control of two of the largest breweries in Poland, Lech and Tyskie, as well as three breweries in Romania and one in Slovakia. In 1994 SAB created a joint venture with Hong Kong-based China Resources Enterprise Limited, which by early 1998 had control of five breweries in China. By 1997 SAB had grown to become the world's fourth largest brewer and had a rapidly expanding international brewing empire. The company thereafter sold the remainder of its non-core businesses in OK Bazaars, Afcol, Da Gama Textiles, Lion Match and footwear manufacturer Conshu Holdings. See http://www.fundinguniverse.com/company-histories/the-south-african-breweries-limited-history/, accessed December 2016.

20 Interview with Michael Macharia, 18 September 2016.

Chapter 8

1 http://www.pewglobal.org/2015/04/15/cell-phones-in-africa-communication-lifeline/.

2 Internet Usage for Africa 2016, http://www.internetworldstats.com/stats1.htm.

3 Internet Development and Internet Governance in Africa, Internet Society, 22 May 2015, http://www.internetsociety.org/sites/default/files/internet%20devlopment%20and20Internet%20governance%20in20africa.pdf.

4 Emmanuel Wanjala, 'Facebook's Mark Zuckerberg makes surprise visit to Kenya', *The Star*, 1 September 2016, http://www.the-star.co.ke/news/2016/09/01/facebooks-mark-zuckerberg-makes-surprise-visit-to-kenya_c1413233, accessed December 2016.

5 Stephan Faris, 'The solar company making a profit on poor Africans', Bloomberg, 2 December 2015, http://www.bloomberg.com/features/2015-mkopa-solar-in-africa/, accessed December 2016.

6 'Inside Kenya's silent tech revolution', *African Business*, 9 December 2015, http://africanbusinessmagazine.com/sectors/technology/kenyas-silent-tech-revolution/#sthash.ckH7dDd8.dpuf, accessed December 2016.

7 Cited in 'Kenyan tech successes Zuckerberg should know about', *Forbes*, 9 September 2016, http://www.forbes.com/sites/tobyshapshak/2016/09/09/kenyan-tech-successes-zuckerberg-should-know-about/#635230d13090, accessed December 2016.

8 Telephonic interview, 14 March 2016.

9 CIA, The World Factbook, Kenya, https://www.cia.gov/library/publications/ the-world-factbook/geos/ke.html, accessed December 2016. This section is, in part, based on two trips to Kenya in February 2013, working with then Prime Minister Raila Odinga's office on a post-election development approach, and again in August and September 2013.

10 Peter Ngau, 'For town and country: A new approach to urban planning in Kenya', Africa Research Institute, 5 December 2013, http://www.africaresearchinstitute. org/publications/policy-voices/urban-planning-in-kenya/, accessed December 2016.

11 See Kenya National Bureau of Statistics, 2009 Kenya population and housing census analytical reports, http://www.knbs.or.ke/index.php?option=com_con- tent&view=article&id=371:2009-kenya-population-and-housing-census-analyti- cal-reports&catid=82&Itemid=593, accessed December 2016.

12 This section draws on a number of publications, including: Martin Ford, *The Rise of the Robots: Technology and the Threat of Mass Unemployment*. London: Oneworld, 2015; 'The rise of big data', *Foreign Affairs*, 92, 3, May/June 2013; the special Davos anthology 'The Fourth Industrial Revolution' of *Foreign Affairs*, January 2016; the special collection 'African farmers in the digital age: How digital solutions can enable rural development', *Foreign Affairs*, 2016; and 'Inequality: What causes it, why it matters, what can be done', *Foreign Affairs*, 95, 1, January/February 2016. See also Viktor Mayer-Schonberger and Kenneth Cukier, *Big Data: A Revolution That Will Transform How We Live, Work and Think*. London: John Murray, 2013; Danny Dorling, *Population 10 Billion: The Coming Demographic Crisis and How to Survive It*. London: Constable, 2013; and the World Economic Forum blog on technology and Africa at https://www. weforum.org/agenda/2016/05/africa-s-digital-revolution-a-look-at-the-technolo- gies-trends-and-people-driving-it, accessed December 2016.

13 Songezo Zibi, 'Unemployment set to threaten SA's welfare system', *Financial Mail*, 12 December 2013, http://www.financialmail.co.za/features/2013/12/12/unemploy- ment-set-to-threaten-sa-s-welfare-system, accessed December 2016.

14 Amogelang Mbatha, 'South African poverty rate drops as government expands welfare', Bloomberg News, 3 April 2014, http://www.bloomberg.com/news/2014- 04-03/south-african-poverty-rate-drops-as-government-expands-welfare.html, accessed December 2016.

15 'Developing countries are cutting fraud and waste from anti-poverty schemes. Deciding who should be eligible is harder', *The Economist*, 8 January 2015, http:// www.economist.com/news/international/21638127-developing-countries-are-cut- ting-fraud-and-waste-anti-poverty-schemes-deciding-who?frsc=dg%7Ca, accessed December 2016.

16 Interview, Nairobi, 8 September 2016.

17 World Bank, 'Africa still poised to become next great investment destination', 30 June 2015, http://www.worldbank.org/en/news/opinion/2015/06/30/africa-still-poised-to-become-the-next-great-investment-destination, accessed December 2016.

18 Kyle Rother, 'Technology can revolutionise university access', *Daily Maverick*, 21 June 2016, http://www.dailymaverick.co.za/article/2016-06-21-op-ed-technology-can-revolutionise-university-access/#.V5H1P03lqM8, accessed December 2016.

19 'Getsmarter: Cape company disrupting world's higher education, one MIT, Cambridge at a time', https://soundcloud.com/biznews-com/getsmarter-cape-company-disrupting-worlds-higher-education-one-mit-cambridge-at-a-time, accessed December 2016.

20 See 'The secret decoder ring: How cell phones let farmers, governments, and markets talk to each other', 'African Farmers in the Digital Age', *Foreign Affairs*, 2016, 89–90.

21 '9 African tech hubs of the future', *CNN*, 11 November 2015, http://edition.cnn.com/2015/06/19/africa/gallery/african-tech-hubs/, accessed December 2016.

22 See, for example, http://www.cnbcafrica.com/news/financial/2016/06/13/factors-that-differentiate-fintech-in-africa/?utm_source=CNBC+Daily+Newsletter&utm_campaign=74209677bf-RSS_EMAIL_CAMPAIGN_Daily&utm_medium=email&utm_term=0_37ea1a8e5e-74209677bf-216248097, accessed December 2016.

23 Interview, Riverside, Nairobi, 13 September 2016.

24 Cited in Tiyambe Zeleza and Ibulaimu Kakoma, *Science and Technology in Africa*. Africa World Press, 2003, https://books.google.co.uk/books?id=x6nVozGjc_IC&pg=PA99&lpg=PA99&dq=africa+telephone+connections+1995&source=bl&ots=5Sp75Ekg-y&sig=T_NnYAsfhzuLvAhE8Ng1uTX5gOY&hl=en&sa=X&ved=0CD8Q6AEwBmoVChMIm4GA3MfLyAIViV0aCh2upAaC#v=onepage&q=africa%20telephone%20connections%201995&f=false, accessed December 2016.

25 See Manuel Castells, *End of the Millennium: The Information Age: Economy, Society, and Culture*. Oxford: Blackwell, 1997, Volume 3, 95.

26 International Telecommunication Union, *World Telecommunication/ICT Development Report* and database, http://databank.worldbank.org/data/reports.aspx?source=world-development-indicators, accessed December 2016.

27 On the details of African internet and cell usage, see http://www.theguardian.com/world/2014/jun/05/internet-use-mobile-phones-africa-predicted-increase-20-fold, accessed December 2016.

28 Patrick Kihara and Juliet Njeri, 'Africa cracks down on social media', BBC News, 10 September 2016, http://www.bbc.com/news/world-africa-37300272, accessed December 2016.

29 Erik Brynjolfsson, Andrew McAfee and Michael Spence, 'New world order: Labor, capital, and ideas in the power law economy', in the special Davos anthology 'The Fourth Industrial Revolution' of *Foreign Affairs*, January 2016.

30 Alex Barinka, 'Blockbuster video rental chain will shut all US stores', *Bloomberg*, 6 November 2013, http://www.bloomberg.com/news/articles/2013-11-06/blockbuster-video-rental-chain-will-shut-remaining-u-s-stores, accessed December 2016.

31 Martin Ford, *The Rise of the Robots: Technology and the Threat of Mass Unemployment*. London: Oneworld, 2015.

32 Cited in Niall Ferguson, Hillary Snafu and Donald Fubar 'It's all about which mess America wants', *The Sunday Times*, 18 September 2016, http://www.thetimes.co.uk/edition/comment/hillary-snafu-and-donald-fubar-its-all-about-which-mess-america-wants-kkhvmbkdg, accessed December 2016.

33 Rhys Blakely, 'Hard-hitting Trump winning on points in key swing states', *The Times*, 24 September 2016, http://www.thetimes.co.uk/edition/world/hard-hitting-trump-winning-on-points-in-key-swing-states-th8fdvznv, accessed December 2016.

34 Caelainn Barr and Shiv Malik, 'Revealed: The 30-year economic betrayal dragging down Generation Y's income', *The Guardian*, 7 March 2016, https://www.theguardian.com/world/2016/mar/07/revealed-30-year-economic-betrayal-dragging-down-generation-y-income, accessed December 2016.

35 Ronald Inglehart, 'Inequality and modernization: Why equality is likely to make a comeback', in 'Inequality: what causes it, why it matters, what can be done', *Foreign Affairs*, 95, 1, January/February 2016.

36 Ibid.

37 This interview was conducted by Greg Mills at Venetia Mine, South Africa in 2015.

38 Interview conducted by Greg Mills, Angloplats, Johannesburg, 21 November 2014.

39 For detailed statistics on the South African deciduous fruit industry, see Key deciduous fruit statistics 2015. Paarl: Hortgro, 2016.

40 See World Apple and Pear Association, World data report, http://www.wapa-association.org/asp/page_1.asp?doc_id=446, accessed December 2016.

41 The visit to Kromco was conducted by Greg Mills in August 2016.

42 This section is partly based on Greg Mills and Dickie Davis, 'Countries as companies; Morocco's use of technology for development', *Daily Maverick*, 11 August 2016, http://www.dailymaverick.co.za/article/2016-08-11-countries-as-companies-moroccos-use-of-technology-for-development/, accessed December 2016.

43 This information was acquired and these interviews were conducted during a research trip to Morocco in July 2016.

44 'Predictions: voLTE/voWiFi – capacity, reach, and capability', Deloitte, http://www2.deloitte.com/rs/en/pages/technology-media-and-telecommunications/articles/tmt-pred16-telecomm-volte-vowifi-capacity-reach-capability.html, accessed December 2016.

45 'Lessons in entrepreneurship from two of Africa's most successful business leaders', World Economic Forum, 5 May 2016, https://www.weforum.org/agen-

da/2016/05/lessons-in-entrepreneurship-from-two-of-africa-s-most-successful-business-leaders, accessed December 2016.

46 'Africa's digital revolution: A look at the technologies, trends and people driving it', World Economic Forum, 4 May 2016, https://www.weforum.org/agenda/2016/05/africa-s-digital-revolution-a-look-at-the-technologies-trends-and-people-driving-it, accessed December 2016.

47 'The notion of leapfrogging poor infrastructure in Africa needs to come back down to earth', *The Economist*, 6 August 2016, http://www.economist.com/news/business/21703399-notion-leapfrogging-poor-infrastructure-africa-needs-come-back-down-earth-look, accessed December 2016.

48 Interview, Nairobi, 8 September 2016.

49 Hanna Ziady, 'Start-up visas: Countries draw top talent', *Financial Mail*, 1 September 2016, http://www.financialmail.co.za/features/2016/09/01/start-up-visas-countries-draw-top-talent, accessed December 2016.

50 World Bank, Research and development expenditure (% of GDP), http://data.worldbank.org/indicator/GB.XPD.RSDV.GD.ZS, accessed December 2016.

Chapter 9

1 UN Conference on Trade and Development, *World Investment Report 2015: Reforming International Investment Governance*, UN 2015, http://unctad.org/en/PublicationsLibrary/wir2015_en.pdf, accessed December 2016.

2 See World Bank, 'Net official development assistance and official aid received', http://data.worldbank.org/indicator/DT.ODA.ALLD.CD, accessed December 2016.

3 This section is based on an article first published in the *Daily Maverick*. Greg Mills and Dickie Davis, 'Decline and regeneration: Zambia's ghosts of development past', *Daily Maverick,* 11 April 2016.

4 See the *KGL Independent Power Project Report*, Burns & McDonnell, The Dahlgren Group, and McKenna & Co, March 1997. For details on Zambia's power constraints, see http://www.dailymaverick.co.za/article/2016-02-29-the-deficits-behind-zambias-power-problems/#.VvLboU3lqM8; http://www.dailymaverick.co.za/article/2015-09-02-zambias-power-woes-all-roads-lead-to-kariba-dam/#.VvLbzk3lqM8, accessed December 2016.

5 World Bank, 'Net official development assistance and official aid received', http://data.worldbank.org/indicator/DT.ODA.ALLD.CD, accessed December 2016.

6 Of so-called country programmable aid, 'the portion of ODA [official development aid] that donors programme for individual countries or regions, and over which partner countries could have a significant say' excludes humanitarian and emergency assistance, administrative costs, and food aid. See https://www.oecd.org/dac/stats/documentupload/2%20Africa%20-%20Development%20Aid%20at%20a%20Glance%202015.pdf, accessed December 2016.

7   Kwame Anthony Appiah and Henry Louis Gates (eds), *Africana: The Encyclopaedia of the African and African American Experience*. US: Basic Civitas, 1999, 142.

8   See, for example, https://www.oecd.org/derec/denmark/Review-of-Budget-Support-Evaluation.pdf, accessed December 2016.

9   Daron Acemoglu and James A. Robinson, 'Why foreign aid fails – and how to really help Africa,' *The Spectator*, 25 January 2014, http://www.spectator.co.uk/2014/01/why-aid-fails/, accessed December 2016.

10   Brad Parks, '10 essential facts about Chinese aid in Africa', The National Interest, 30 November 2015, http://nationalinterest.org/feature/10-essential-facts-about-chinese-aid-africa-14456, accessed December 2016.

11   Paul Adams, 'Africa debt rising', Africa Research Institute, 22 January 2015, http://www.africaresearchinstitute.org/publications/africa-debt-rising-2/, accessed December 2016.

12   World Bank, 'Foreign direct investment flows into sub-Saharan Africa', March 2014, http://www-wds.worldbank.org/external/default/WDSContentServer/WDSP/IB/2014/03/18/000456286_20140318105721/Rendered/PDF/860600BRI0WB0H00Box382147B00PUBLIC0.pdf, accessed December 2016.

13   UN Conference on Trade and Development, *World Investment Report 2015: Reforming International Investment Governance*, UN 2015, http://unctad.org/en/PublicationsLibrary/wir2015_en.pdf.

14   Mikolaj Radlicki, 'The 30m-strong Africa diaspora likely sends $160bn home every year: Where does it go?', *Mail & Guardian Africa*, 29 May 2015, http://mgafrica.com/article/2015-05-29-remittance-in-africa-where-does-it-go, accessed December 2016.

15   'Africa losing billions from fraud and tax avoidance', *The Guardian*, 2 February 2015, https://www.theguardian.com/global-development/2015/feb/02/africa-tax-avoidance-money-laundering-illicit-financial-flows; see also Caroline Kende-Robbe, 'Africa is rich in resources but tax havens are keeping its people poor', World Economic Forum, 17 May 2016, https://www.weforum.org/agenda/2016/05/africa-is-rich-in-resources-but-tax-havens-are-keeping-its-people-poor, accessed December 2016.

16   'Overview of ODA and international NGOs in Vietnam', Danske Vietnamesisk Forening, http://www.davifo.dk/userfiles/file/pdf/International%20NGOs%20in%20Vietnam8.pdf, accessed December 2016.

17   World Bank, 'Foreign direct investment, net inflows', http://data.worldbank.org/indicator/BX.KLT.DINV.CD.WD?locations=VN, accessed December 2016.

18   World Bank, 'Net official development assistance and official aid received', http://data.worldbank.org/indicator/DT.ODA.ALLD.CD, accessed December 2016.

19   World Bank, 'Mozambique', http://data.worldbank.org/country/mozambique, accessed December 2016.

20   David Smith, 'Boom time for Mozambique, once the basket case of Africa', *The Guardian*, 27 March 2012, https://www.theguardian.com/world/2012/mar/27/mozambique-africa-energy-resources-bonanza, accessed December 2016.

21 Alex Court and Dianne McCarthy, 'Massive gas discovery transforms Mozambique backwater into boomtown', CNN, 3 February 2015, http://edition.cnn.com/2015/02/03/africa/pemba-port-mozambique-gas/, accessed December 2016.

22 David Smith, 'Boom time for Mozambique, once the basket case of Africa', *The Guardian*, 27 March 2012, https://www.theguardian.com/world/2012/mar/27/mozambique-africa-energy-resources-bonanza, accessed December 2016.

23 'World Bank delays aid to Mozambique pending debt analysis: spokesman', CNBC Africa, 28 April 2016, http://www.cnbcafrica.com/news/southern-africa/2016/04/28/world-bank-delays-aid-to-mozambique/, accessed December 2016.

24 Tom Bowker and Michael Cohen, 'Mozambique resorts to foreign exchange curbs as metical dives', Bloomberg, 8 December 2015, http://www.bloomberg.com/news/articles/2015-12-08/mozambique-resorts-to-foreign-exchange-curbs-as-metical-dives, accessed December 2016.

25 'Mozambique is floundering amid corruption and conflict', *The Economist*, 18 March 2016, http://www.economist.com/news/middle-east-and-africa/21695203-scandals-and-setbacks-gas-and-fishing-industries-darken-mood-mozambique, accessed December 2016.

26 World Bank, 'Mozambique, overview', http://www.worldbank.org/en/country/mozambique/overview, accessed December 2016.

27 'Mozambique: Foreign aid dependency necessary for growth and not the other way around', Econ 488 at JMU, 3 November 2014, http://econ488.com/2014/11/03/mozambique-foreign-aid-dependency-necessary-for-growth-and-not-the-other-way-around/, accessed December 2016.

28 World Economic Forum, 'Mozambique', http://reports.weforum.org/global-competitiveness-report-2015-2016/economies/#economy=MOZ, accessed December 2016.

29 See Transparency International Corruption Perceptions Index, http://www.transparency.org/research/cpi/overview, accessed December 2016.

30 'Overview of corruption and anti-corruption in Mozambique', U4 Anti-Corruption Resource Centre, http://www.u4.no/publications/overview-of-corruption-and-anti-corruption-in-mozambique/, accessed December 2016.

31 Paul Collier, 'The role of donors in fragile African states', paper presented to the African Development Bank high-level panel on fragile states, August 2013.

32 See, for example, the China in Africa project of the South African Institute of International Affairs, http://www.saiia.org.za/news/china-in-africa-project, accessed December 2016.

33 Kevin Bloom and Richard Poplak, *Continental Shift: A Journey into Africa's Changing Fortunes*. Cape Town: Jonathan Ball, 2016.

34 '5 myths about Chinese investment in Africa', Foreign Policy, http://foreignpolicy.com/2015/12/04/5-myths-about-chinese-investment-in-africa/, accessed December 2016.

35 World Bank, 'GDP per capita', http://data.worldbank.org/indicator/NY.GDP. PCAP.CD?order=wbapi_data_value_2013+wbapi_data_value&sort=asc, accessed December 2016.

36 Joe Bavier, 'China's DRC investment $9 billion – $3 billion for mining', Mineweb, 16 February 2008, http://www.mineweb.com/archive/chinas-drc-investment-9-billion-3-billion-for-mining/; see also 'China and Congo: Friends in need', Global Witness, March 2011, https://www.globalwitness.org/sites/default/files/library/friends_in_need_en_lr_1.pdf, accessed December 2016.

37 Wenjie Chen, David Dollar and Heiwei Tang, 'China's direct investment in Africa: Reality versus myth', Brookings Institute, 3 September 2015, http://www.brookings.edu/blogs/africa-in-focus/posts/2015/09/03-china-africa-investment-trade-myth-chen-dollar-tang, accessed December 2016.

38 This interview was conducted in Como, Italy, on 2 August 2016.

39 Paul Collier, 'The case for investing in Africa', McKinsey, June 2010, http://www.mckinsey.com/global-themes/middle-east-and-africa/the-case-for-investing-in-africa, accessed December 2016.

40 Makhtar Diop, 'Africa still poised to become the next great investment destination', World Bank, 30 June 2015, http://www.worldbank.org/en/news/opinion/2015/06/30/africa-still-poised-to-become-the-next-great-investment-destination, accessed December 2016.

41 This is taken from a discussion at a London-based investment club, 27 September 2016.

42 The term 'loss given default' refers to the share of an asset that is lost if a borrower defaults, which reflects collateral and degree of debt subordination.

43 Discussion at UBS, London, 21 September 2016.

44 Joe Brock, 'Weak economy takes gloss of "Africa Rising" optimism', CNBC Africa, 16 September 2016, http://www.cnbcafrica.com/news/special-report/2016/09/16/private-equity-in-africa-loses-its-shine/?utm_source=CNBC+Daily+Newsletter&utm_campaign=d0f3c17366-RSS_EMAIL_CAMPAIGN_Daily&utm_medium=email&utm_term=0_37ea1a8e5e-d0f3c17366-216248097, accessed December 2016.

45 'Listing in Africa – extractive industries', KPMG, 2015, https://www.kpmg.com/Africa/en/IssuesAndInsights/Articles-Publications/Documents/KPMG%20Listing%20in%20Africa-extractive%20industries.pdf, accessed December 2016.

Chapter 10

1 See World Bank, Worldwide Governance Indicators, http://info.worldbank.org/governance/wgi/index.aspx#reports, accessed December 2016.

2 'Where to start? Aligning sustainable development goals with citizen priorities', Afrobarometer, http://afrobarometer.org/sites/default/files/publications/

Dispatches/ab_r6_dispatchno67_african_priorities_en.pdf, accessed December 2016.

3   This section is based on an article first published in the *Daily Maverick*. See Greg Mills, 'Inside the house Namibia built: Open windows and a breath of fresh air', *Daily Maverick*, 12 September 2016, http://www.dailymaverick.co.za/article/2016-09-12-inside-the-house-namibia-built-open-windows-and-a-breath-of-fresh-air/#.WEY5SXecbJI, accessed December 2016.

4   Interview, 6 September 2016.

5   World Bank, Namibia, http://data.worldbank.org/country/namibia, accessed December 2016.

6   Republic of Namibia, Harambee Development Plan, http://www.gov.na/documents/10181/264466/HPP+page+70-71.pdf/bc958f46-8f06-4c48-9307-773f242c9338, accessed December 2016.

7   For more detail on the costs of the civil service, see http://www.namibian.com.na/index.php?id=138292&page=archive-read, accessed December 2016.

8   For example, one of the brains behind Singapore's national economic development strategy was Dutch economist Albert Winsemius, who had played a key role in industrial planning in his own country's economy after World War II. An early act of the new government of Singapore was to request advice from the UN Technical Assistance Programme (now the United Nations Development Programme). The mission, which took place in 1960, was led by Winsemius. At its conclusion, he presented an outline 10-year economic development plan, which Singapore broadly adopted. He went on to serve as chief economic advisor to the government from 1961 to 1984, playing a vital role in the transformation of the country. By 1985 the UN had provided the services of 744 technical experts and, between 1950 and 1985, awarded 2 029 fellowships to students from Singapore. For more detail on the roles of Winsemius and the UNDP, see https://issuu.com/undppublicserv/docs/booklet_undp-sg50-winsemius_digital, accessed December 2016.

9   'Remembering Lee Kuan Yew', Channel News Asia, http://www.channelnewsasia.com/news/specialreports/rememberingleekuanyew/features/team-s-pore-strong/1740616.html, accessed December 2016.

10   Vision 2020, the National Long-Term Development Perspective, National Economic Council, Malawi, http://www.africanchildforum.org/clr/policy%20per%20country/malawi/malawi_vision2020_en.pdf.

11   Malawi Growth and Development Strategy 2006–2011, 3–4, http://api.ning.com/files/R9O3ej52zzLO0AZVM*p7O9s7bOPX2Adsbc8Mq942QLrYOepESAv*mIff1PT8dEtl9wPkGQ16q7XP8QGOGOuKLq8rBqwNHWAe/MalawiGrowthandDevelopmentStrategy20062011.pdf, accessed December 2016.

12   Second Malawi Growth and Development Strategy Joint Staff Advisory Note, International Development Association and the IMF, 5 July 2012, 2, http://www-wds.worldbank.org/external/default/WDSContentServer/WDSP/IB/2012/07/18

/000386194_20120718044147/Rendered/PDF/691340PRSP0P120Official0Use0 Only090.pdf, accessed December 2016.

13 For details, see World Bank, Senegal, Overview, http://www.worldbank.org/en/ country/senegal/overview, accessed December 2016.

14 'Blueprint for coming generation in store, says Lee', *The Straits Times*, 9 April 196.

15 'Seizing the moment: Liberia's 150-day plan', Tony Blair Africa Governance Initiative, http://www.africagovernance.org/article/case-study-delivering-liberias-150-day-plan, accessed December 2016.

16 Kishore Mahbubani, 'Why Singapore is the world's most successful society', *The World Post*, 8 April 2015, http://www.huffingtonpost.com/kishore-mahbubani/singa-pore-world-successful-society_b_7934988.html, accessed December 2016.

17 Ian Lienert and Jitendra Modi, 'A decade of civil service reform in sub-Saharan Africa', IMF working paper, 4, https://www.imf.org/external/pubs/ft/wp/ wp97179.pdf, accessed December 2016.

18 World Bank, Worldwide Governance Indicators, http://info.worldbank.org/ governance/wgi/index.aspx#home, accessed December 2016.

19 World Bank, Factbook 2016, Countries glossary, http://siteresources.worldbank. org/INTPROSPECTS/ Resources/334934-1199807908806/4549025-1450455807487/Factbook2016_ Countries_M-Z_Glossary.pdf, accessed December 2016.

20 Office of the President of the Republic of Zambia, 'Zambian diaspora survey', https://www.iom.int/jahia/webdav/shared/shared/mainsite/activities/countries/ docs/zambia/Zambian-Diaspora-survey-Report.pdf, accessed December 2016.

21 Greg Mills, *Why States Recover*. Johannesburg: Pan Macmillan, 2014, 272.

22 UN Sustainable Development Knowledge Platform, https://sustainabledevelopment. un.org/content/documents/1431Singapore.pdf, accessed December 2016.

Chapter 11

1   These are Somalia, South Sudan, Central African Republic, Sudan, Chad, DRC, Guinea, Nigeria, Burundi and Zimbabwe.

2   The other six being Yemen, Syria, Afghanistan, Haiti, Iraq and Pakistan.

3   The Fund for Peace, Fragile States Index 2016, http://fsi.fundforpeace.org/, accessed December 2016.

4   In order (bottom ranked first): Somalia, Sudan, South Sudan, Angola, Libya and Guinea-Bissau.

5   The others being North Korea, Afghanistan, Venezuela and Iraq.

6   Transparency International, Corruption Perceptions Index 2015, http://www. transparency.org/cpi2015, accessed December 2016.

7   In order (from the bottom): Guinea, Chad, Mauritania, Sierra Leone, Burundi, Malawi, Haiti, Mozambique, Venezuela, Myanmar, Madagascar, Liberia, Swaziland, Mali, Pakistan, Zimbabwe, Nigeria, The Gambia, Benin, Guyana and Tanzania. See

https://www.weforum.org/agenda/2015/09/what-are-the-10-most-competitive-economies-in-sub-saharan-africa/, accessed December 2016.

8 The Paris Club was established in 1956 when negotiations between Argentina and its public creditors took place in Paris. It comprises 21 permanent members as major creditor countries, whose aim is to coordinate and find sustainable solutions to debt payment difficulties of debtor countries. The permanent members of the Paris Club are Australia, Austria, Belgium, Canada, Denmark, Finland, France, Germany, Ireland, Israel, Italy, Japan, the Netherlands, Norway, the Russian Federation, South Korea, Spain, Sweden, Switzerland, the UK and the US.

9 Freedom House, *Freedom in the World, 2015*. New York: Freedom House, 2015, www.FreedomHouse.org, accessed December 2016.

10 This section is based on an article first published in the *Daily Maverick*. See Greg Mills, 'Ethiopia's Hailemariam Desalegn: Growth has to be shared to be sustainable', *Daily Maverick*, 7 June 2016, http://www.dailymaverick.co.za/article/2016-06-07-ethiopias-hailemariam-desalegn-growth-has-to-be-shared-to-be-sustainable/, accessed December 2016.

11 One of the nine ethnically based regional states of Ethiopia.

12 Ethiopia's population in 2016 was 94 million.

13 World Bank, 'Ethiopia, Overview', http://www.worldbank.org/en/country/ethiopia/overview, accessed December 2016.

14 World Bank, 'Ethiopia', http://data.worldbank.org/country/ethiopia, accessed December 2016.

15 With thanks to Christopher Clapham for this observation.

16 'Chinese shoe factory Huajian now employs 3 200 people', Addis Ababa Online, http://addisababaonline.com/chinese-shoe-factory-huajian-now-employs-3200-people/, accessed December 2016.

17 'Economic development: The good news from Ethiopia and what might make it even better', UK Department for International Development, https://www.gov.uk/government/speeches/economic-development-the-good-news-from-ethiopia-and-what-might-make-it-even-better, accessed December 2016.

18 This section is based on an article first published in the *Daily Maverick*. Greg Mills, 'Botswana's President Ian Khama: "Diamonds are not forever"', *Daily Maverick*, 29 June 2016, http://www.dailymaverick.co.za/article/2016-06-29-botswanas-president-ian-khama-diamonds-are-not-forever/, accessed December 2016.

19 Leah Granof, 'DTC sight week revealed', *Rapaport Magazine*, January 2008, http://www.diamonds.net/Magazine/Article.aspx?ArticleID=20171&RDRIssueID=21, accessed December 2016.

20 World Bank, 'International tourism, number of arrivals', http://data.worldbank.org/indicator/ST.INT.ARVL, accessed December 2016.

21 Victor Baatweng, 'Botswana loses up to 90% of tourism revenue', *Sunday Standard*, 10 July 2014, http://www.sundaystandard.info/botswana-loses-90-tourism-revenue, accessed December 2016.

22 This section was researched during a visit to Mauritania in October 2016 by Greg Mills and is based on an article first published in the *Daily Maverick*. See Greg Mills, 'Reform in the Sahel: Mars, Mauritius or Mauritania', *Daily Maverick,* 19 October 2016, http://www.dailymaverick.co.za/article/2016-10-19-reform-in-the-sahel-mars-mauritius-or-mauritania/, accessed December 2016.

23 This section is based on two trips to Côte d'Ivoire, in 2012 and 2016, including an interview with President ADO by Greg Mills on 16 December 2016.

24 This figure was supplied by Fidèle Sarassoro, Counsellor to the President, 15 December 2016.

25 Cited in Martin Meredith, *The Fortunes of Africa: A 5,000-Year History of Wealth, Greed and Endeavour*. London: Simon & Schuster, 2015, 619.

26 World Bank, GDP per capita growth, http://data.worldbank.org/indicator/NY.GDP.PCAP.KD.ZG?locations=CI, December 2016.

27 World Bank, Country overview, http://www.worldbank.org/en/country/cote-divoire/overview, December 2016.

28 We are grateful for Stephan Malherbe's insights in this regard.

29 Email correspondence with Ambassador (rtd) Phil Carter, 17 December 2016.

30 World Bank, Country overview, http://www.worldbank.org/en/country/cote-divoire/overview, December 2016.

31 Discussion, Abidjan, 14 December 2016.

32 The example of the Colombian government's fight this century against the guerrilla movement the FARC and its ideological offspring may be relevant. The backfilling behind the military effort through the provision of improved governance and basic infrastructure, especially roads and cellular communications, has been largely successful. Delivering improved governance has been a presidentially led initiative, throughout the country's 1 100 municipalities. See Dickie Davis, David Kilcullen, Greg Mills and David Spencer, *A Great Perhaps? Colombia: Conflict and Convergence*. London: Hurst, 2015.

33 Discussion with Greg Mills and Dickie Davis, Gauteng Legislature, 24 November 2016.

34 With thanks to General (rtd) George Casey Jnr for his thoughts in this regard.

Conclusion

1   UN FAO, 'Nigeria at a glance', http://www.fao.org/nigeria/fao-in-nigeria/nigeria-at-a-glance/en/, accessed December 2016.

2   Central Intelligence Agency, *The World Factbook*, https://www.cia.gov/library/publications/the-world-factbook/geos/id.html, accessed December 2016.

3   For the Gini coefficient, see http://hdr.undp.org/en/content/income-gini-coefficient, accessed December 2016.

4   For a detailed examination of the parallels with Africa, see Greg Mills, 'A new Bandung Consensus? What Africa and Indonesia can learn from each other', *Daily Maverick*, 9 March 2016, http://www.dailymaverick.co.za/article/2016-03-09-a-new-bandung-consensus-what-africa-and-indonesia-can-learn-from-each-other/; and Greg Mills, 'Indonesia: A messy democracy that somehow works', *Daily Maverick*, 1 September 2014, http://www.dailymaverick.co.za/article/2014-09-01-indonesia-a-messy-democracy-that-somehow-works/#.WEQeL03lqM8, accessed December 2016.

5   In order of increasing size: Seychelles, São Tomé and Príncipe, Cape Verde, Comoros, Djibouti, Swaziland, Mauritius, Guinea-Bissau, Gabon, Lesotho, Equatorial Guinea, Gambia, Botswana, Namibia and Mauritania.

Index